Gaslighting

SUNY series in Gender Theory
―――――――
Tina Chanter, editor

Gaslighting

Philosophical Approaches

Edited by

KELLY OLIVER, HANNA KIRI GUNN,
and HOLLY LONGAIR

SUNY PRESS

Published by State University of New York Press, Albany

© 2025 State University of New York

All rights reserved

Printed in the United States of America

No part of this book may be used or reproduced in any manner whatsoever without written permission. No part of this book may be stored in a retrieval system or transmitted in any form or by any means including electronic, electrostatic, magnetic tape, mechanical, photocopying, recording, or otherwise without the prior permission in writing of the publisher.

Links to third-party websites are provided as a convenience and for informational purposes only. They do not constitute an endorsement or an approval of any of the products, services, or opinions of the organization, companies, or individuals. SUNY Press bears no responsibility for the accuracy, legality, or content of a URL, the external website, or for that of subsequent websites.

EU GPSR Authorised Representative:
Logos Europe, 9 rue Nicolas Poussin, 17000, La Rochelle, France
contact@logoseurope.eu

For information, contact State University of New York Press, Albany, NY
www.sunypress.edu

Library of Congress Cataloging-in-Publication Data

Names: Oliver, Kelly, editor. | Gunn, Hanna Kiri, editor. | Longair, Holly, editor.
Title: Gaslighting : philosophical approaches / edited by Kelly Oliver, Hanna Kiri Gunn, and Holly Longair.
Description: Albany : State University of New York Press, [2025] | Series: SUNY series in Gender Theory | Includes bibliographical references and index.
Identifiers: ISBN 9798855801309 (hardcover : alk. paper) | ISBN 9798855801323 (ebook)
Further information is available at the Library of Congress.

Contents

Acknowledgments   vii

Introduction   1
   Hanna Kiri Gunn and Holly Longair

Part I: What Is Gaslighting?

CHAPTER 1
Structural Gaslighting   23
   Nora Berenstain

CHAPTER 2
Theorizing Structural Gaslighting as Gaslighting   65
   Holly Longair

CHAPTER 3
Gaslighting and Social Power: Mills, Medina, and Moi on Knowledge and the Social Imaginary   87
   Sabrina L. Hom

CHAPTER 4
Moral Gaslighting   103
   Kate Manne

CHAPTER 5
Affective Gaslighting   127
   Kelly Oliver

CHAPTER 6
Anger Gaslighting as Affective Injustice — 147
Shiloh Whitney

Part II: Experiences of Gaslighting

CHAPTER 7
Allies Behaving Badly: Gaslighting as Epistemic Injustice — 177
Veronica Ivy [Rachel McKinnon]

CHAPTER 8
Racial Gaslighting — 193
Angelique M. Davis and Rose Ernst

CHAPTER 9
Varieties of Gaslighting — 213
Cynthia A. Stark

CHAPTER 10
Giving an Account of the Harms of Medical Gaslighting — 231
Lilyana Levy

CHAPTER 11
Structural Gaslighting: Hurricane María and Recovery in Puerto Rico — 249
Taína M. Figueroa

LIST OF CONTRIBUTORS — 275

INDEX — 281

Acknowledgments

An earlier version of chapter 4 was originally published as Kate Manne, "Moral Gaslighting," *Aristotelian Society Supplementary Volume 97*, no. 1 (2023): 122–45, https://doi.org/10.1093/arisup/akad006.

An earlier version of chapter 7 is a reprint of Veronica Ivy [Rachel McKinnon], "Allies Behaving Badly: Gaslighting as Epistemic Injustice," in *The Routledge Handbook of Epistemic Injustice*, ed. Ian James Kidd, José Medina, and Gaile Polhaus Jr., 167–74 (New York: Routledge, 2017).

An earlier version of chapter 8 was originally published as Angelique M. Davis and Rose Ernst, "Racial Gaslighting," *Politics, Groups, and Identities* 7, no. 4 (2017): 761–74, https://doi:10.1080/21565503.2017.1403934.

Introduction

Hanna Kiri Gunn and Holly Longair

This volume brings together an instructive selection of foundational and new work on the concept of gaslighting in philosophy as a resource for those interested in an introduction to a relatively recent but quickly growing field of study. Gaslighting has become a powerful concept in popular culture and in academic contexts for analyzing and evaluating how the exercise of social power can lead to isolation and estrangement, both for individual persons and for identity groups. The pieces in this volume contribute to several lines of inquiry into gaslighting including conceptual clarity between gaslighting and related phenomena, theorizing the nature of gaslighting in several distinct forms, and analyzing the impact of gaslighting on its victims. To do so, and using different methodological approaches, the work in this collection examines gaslighting as it affects the epistemic, moral, political, social, and emotional dimensions of our lives. One significant contribution of the essays in this collection is a commitment to not only examining cases of gaslighting between individuals, but also beginning to theorize how gaslighting occurs at a structural level and thereby targets specific groups.

Within feminist philosophy, analyses of *gaslighting* specifically are a recent topic. However, they are in a continuum with a long history of feminist analyses into how norms, stereotypes, and forms of social injustice lead to exclusion and marginalization across significant domains of life. Another important point of connection is with preexisting work in feminist epistemic phenomenology including, for example, gaslighting as a form of epistemic injustice and gaslighting as it relates to psychoanalysis. Feminist social epistemology and psychoanalysis share an interest in the causal connections between social injustices and unconscious attitudes—including fears, desires, and prejudicial conceptual associations (commonly referred to as implicit biases). One pertinent question about gaslighting concerns whether it must be an intentional act or process or if gaslighting can, at least in some cases, occur unintentionally. This question points not only to the unconscious and intersubjective dimensions of gaslighting but also, and more importantly, to the social and structural components of gaslighting.

The relevant sense of the term "gaslighting" comes to us from Patrick Hamilton's 1938 play, *Gas Light* (in the United States, the play was known as *Angel Street*). This Victorian thriller, in very brief, follows the story of a man determined to drive his newlywed wife mad to steal her inheritance. The concept of gaslighting that emerges refers to the husband's actions and their consequences for his wife: to gaslight is to intentionally manipulate someone to make them believe they are mentally ill as a means of achieving some other end. *Gas Light* was a major success as a play, resulting in many re-creations in other forms of media (which made various changes in how the story unfolds while keeping the main manipulative features of the plot intact).

In 1940 and 1944, *Gas Light* was made, respectively, into a British film and an American one (both titled *Gaslight*). Alongside stage plays and films, *Gas Light* was also reproduced as several radio plays and television adaptations. And in 2019, its legacy in media still enduring, a modern adaption was released as a podcast ("Gaslight," QCode 2019). The American film, directed by George Cukor and starring Ingrid Bergman, Joseph Cotten, and Charles Boyer, is now the better known of the many incarnations of the original. (For the remainder of this discussion, we refer to Cukor's film.)

The plot of this version of *Gaslight* follows Paula Alquist Anton, who, as a teenager, is witness to the murder of her aunt, Alice Alquist, a world-famous opera singer whose death results in her London townhouse passing on to Alice. After Alice's death, Paula follows in her stead and leaves London for Italy to train in opera. Enter Gregory Anton, the love-affair-turned-husband of Paula. After only a two-week romance, the pair marry and return to London to live in Paula's aunt's townhouse. In reality, Gregory is a liar and a cheat who only married Paula to finish off a heist he had begun years earlier, during which Alice was killed. There is a temptation to view Gregory as guileful, but this understates his abusive actions and their impact: he socially isolates Paula, emotionally manipulates her to gain control over her, and temporarily succeeds in causing her to believe that she has become mentally ill. In exchange for Paula's social and material connection to the world—her sanity—Gregory's measly desire is to gain jewels and riches.

Accomplishing this insidious task requires both public and private work on Gregory's behalf. He publicly challenges Paula's sense of reality on the rare occasions that he allows her to leave the house. At home, Gregory hides belongings and convinces Paula that their maid hates her—all trickery and lies. The eponymous gaslights throughout the house dim when Gregory turns on the lights in the attic to search for Alice's hidden jewelry. Paula, quite naturally, notices the dimming lights, but when she questions Gregory about them, he turns her observation into merely another symptom. Deeply unsettling and morbidly thrilling, *Gaslight* forces us to confront the power that those we love have over our sense of reality. As such, it illustrates the relationship between knowledge, affect, and power that informs the feminist philosophical approaches of this volume.

Gaslighting and Psychoanalysis

About four decades after the original play, in the 1980s, "gaslighting" became a technical term in psychology and psychiatry. In keeping with Gregory's behavior, "to gaslight" describes the action of intentionally manipulating someone else to make them think that they are mentally ill. An early piece, for example, is Victor Calef and Edward M. Weinshel's (1981) paper on gaslighting and introjection. They propose that gaslighting is a possible consequence of introjection, which is the unconscious process of taking on someone else's attitudes or dispositions. Calef and Weinshel propose that gaslighting revolves around a particular "human potential": "the ability to disavow (with the help of a variety of defenses) that which has been introjected and/or the ability to incorporate and to assimilate that which others externalize and project onto them" (1981, 45).

Calef and Weinshel note that "gaslighting" had been used to label a wide range of psychological and psychiatric cases. These include cases when someone, the gaslighter, attempts to have another, the gaslightee, institutionalized by making those around them view the gaslightee as "crazy"; cases when there is an attempt to actually cause mental illness in another; and cases when untrained psychoanalysts may in fact "drive a patient psychotic."

One significant conceptual connection in their discussion is between gaslighting and the work of Melanie Klein (and others) on projective identification. Projective identification is a Freudian concept that describes a process of attributing some dispositions or attitude of one's own onto an object, for example, projecting one's own insecurity onto another and perceiving them as insecure rather than oneself. At the time of publication, Calef and Weinshel propose a need for careful analysis of the cases they are interested in as instances of gaslighting and those examined under the rubric of projective identification because "the clinical phenomena may be similar, if not identical, while our formulations may differ" (47). The development of this connection in the psychological literature is an interesting historical note given that one of the seminal pieces on gaslighting in the philosophical literature by Kate Abramson (2014) develops the view that gaslighting *is* projective identification. The early uses of the term in the psychological and psychiatric context still influences the ways in which it is conceptualized and theorized today.

This connection between projective identification and gaslighting is also important because gaslighting was not a term used widely outside clinical settings until recent decades. In popular circles, it is still most familiarly a term for describing emotional abuse, narcissistic personalities, and other forms of abusive manipulation in relationships. However, gaslighting is also now commonly found in self-help literature and has even become a part of political debate and social critique as well.[1] The conceptual bridge with projective identification helped to bring it into those other spaces.

Philosophical treatment of the term is much more recent and its application far more varied than its original use in psychological contexts. In the remainder of this introduction, we first situate gaslighting in relation to some other ongoing and relevant conversations both in philosophy and popular culture, namely, those about post-truth, the epistemological crisis, and the #MeToo movement. We then contextualize current analyses of gaslighting in relation to prior philosophical work on the topics of epistemic injustice, epistemic violence, and silencing speech. As already noted, within philosophy, discussions of gaslighting began with feminist analyses of relations between knowledge, affect, and power. And, as such, so does this collection. We hope that the analyses of gaslighting in these chapters will be instructive to other philosophical approaches and broader considerations of gaslighting as well.

One problematic feature of both psychological, psychoanalytic, and early philosophical treatments of gaslighting is the way these express how targets of gaslighting may come to question their own mental states. Often this is framed in terms of the person who is being gaslighted being accused of being "crazy" or "insane" and "questioning their own sanity" (for examples in key texts on gaslighting, see Calef and Weinshel 1981 and Abramson 2014). These terms carry negative normative implications, or negative value judgments of those to whom they are applied, thus expressing an ableist judgement about those who have experienced gaslighting (see Chappell 2021 for a discussion of similar implications of mental illness–related slurs in areas of popular discourse). This particular variety of ableist judgment brings forward a common connection between rationality and autonomous agency and denies these capacities to those who are, in this case, gaslit. However, it is important to interrogate that assumed connection. Sophia Jeppson's argument for the intelligibility of experiences that are labeled psychotic or delusional is particularly useful in breaking down ableist implications often assumed by using terms such as "crazy" or "insane" to describe the victims of gaslighting (2021). Although throughout this introduction we have avoided these terms and made an effort to frame the discussion in terms of making someone think they are mentally ill, it is important to interrogate that language use as well. Those theorizing gaslighting must always be careful to avoid ableist (and particularly saneist) language, assumptions, and implications in the course of describing this phenomenon and pay close attention to the context in which it is being discussed.

The essays in this collection give us not only different ways of understanding the urgency and relevancy of the concept of gaslighting, but also a set of tools of analysis for future discussions both within philosophy and in other disciplines as well. Several pieces in this volume demonstrate the relevance of insights from within those subfields to wider scholarly and popular discussions of gaslighting. In addition, insofar as they investigate the relationships between knowledge, affect, and power, the feminist philosophical approaches set forth in this volume demonstrate why gaslighting recently has become such a prevalent term in public life. In other words, gaslighting is a concept that speaks to the conjunction of knowledge, affect, and power, and the manipulation thereof.

The philosophical approaches—including both individual or transactional and structural analyses—employed in this volume are evidence not only of the usefulness of a philosophically robust conception of gaslighting, but also of the importance of considering gaslighting from different perspectives. Furthermore, they point to the importance of theorizing gaslighting beyond the context of philosophy to better understand the changing landscape of contemporary power relations.

Gaslighting and Salience

In investigating why gaslighting is experiencing such a boost as a topic of theoretical inquiry, we should consider its relationship to conversations, both academic and public, about both trust and truth. We here propose two important connections: the popularization of Tarana Burke's #MeToo movement about sexual abuse and assault and the "post-truth" political culture debate. As a feminist political movement, #MeToo is part of a resurgence of activism that seeks to establish solidarity between victims of sexual assault and abuse while actively challenging their silencing through public campaigns. An important element in the #MeToo movement involves explicit awareness raising about how sexist norms set expectations that disable victims from speaking out about their experiences while helping perpetrators and bystanders to doubt their testimony. Focusing on this dynamic is something that feminist theorists have both studied and called out in practice, and one that is key to many analyses of transactional instances of gaslighting.

The idea of post-truth fits in a broader network of terms describing what has been called the "epistemological crisis,"[2] a crisis of destabilization of epistemic networks, norms, and social epistemic practices like testimony that are, respectively, usually moderated by a commitment to the shared value of truth. It is interesting from an etymological perspective that both "post-truth" and "gaslighting" recently have seen sharp increases in usage.

Use of the term "post-truth" spiked in frequency alongside a series of major political events including both the British exit from the European Union ("Brexit") and the 2016 US presidential election. Post-truth became the Oxford English Dictionary "Word of the Year" in 2016 and was defined in the following way: "relating or denoting circumstances in which objective facts are less influential in shaping public opinion than appeals to emotion and personal belief." Alongside this adjectival usage, "post-truth politics" arrived as a counterpart to name an apparently new phase of political culture with a shift away from reasons-based political persuasion. And, indeed, if we look at Google Trends data on the rate of searches including "gaslighting" from 2004 (the earliest Trends data available) onward we see a telling picture. Google Trends data report the popularity of a search, with 100 indicating that the term is at its most "popular" (or searched) point and 0 indicating the lowest. Searches for gaslighting were flat from 2004 until 2016, with a sharp increase (to 25) in 2017 when the #MeToo movement rapidly gained popular salience.

The term "gaslighting" was shortlisted in the 2018 Oxford English Dictionary Word of the Year competition ("toxic" took the title). In its discussion of the rise of gaslighting, Oxford explains that it has become prominent in both discussions about domestic abuse and in political discussions about the same kinds of events that caused the term post-truth to become ubiquitous.

Discussions of #MeToo, post-truth, and gaslighting, then, indicate a broad trend in public sentiment about our epistemic relationships with one another and our political institutions. The concept of gaslighting, however, has taken on a stronger moral valence than post-truth. While the latter focuses on, in part, the erosion of epistemic authority, discussions of the former almost always include a discussion of how such erosion hurts people and their relationships. This can be seen by the way in which many entries into the literature on gaslighting (both in this volume and elsewhere) focus on the harms and wrongs of the phenomenon.

The etymological story of gaslighting tracks, roughly, a progression in how it is being theorized within philosophy. The concept, as the contributions to this volume demonstrate, continues to be one for exploring abuse within personal relationships. However, it is also being actively developed into a concept for analyzing and describing oppressive social structures. Research into gaslighting is still finding its place in the broader structure of feminist philosophical work, but it seems clear, at this stage, that it provides the feminist theorists a new lens for describing and challenging the weaponization of oppressive social norms and expectations at the local and collective levels. Importantly, gaslighting provides a distinctive investigation of how our emotional lives can be used and abused to distort our own understanding of our lived experiences and, similarly, how it can be used to control the receptiveness of those around us to our plight.

In the last ten years, feminist philosophers, including those working in social epistemology, have analyzed gaslighting in relation to gender norms (for example, see Abramson 2014, Ivy [McKinnon] 2017, and Stark 2019). Related to such discussions there has also emerged deeper intersectional analysis of how similar manipulations can be identified in relation to race, colonization, and in medical settings (for example, Ruíz 2014, Davis and Ernst 2019, and Berenstain 2020). Increasingly, gaslighting is being used to describe the ways in which a wide variety of oppressed and marginalized peoples are manipulated into not trusting their own feelings, beliefs, or experience. This multitude of uses has sparked conversations about where and when gaslighting occurs, as well as what makes something a case of gaslighting, debates that continue to grow and evolve alongside the colloquial uses of the term.

Feminist philosophers, critical race theorists, and many others within philosophy concerned with those who are marginalized and oppressed have consistently paid attention to the effect of social power, both at the individual and collective levels, on our lives. At a minimum, social power is a term that refers to the social and political forces that determine what actions, choices, emotions, and beliefs are open to us.[3] Those with high levels of social power have high levels of control over their actions and a wide range of attitudes open to them, while those with low levels of social power face restricted control over action and a depressed range of attitudes and choices available to them. Thus, and despite meritocratic mythology, such philosophers have remained committed to the idea that social power is neither evenly nor fairly spread. Gaslighting is rapidly gaining traction as a concept for analyzing such processes of social power, both at individual and structural levels. It has been particularly powerful for an elucidation of how the exercise of social power can lead to isolation and estrangement, both for individual persons and for identity groups.

Theoretical Context and Approaches to Gaslighting

It is an unusual trajectory for a concept to arise as a visual metaphor in film, then to have such power over the public imagination that it is adapted into the technical terminology of psychology. From there, it was taken up by philosophers with the goal of explaining the nature of the harm or wrong done by gaslighters to gaslightees, while still relying on these psychological theories of the concept. However—as seen in several essays in this collection—philosophical work on gaslighting is no longer always committed to these psychological treatments of the concept.

With an eye to the salience of the #MeToo movement and the "epistemological crisis" outlined in the previous section, it is useful to think about current philosophical work on gaslighting through the lens of preceding work on both epistemologies of ignorance and epistemic injustice, two related areas of inquiry into how social power structures our epistemic lives.[4] Further, and somewhat adjacent to the epistemic inquiries, feminist philosophers of language have explored how social power can silence some voices, typically those of marginalized groups, while amplifying the voices of others (for example Langton 1993, and Hornsby 1995). Silencing works in part because of stereotypes and assumptions about persons or groups in the wider social imaginary (Dotson 2011). Other philosophers working in the Black feminist tradition and in critical race theory have developed lines of inquiry critically exploring the gaps in these dominant understandings of such power structures, with important implications for the discussion of gaslighting both within and outside disciplinary confines we have focused on here (such as Doston 2012, Ruíz 2014, and Berenstain 2020). The chapters in this collection situate themselves with respect to different facets of the relevant existing literature, with insights useful for furthering existing dialogues on social power in a variety of philosophical domains.

In mainstream social epistemology, gaslighting is often discussed in combination with Miranda Fricker's (2007) work on epistemic injustice and, in particular, her concept of testimonial injustice. Fricker defines testimonial injustice as a faulty perceptual capacity that has been trained by prejudicial attitudes in the wider society. When operating well, the "virtue of testimonial justice" enables hearers to accurately perceive the credibility of a speaker. Testimonial injustice, then, leads to deflated credibility assessments of speakers resulting in communicative and epistemic marginalization. If we consider the characters of Paula and Gregory from *Gaslight*, it is in part owing to the stereotypes about women and "hysteria" that Gregory is able to so effectively challenge her experience of events. Some, then, understand testimonial injustice to be a means by which gaslighting can be achieved.

Although many have found Fricker's conceptual framework useful in analyzing gaslighting, others have been critical of her approach. Nora Berenstain (2020), for example, argues that Fricker's methodology and virtue theoretic framework of epistemic injustice constitutes structural gaslighting—and in so doing, she first introduces an account of structural gaslighting into the philosophical literature. Berenstain's argument applies most directly to Fricker's account of hermeneutical injustice, wherein Fricker traces a history of the concepts "sexual harassment" and "postpartum depression" while not explicitly engaging with the history of Black women's movements in raising awareness of the former or the role of ableism for the latter. A similar critique comes from Kristie Dotson, who argues that Fricker unintentionally engages in epistemic oppression. Dotson defines epistemic oppression as occurring when social knowledge is deficient as a result of excluding certain positions and communities from participating in the relevant epistemic community, infringing on epistemic agency (Dotson 2012, 24), providing a broader concept of an epistemic wrong than Fricker's concept of epistemic injustice. Dotson argues that Fricker perpetuates an epistemic oppression because she uses a closed conceptual structure that "prematurely forecloses the possibility of alternative forms of epistemic injustice" (Dotson 2012, 25).

Although the literature has often focused on epistemic injustice, other concepts in feminist social epistemology have proved useful in theorizing gaslighting. Dotson's (2011) concept of epistemic violence has been particularly useful to understand the kind of social and epistemic power at play in gaslighting (for example, by Ruíz 2020 and Berenstain 2020, as well as in several chapters of this volume). Central to Dotson's notion of epistemic violence is the concept of "pernicious ignorance" (2011, 238). Pernicious ignorance describes a gap in cognitive resources that manifests reliably and leads to consistent failures to correctly uptake a speaker's testimony. This ignorance gap is brought about by the existence of stereotypes or controlling images of groups that lead to these failures in uptake (for discussion of "controlling images," see Collins 2000). The account of epistemic violence presents two forms of silencing that result from pernicious ignorance: testimonial quieting of a speaker by an audience and testimonial smothering of oneself as a speaker in the face of a perniciously ignorant audience. Like testimonial injustice, epistemic violence is another process by which gaslighting can be understood to come about.

Similar to the above social epistemic frameworks—though preceding them—the idea of silencing speech also draws on the significance that stereotyping and prejudicial representations have for enabling and disabling communicative acts. Feminist philosophers of language in the early 1990s applied the tools of Austinian speech act theory to explain how performative speech can be silenced (Austin 1975). Rae Langton (1993) presented the first analysis of illocutionary silencing as a development of Catherine Mackinnon's (1987) position that pornography can both silence and subordinate women.

J. L. Austin's theory of speech acts allows us to distinguish between the locutionary content of an utterance, the illocutionary act that is performed in making the utterance with a specific performative force, and the typical perlocutionary consequences that result by an utterance with that force. Theories of silencing attend to the ways that our ability to perform speech acts is in part determined by the willingness of our audience to uptake our communicative acts and intentions, and if they refuse, they explain a unique way that one's ability to act can be curtailed by others' beliefs about one.

Langton was concerned primarily with pornographic depictions of women that recoded their refusals for sex as misleading—women are not *really* performing an act of refusal, they are instead being shy or coy. Langton proposed, then, that the locutionary content of this form of pornography depicted women's subordination to men, that the illocutionary force constituted a form of subordination, and that its perlocutionary consequences were to cause the further subordination of women. Thus, pornographic speech can systematically silence women's illocutionary acts of refusal by leading men to take them as mere coyness and to further maintain a system of subordination. Dotson's concept of pernicious ignorance is developed in part in connection with this earlier work on silencing speech, in particular, Jennifer Hornsby's (1995) discussion of the significance of reciprocity for the successful performance of a speech act.

Theories of gaslighting, then, continue to build on a series of approaches to understanding our epistemic and communicative interdependence. Silencing debates highlight the ways that our very ability to speak and perform actions with our speech can be undermined by prejudicial attitudes that lead to systematic and pervasive failures of uptake. Testimonial injustice, as a form of epistemic injustice, further develops the basic idea in the silencing literature along the lines of our epistemic agency: what kinds of epistemic actions are open to us, who can earn epistemic statuses like credibility. The framework of epistemic violence draws our attention to ways that prejudicial attitudes lead not only to problems of uptake, but also to the ways that individuals targeted by such prejudices experience epistemic and communicative forms of alienation. Each highlights a different way that our ability to act and speak is enabled or disabled by how others are willing to understand and perceive us. Gaslighting, it would seem, is parasitic on these kinds of processes and extends their harmful consequences.

Much of the prior work on gaslighting that has received attention in mainstream philosophy has been done primarily as a topic within social epistemology. A notable outlier is Kate Abramson's (2014) paper "Turning Up the Lights on Gaslighting." Abramson analyzes gaslighting as a moral phenomenon and presents an account of the wrong of gaslighting someone. Abramson uses a psychoanalytic understanding of gaslighting as projective identification and argues that its harm can be explained as a form of emotional manipulation where the gaslighter tries (intentionally or not) to cause the gaslightee to lose their sense of reality. As one of the earliest treatments of gaslighting within philosophy, Abramson's account creates a clear bridge between the early technical definitions in psychology and the normative discussions of the concept that have followed in philosophy, while placing the moral question front and center.

Contra Abramson, Andrew Spear (2018) argues that a full account of gaslighting must place epistemic factors centrally to the phenomenon. Key to Spear's analysis is the psychological concept of "confabulation." Though this is a complicated cluster of phenomena in their own right, for simplicity, we can understand confabulation as the tendency to offer reasons in response to questions that, while not intentionally deceptive or misleading, are the product of motivated reasoning rather than evidence. Spear argues that paradigm cases of gaslighting involve confabulation by both the gaslighter and gaslightee.

Other discussions of gaslighting have balanced the focus on the moral and epistemic features of gaslighting. A useful collection can be found in a special issue of *Hypatia* (2020, 35[4]) on gaslighting and epistemic injustice, and the articles within the collection employ the concept to understand many different phenomena and contexts. For instance, work on structural gaslighting is a recent shift in philosophical discussions of gaslighting, and several papers published in 2020 begin to develop this collective form of gaslighting. In her introduction to a cluster of articles on the topic, Alison Bailey (2020) describes structural gaslighting as a social epistemic phenomenon and uses the metaphor of an "unlevel knowing field" to elucidate the concept, while Nora Berenstain describes it as "any conceptual work that functions to obscure the nonaccidental connections between structures of oppression and the patterns of harm that they produce and license" (2020, 734).

A particularly important piece for many contributors to this volume is Elena Ruíz's (2020) paper on "cultural gaslighting." Ruíz argues that gaslighting is a structural phenomenon, which has been a powerful tool of abuse and control in settler colonial societies by creating asymmetric harms depending one's position in relation to and within the settler colonial state. It serves to both consolidate the settler colonial project and control the experiences of settler violence through one culture undermining another on a collective level of sense and belief. Ruíz is particularly critical of the prior focus on gaslighting exclusively at the individual level, arguing that this actually has been an instance of the phenomenon obscuring its structural nature in order to maintain it. Her focus on the pervasiveness of the structural elements of gaslighting has opened up new avenues of inquiry, some of which are explored in this volume.

In the course of the time it has taken to put together this volume, several new contributions have been made to the literature in philosophy on gaslighting. Of particular note are Carla Bagnoli's "Normative Isolation: The Dynamics of Power and Authority in Gaslighting" and Kate Manne's "Moral Gaslighting," both published in 2023. Manne's article has been reprinted in this volume, as it makes a significant contribution to elaborating the kinds of gaslighting that are of particular concern to feminist theorizing and activism. However, it should be noted that these articles had not yet been published at the time when the contributions to this volume were written, so the authors had not yet had the opportunity to engage with their theories.

Contributions to the Volume

The first part of the volume presents six essays exploring the nature of gaslighting. While the paradigmatic case of gaslighting is instances of emotional manipulation in interpersonal relationships, several contributors to this collection develop a collective analogue: structural gaslighting. The notion of structural gaslighting raises the possibility of gaslighting-at-scale: the possibility that whole societies, or proper subsets thereof, experience gaslighting processes in the routine course of their lives. Another line of inquiry taken up by contributors to the volume questions the primary domain of gaslighting. We have explained in the previous section that gaslighting has received both moral and epistemic analyses. Several contributors to this collection propose a further, arguably essential, analysis of gaslighting as an affective phenomenon.

Kate Abramson's essay, while not reprinted in this volume, is a canonical piece in the philosophical literature on gaslighting and thus is an important resource for a full understanding of the development of this area of research. As previously introduced, Abramson's approach to the topic is from the moral perspective and proposes an account of the wrong of gaslighting. Her discussion focuses on transactional cases of gaslighting as in the prototypical case of the phenomenon from *Gaslight*. Gaslighters, in her view, seek to exclude their targets from the moral community to dominate them. Many of the pieces in this collection respond to Abramson's analysis or use it as the starting place for developing their own accounts.

Nora Berenstain argues for a structural account of gaslighting that takes the phenomenon to be, at its core, about conceptual resources that maintain systems of oppression. Berenstain proposes that gaslighting is an important part of the epistemological project of oppressive domination, both in establishing relationships of domination and in maintaining them. As illustrated by the range of cases—scientific racism, ableist violence, and colonial land theft—structural gaslighting in her analysis is a pervasive and widespread phenomenon.

Holly Longair's contribution to the volume raises important theoretical questions about the relationship between accounts of transactional gaslighting and structural gaslighting. She notes that there are competing theories of each type of gaslighting and, importantly, that there are also noncompeting accounts of gaslighting simply theorizing different phenomena. A central question for Longair is what unites transactional and structural accounts such that they can be understood as theories of the same, broad phenomenon. Longair proposes a unifying conception of structural gaslighting that aims to show what these accounts have in common.

Sabrina Hom proposes an account of structural gaslighting as a form of epistemic violence that is grounded in control over the social imaginary. Hom adopts the position that gaslighting is a form of epistemic injustice, but, finding the transactional character of Fricker's account insufficient for generalizing to structural cases, she proposes instead that we adopt a view of gaslighting as about the collective social imaginary rather than personal identity prejudices.

Kate Manne's recently published piece on moral gaslighting has been reprinted here. For Manne, *moral* gaslighting targets one's own sense of one's moral agency such that one is "made to feel morally defective." Manne contests the idea that it is only one's rational or epistemic agency that is targeted by gaslighters. Instead, she proposes that gaslighting targets one's sense of self such that one begins to feel defective fundamentally, be it morally, epistemically, affectively, and so forth. Manne takes gaslighting to essentially depend on norms and preexisting power structures, discussing, for example, how misogyny facilitates moral gaslighting. One of the strengths Manne proposes for her account is that moral gaslighting, as she understands it, is not necessarily a transactional process but one that can occur for groups.

In one of two pieces on affective gaslighting, Kelly Oliver argues that we cannot adequately explain cases of gaslighting if we only attend to their moral and epistemic qualities. She argues that the affective dimension of gaslighting is what enables the epistemic and moral harms that other writers have identified. Oliver draws on her previous work on the colonization of psychic space to explain how the internalization of affective norms and expectations enables gaslighting. Oliver's analysis draws our attention to the ways that gaslighting can operate unconsciously through the use of implicit biases and prejudices.

Shiloh Whitney argues that gaslighting presents a form of affective injustice. Whitney proposes a broad category of "uptake injustices" that may be epistemic, communicative, and, she argues, affective. Through an analysis of anger gaslighting, she proposes that refusals to uptake someone's anger challenges the "aptness" of their emotional response. The result is that someone may come to question whether their anger, or emotional responses more generally, are appropriate or if they are, instead, affectively incompetent.

The second part of the volume includes papers that explore particular experiences of gaslighting. The chapters in this section demonstrate the analytical potential of gaslighting as a concept for understanding forms of social power and control across a wide range of cases.

Veronica Ivy's essay is a second canonical piece in the philosophical literature on gaslighting. It is reprinted here with a substantive new preface that relocates gaslighting in theoretical space from epistemic injustice, that is, testimonial injustice, to epistemic violence. Ivy elucidates another harm of gaslighting by identifying a dynamic between trans persons and their alleged allies. Ivy proposes that skepticism on behalf of purported allies when presented with first-personal accounts of anti-trans experiences constitutes gaslighting of the trans person.

Cynthia Stark considers the idea that citizens of the United States may be facing an epidemic of gaslighting in political life. Stark presents a variety of cases of political deception from lying to whataboutism and poses the question: what makes each of these an instance of gaslighting?

Stark proposes that gaslighting is a coercive practice that aims at getting other people to adopt one's view—whether that view is a lie, some kind of Frankfurtian bullshit, or is otherwise misleading. Stark's unifying analysis of gaslighting not only entails a verdict on essential properties of transactional gaslighting, but can be extended to structural cases as well.

Angelique Davis and Rose Ernst's reprinted paper, "Racial Gaslighting," takes up the role of gaslighting for white supremacy in the United States. Davis and Ernst argue that gaslighting is a means for sustaining white supremacy because of the power that gaslighting processes have for creating racial spectacle. They propose that racial gaslighting is a multifaceted process that normalizes white supremacy while simultaneously pathologizing the acts of those who resist it. This process of domination occurs through the narrative control that racial gaslighting can produce, creating prejudicial myths that enable forms of epistemic and communicative injustice.

Lilyana Levy's contribution to the volume concerns medical gaslighting. Levy understands medical gaslighting as a form of testimonial injustice that depends on both interpersonal and structural enabling factors. Levy discusses the ways that an absence of an underlying physiological explanation for one's symptoms can cause patients to be labeled as unreliable, overly emotional, and, perhaps, responsible for their illnesses. One of the primary harms that results from this form of testimonial injustice, Levy argues, is a radical form of self-doubt about one's own experiences.

Taína Figueroa discusses the role played by structural gaslighting in the response to the devastation wrought by Hurricane María in Puerto Rico in 2017. Figueroa proposes that the United States government used explicit denial alongside fictitious and harmful narratives about Puerto Rico to mislead the wider public about the damage of the storm, shift blame for an ineffective relief effort, and deflect other public challenges. Figueroa discusses the connection between structural gaslighting and settler colonialism and argues that structural gaslighting can be used to protect racio-colonial capitalist power.

The contributions to this volume demonstrate the presently elastic nature of the concept of gaslighting. Approaches to theorizing about the concept of gaslighting are frequently ameliorative, aiming to propose accounts of the concept that help us to make sense of the maul-like potential of social power to be used as a tool to maintain and create harmful divisions that contribute to marginalization and oppression. Social and political divisions can be a source not only of inequality, but also of deep forms of isolation and distrust. The contributions to this collection converge on the idea that gaslighting processes, be they transactional or structural, often serve to create siloes where such isolation and distrust can flourish and contribute to ongoing wrongs.

In articulating both transactional and structural accounts of gaslighting, the contributors to this volume challenge our existing resources for making sense of a variety of epistemic, moral, political, and affective harms. They enrich ongoing discussions of social power, prejudicial stereotyping, and structurally unjust social institutions by introducing new ways of conceiving of the harms these phenomena bring about. Gaslighting has fast become an important theoretical lens through which to approach familiar problems within socially applied philosophy, and one that we anticipate will continue to develop as a robust conceptual resource for future work in these areas.

Notes

1. See, for example, titles such as *The Gaslighting Recovery Workbook: Healing from Emotional Abuse* by Amy Marlow-MaCoy, and *Gaslighting America: Why We Love It When Trump Lies to Us* by Amanda Carpenter.

2. E.g., see "The Internet, Epistemological Crisis and the Realities of the Future, special issue of *Journal of Future Studies*, June 2020.

3. For an overview of feminist engagements with social power, see Amy Allen, "Feminist Perspectives on Power," in *The Stanford Encyclopedia of Philosophy* (Fall 2022 edition), ed. Edward N. Zalta and Uri Nodelman, https://plato.stanford.edu/archives/fall2022/entries/feminist-power/.

4. See Mills 1997 and Fricker 2007 for the origins of epistemologies of ignorance and epistemic injustice, respectively, and Sullivan and Tuana 2007 and Kidd et al. 2017 for collections of work on these topics from a variety of authors.

Works Cited

Abramson, Kate. 2014. "Turning Up the Lights on Gaslighting." *Philosophical Perspectives* 28: 1–30.

Allen, Amy. 2022. "Feminist Perspectives on Power." In *The Stanford Encyclopedia of Philosophy*, edited by Edward N. Zalta and Uri Nodelman. https://plato.stanford.edu/entries/feminist-power/.

Austin, John. L. 1975. *How to Do Things with Words*. Oxford: Clarendon Press.

Bailey, Alison. 2020. "On Gaslighting and Epistemic Injustice: Editor's Introduction." *Hypatia* 35 (4): 667–73.
Berenstain, Nora. 2020. "White Feminist Gaslighting." *Hypatia* 35: 733–58.
Calef, Victor, and Edward M. Weinshel. 1981. "Some Clinical Consequences of Introjection: Gaslighting." *Psychoanalytic Quarterly* 50 (1): 44–66.
Carpenter, Amanda. 2018. *Gaslighting America: Why We Love It When Trump Lies to Us*. New York: HarperCollins.
Chappell, Zsuzsanna. April 2021. "It's So Crazy That You Called Me a Psycho: Why Are We Still Using Mental Illness Slurs?" *Justice Everywhere blog*. https://justice-everywhere.org/health/its-so-crazy-that-you-called-me-a-psycho-why-are-we-still-using-mental-illness-slurs/.
Collins, Patricia Hill. 2000. *Black Feminist Thought: Knowledge, Consciousness, and the Politics of Empowerment*. New York: Routledge.
Davis, Angelique M., and Rose Ernst. 2019. "Racial Gaslighting." *Politics, Groups and Identities* 7 (4): 761–74.
Dotson, Kristie. 2011. "Tracking Epistemic Violence, Tracking Practices of Silencing." *Hypatia* 26 (2): 236–57.
———. 2012. "A Cautionary Tale: On Limiting Epistemic Oppression." *Frontiers: A Journal of Women Studies* 33 (1): 24–47.
Fricker, Miranda. 2007. *Epistemic Injustice: Power and the Ethics of Knowing*. Oxford: Oxford University Press.
Hornsby, Jennifer. 1995. "Disempowered Speech." *Philosophical Topics* 23 (2): 127–47.
Ivy, Veronica [Rachel McKinnon]. 2017. "Allies Behaving Badly." In *The Routledge Handbook of Epistemic Injustice*, edited by Ian James Kidd, José Medina, and Gaile Pohlhaus Jr., 167–74. New York: Routledge.
Jeppson, Sophia. 2021. "Psychosis and Intelligibility." *Philosophy, Psychiatry, and Psychology* 28 (3): 233–49.
Langton, Rae. 1993. "Speech Acts and Unspeakable Acts." *Philosophy and Public Affairs* 22 (4): 293–330.
Kidd, Ian James, José Medina, and Gaile Pohlhaus Jr. 2017. *The Routledge Handbook of Epistemic Injustice*. New York: Routledge.
MacKinnon, Catherine. 1987. *Feminism Un-modified*. Cambridge, MA: Harvard University Press.
Marlow-MaCoy, Amy. 2020. *The Gaslighting Recovery Workbook: Healing from Emotional Abuse*. Emeryville, CA: Rockridge Press.
Mills, Charles. 1997. *The Racial Contract*. Ithaca, NY: Cornell University Press.
QCode. 2019. *Gaslight*. https://qcodemedia.com/gaslight.
Ramos, José, and Michael Nycyk. 2020. "The Internet, Epistemological Crisis and the Realities of the Future." *Journal of Future Studies* 24 (4): 1–4.
Ruíz, Elena. 2014. "Musing: Spectral Phenomenologies: Dwelling Poetically in Professional Philosophy." *Hypatia* 29 (1): 196–204.

———. 2020. "Cultural Gaslighting." *Hypatia* 35 (4): 687–713.
Spear, Andrew. 2018. "Gaslighting, Confabulation, and Epistemic Innocence." *Topoi* 39: 229–41.
Stark, Cynthia. 2019. "Gaslighting, Misogyny, and Psychological Oppression." *Monist* 102 (2): 221–35.
Sullivan, Shannon, and Nancy Tuana. 2007. *Race and Epistemologies of Ignorance*. Albany: State University of New York Press.

Part I
What Is Gaslighting?

1

Structural Gaslighting

Nora Berenstain

> Because keeping oppressed peoples in the dark about the social formation of psychological toolkits for understanding violence is a cultural, counterrevolutionary strategy designed to manipulate social understanding of colonial violence and its structural prevalence, the greatest success of the gaslighting paradigm is that it provides cover for the structural dimensions of gaslighting.
>
> —Elena Ruíz, *Cultural Gaslighting*

Gaslighting is an epistemic form of abuse that aims to facilitate further abuse by interrupting its targets' ability to name and resist abuse. It involves calculated distortions of reality and production of doubt, and it relies on and solicits complicity from those who have the power to interrupt the abuse. This is true of gaslighting at both the interpersonal scale and the broader structural scale. Interpersonal gaslighting and structural gaslighting are isomorphic forms of abuse. Beyond sharing a name, they share the same goals, functions, mechanisms, and success conditions. They also share the same purpose of undermining resistance to the abuse while simultaneously creating plausible deniability that the abuse is even happening.

While gaslighting is often understood solely at the scale of interpersonal relationship dynamics, structurally produced gaslighting that produces population-level harms has recently been receiving greater focus.

This is a much-needed attentional shift. As I noted when first introducing the concept, structural gaslighting is significantly more pervasive than interpersonal gaslighting and produces harm well beyond the scale of the individual (Berenstain 2020). Population-level harms produced by the violence of structural oppression are vast, and scholars who are working to reveal the operations of structural gaslighting projects are invested in their disruption. Tremain (2021, 13), for example, reveals how narratives that naturalize and medicalize disability by portraying disabled people as "defective, unreliable, and suboptimal" contribute to the structural gaslighting that frames nursing homes as sites of love and care rather than as carceral facilities of institutionally enabled abuse and maltreatment. Hatch (2020, 2) invokes structural gaslighting to describe how the collection of data on racial disparities during the COVID-19 pandemic "keeps scientists in an endless search for more and more refined measurements of racism's harms, while the political and economic systems that comprise the fundamental causes of those harms are given a pass until all the data are counted." Davis and Ernst (2019) outline an innovative notion of racial gaslighting, which perpetuates and normalizes white supremacy by pathologizing resistance to it. Abu Laban and Bakan (2022) extend the notion of racial gaslighting to Israel's ongoing occupation of Palestine, including through the denial of the 1948 Nakba, the obscuring of the violence Palestinians face under apartheid rule, and the distortion and erasure of Palestinian history. Ruíz's (2020) notion of cultural gaslighting further analyzes the epistemic violence and attempted destruction of Indigenous epistemologies that are foundational to the settler colonial project and endure within settler colonial societies. These examples reflect the incredibly high stakes of the material realities that structural gaslighting enables and provides cover for. The violence that structural gaslighting protects and makes possible includes political and economic violence, racialized terror, rape and sexual abuse, land theft, forced displacement, and genocide. As each of the examples discussed here makes clear, the victims of structural violence are not the only ones who are targeted by structural gaslighting. The complicity of bystanders is just as important (and sometimes even more so) to the success conditions of structural gaslighting.[1] I explore this dimension of structural gaslighting in section 2 on what I term *narrative complicity*.

Interrupting structural violence requires a shift of attention to gaslighting at the scale of the structural and a focus on its inherent connections to systems of oppression and the population-level harms they reliably produce.[2] As Ruíz notes in her (2020) account of cultural gaslighting, a conception of gaslighting that frames the phenomenon as *primarily* an interpersonal phenomenon to which we are all equally susceptible actually works to cover over the structured epistemic violence linked to death-by-design for certain populations in settler colonial societies. Revealing the function and operation of structural gaslighting aids in understanding large-scale justifications for structural oppression and the narrative myths that obscure the violence they produce. In societies that are fundamentally structured by oppression, structural gaslighting is not the exception but the rule.

Structures of oppression in settler colonial societies rely on epistemological foundations to orient themselves toward their goals of containment, white supremacy, population control, racial capitalism, gendered domination, and land dispossession. Structural gaslighting encompasses the justifying stories and mythologies produced in these societies to normalize, obscure, and uphold structures of oppression, as well as the sleight of hand used to conceal the non-accidental connections between structures of oppression and the population-level harms they produce. Among other conjurings, these epistemic practices include "systems of justification that locate the causes of pervasive inequalities in flaws of the oppressed groups themselves while obscuring the social systems and mechanisms of power that uphold them" (Berenstain 2020, 734). Such epistemic legwork often works by naturalizing socially produced inequalities through positing biological or cultural deficiencies in targeted populations. Structural gaslighting can be found in numerous narratives and is produced by many different entities and actors—people, institutions, academic disciplines.[3] It is built into a range of conceptual practices, theoretical systems, methodologies, and epistemologies.[4] This chapter further develops my concept of structural gaslighting (Berenstain 2020) and explores its relationship to scientific and philosophical knowledge production. I investigate the mechanisms of structural gaslighting at play within the practices of "racecraft" (Fields and Fields 2022) and scientific racism, the naturalization of disability, philosophical justifications for ableist violence, and the use of disablement as a tool of settler colonialism. I draw heavily from the work of Dorothy Roberts (2011, 2011b) and Shelley Tremain (2017) to illustrate how structural gaslighting in the sciences often works by characterizing an oppressed group as inherently biologically flawed in a way that detaches from and obscures the production of marginalization via social structure. I analyze paradigmatic instances of structural gaslighting with a focus on the epistemic and material functions they perform for the systems they uphold, and I do this with the hope of providing tools for intervening into the pervasive and death-producing forms of violence they license.

What Is Structural Gaslighting?

Structural gaslighting refers to "any conceptual work that functions to obscure the non-accidental connections between structures of oppression and the patterns of harm that they produce and license" (Berenstain 2020). As such, it is found in an enormous range of western academic and scientific narratives. The stories that structural gaslighting comprises often have a scientific component or dimension. Sometimes they are theoretical without purporting to be scientific. Science provides a wealth of examples of structural gaslighting because it is often presumed to possess dispassionate authority despite its embeddedness within social structures and cultural value systems. Scientific racism is one such form of structural gaslighting. The naturalization of disability is another. Both are effective strategies of structural gaslighting that justify and uphold structurally and institutionally violent forms of settler colonial white supremacy and ableism—along with patriarchy, cisheterosexism, and capitalism—while simultaneously obscuring the nature of that violence. Ruíz's (2024) work on "structural trauma" offers an insightful look into the mechanics of structural gaslighting through an investigation of the origins and effects of the western concept of *trauma*. At its core, this concept produces structural gaslighting by framing intentionally designed structural harms as tragic and unforeseeable acts of fate.

Ruíz argues that the failure to understand trauma as a phenomenon that is *unevenly distributed by design* in settler colonial societies is itself a functional tool of settler colonialism, which compounds the effects of trauma on the populations it harms. Trauma and harm are reliably and predictably produced for Indigenous women and women of color in settler societies. Consider the well-documented phenomenon in which industries such as fossil fuels, mining, and fracking bring transient male laborers to rural and often Indigenous locations, where they set up temporary "man camps" for out-of-state workers (Finn et al. 2017). The influx of male workers for extractivist colonial projects like building pipelines reliably leads to soaring rates of violence against Native women (First Peoples Worldwide 2020). This violence includes kidnapping, assault, rape, sex trafficking, and homicide (Morin 2020). Yet the non-accidental links between settler colonialism and the production of violence against Native women is obscured by the western notion of trauma, which frames the phenomenon not as something systemically produced for certain populations *by design* but as rooted in the Greek conception of tragedy as the "unavoidable casualty of individual fate." The western construction of trauma as depoliticized, unavoidable, and impossible to predict produces structural gaslighting by disconnecting the intentional and systematic production of trauma for Indigenous women as a strategy of settler colonialism (Ruíz and Berenstain 2018).

Ruíz shows that the depoliticized construction of trauma functions to deflect attention and knowability away from the reality that populations of color and Indigenous peoples are reliably subjected to violence and trauma, by design, at a structural scale. A primary function of this is "exonerating white settler culpability through cultural apparatuses like law, policy, law enforcement, governance, and the concepts that uphold them." As such, this conceptual framework of trauma secures the underlying "blamelessness" of those who benefit from domination—a key function of structural gaslighting. This underlying blamelessness depends on the idea that tragedy itself is "built into the very fabric of being in a gambled trade-off for living self-determined lives" and is therefore merely the result of inevitable "bad luck." This etiology disconnects *trauma* from "organized coordinated efforts structured to bring harm and injury to some people but not others."

In this case, structural gaslighting is achieved through the illusion that the instances of systemically produced trauma are i) purely individualized, ii) impossible to predict, and iii) unevenly distributed by accident and without culpability for the populations who constructed the oppressive structures and whose descendants continue to benefit from them while also actively maintaining them. It is further achieved by disrupting the ability to name and identify the structurally produced violence and death. Ruíz writes, "For Indigenous women and women of color living in settler colonial societies like the United States, Canada, and The United Mexican States (Etados Unidos Méxicanos), these founding myths have had a lasting and damaging impact for the role they play in maintaining conceptions of trauma that preclude the identification of ongoing structural oppressions and systemic femicidal violence in our communities."

Structural gaslighting, here, is a counterrevolutionary strategy that aims to disrupt the ability to name and resist this abuse by those for whom settler colonialism produces trauma by design.

While structural gaslighting is primarily about disappearing and obscuring the *actual* causes, mechanisms, and harms of oppression, it frequently does this by manufacturing alternative explanations for the harm that are rooted in oppressive ideologies, and which are often created simultaneously with the production of said harm. As such, structural gaslighting is an essential component of the gearwork of structural oppression. As Black feminist theorist Patricia Hill Collins notes, "Within U.S. culture, racist and sexist ideologies permeate social structure to such a degree that they become hegemonic, namely, seen as natural, normal, and inevitable" (2000, 5). Structures of oppression depend on authoritative justifications for their continued maintenance because "[i]ntersecting oppressions of race, class, gender, and sexuality could not continue without powerful ideological justifications for their existence." Citing Hazel Carby, Collins emphasizes that the purpose of controlling images produced within a society structured by white supremacist capitalist cisheteropatriarchy is "not to reflect or represent a reality but to function as a disguise, or mystification, of objective social relations." The function of disguising or mystifying objective social relations is the ultimate aim of structural gaslighting, Controlling images serve to make "racism, sexism, poverty, and other forms of social injustice appear to be natural, normal and inevitable parts of everyday life" (Collins 2000, 77). Controlling images are thus one tool in the structural gaslighting toolbox, which works to hide and conceptually sever the effects of structural oppressions from the systems that produce them.

Covering stories for violent systems of oppression often locate the causes of pervasive inequalities in the purported "flaws" of the oppressed groups themselves while simultaneously obscuring the social systems and mechanisms of power that uphold them. Consider Collins's incisive explanation of the "Matriarch" controlling image and its service to US capitalism—an example of the extensive and powerful structural gaslighting accomplished by controlling images. The racist, misogynistic "Matriarch" image portrays Black women as unfeminine, aggressive, and masculine. The "Matriarch" is a bad mother because she works outside the home and is unavailable to nurture and tutor her children, thus raising offspring who have no work ethic or educational support outside of school. She is responsible for destroying Black families because she drives away Black men by emasculating them.[5] In the following quote, Collins uncovers the conceptual work that the image does to hide the objective social relations that structurally produce harmful educational outcomes for Black children.

> While at first glance the matriarch may appear far removed from issues in U.S. capitalist development, this image is actually important in explaining the persistence of Black social class outcomes. Assuming that Black poverty in the United States is passed on intergenerationally via the values that parents teach their children, dominant ideology suggests that Black children lack the attention and care allegedly lavished on White, middle-class children. This alleged cultural deficiency seriously retards Black children's achievement. Such a view diverts attention from political and economic inequalities that increasingly characterize global capitalism. It also suggests that anyone can rise from poverty if he or she only received good values at home. Inferior housing, underfunded schools, employment discrimination, and consumer racism all but disappear from Black women's lives. In this sanitized view of American society, those African-Americans who remain poor cause their own victimization. In this context, portraying African-American women as matriarchs allows White men and women to blame Black women for their children's failures in school and with the law, as well as Black children's subsequent poverty. Using images of bad Black mothers to explain Black economic disadvantage links gender ideology to explanations for extreme distributions of wealth that characterize American capitalism. (84)

The "Matriarch" controlling image provides a scapegoat for US social problems in order to deflect from the structural inequalities produced by white supremacy and US capitalism. Instead of identifying any of the real causes of poor educational outcomes of Black schoolchildren—such as the racist-by-design practice of funding public education through property taxes, the practice of majority-white municipalities extracting assets and resources from majority-Black ones (Seamster 2016), the destruction of Black families by the child-welfare system (Roberts 2002), the increasing practice of criminalization-as-punishment in predominantly Black schools, and the ever-expanding school-to-prison pipeline (Morris 2016)—whites can attribute them to the presumed moral failings of Black mothers and their purportedly inadequate parenting. The "Matriarch" image covers over the ongoing choices we make as a white supremacist society to deny equal education to Black children and assign the blame to Black mothers.[6]

In this case of structural gaslighting, the *targets* of racism and misogynoir are scapegoated as the *cause* of their own oppression (as well as the oppression of their children) via the intergenerational transmission of professional, educational, and moral failure. Meanwhile, those who are actually responsible fall out of the picture completely. White preservation of white supremacist institutions and the wealth they accumulate[7] are protected by the structural gaslighting that these controlling images accomplish. This deflection of attention away from the architects and beneficiaries of racial capitalism and onto its exploited targets is an example of what Karen and Barbara Fields refer to as *racecraft*, which they characterize in part as a "conjurer's trick of transforming racism into race" (2014, 26). The next section explores how this insightful notion can offer another informative look into the mechanics of structural gaslighting.

"Racecraft" as Structural Gaslighting

> Racecraft daily performed its conjurer's trick of transforming racism into race, leaving black persons in view while removing white persons from the stage. To spectators deceived by the trick, segregation appeared to be a property of black people, not something white people imposed on them.
>
> —Karen Fields and Barbara Fields

The trick of disappearing white people, the architects and beneficiaries of white supremacy, from view while making racist segregation appear "to be a property of black people" is emblematic of the structural gaslighting that racecraft accomplishes. For Karen Fields and Barbara Fields, racecraft is a significant force, akin to witchcraft, that permeates the American social and political landscape. It is distinct from both race and racism. Fields and Fields explain that racecraft involves transforming the *doings* of *racism* into the objectual features of *race*. This happens, for instance, when "race" or racialized physical features are identified as the primary cause of racist actions, policies, institutions, or mechanisms of white supremacy.[8] "The shorthand transforms racism, something an aggressor does, into race, something the target is, in a sleight of hand that is easy

Structural Gaslighting | 31

to miss" (Fields and Fields 2014, 17). This sleight of hand, switching out the oppressor for the oppressed as the cause of their own oppression, is one of the central mechanisms of structural gaslighting. Notice how it operates in the following example of a mundane yet hardly innocuous expression: "Consider the statement 'black Southerners were segregated because of their skin color'—a perfectly natural sentence to the ears of most Americans, who tend to overlook its weird causality. But in that sentence, segregation disappears as the doing of segregationists, and then, in a puff of smoke—paff—reappears as a trait of only one part of the segregated whole" (Fields and Fields 2014, 17). The sleight of hand involved in ascribing acts of racism to "skin color" is an act of structural gaslighting. In magic, sleight of hand is a practice of attention manipulation that works to hide human action from view to produce a sense of mystical causation. Racecraft too involves deflecting attention from agential actions, background structures of oppression, and the causal roles of both in the production of consequences—the definition of structural gaslighting. The magician hides from view what allows the ball to be suspended in mid-air so that it appears to be floating on its own. Similarly, racecraft removes the perpetrators of racism—both individual and systemic—from view so that the targets of racism appear to have *themselves* caused the harmful social conditions they inhabit. To say that racism occurs as a result of "skin color" implies that racism follows naturally from the features of those targeted by it. This naturalization of racism is the work of structural gaslighting. There are many additional steps in the causal chain between having a certain "skin color" and being targeted by racism, but these steps fall out of view when the consequences of racism are causally attributed to the color of one's skin. It is no coincidence that the steps that are obscured by such a locution are those that involve the *perpetrators* of racism—the creators, facilitators, and beneficiaries of white supremacy—as well as the structures of white supremacy itself.

This subtle blaming of the target of violence in this form of causal reasoning finds consonance with the kind of gaslighting used to cover abuse at the interpersonal scale. In both cases, there is a causal inversion at play—the perpetrator finds reasons to justify the abuse, and these reasons are repeated by the larger community, sometimes even in the context of *condemning* the abuse (as is often the case when switching out a perpetrator's racial animus for a target's skin color in a causal locution). This functions to remove attention and culpability from the perpetrator of abuse and either place it on the target of the abuse or simply diffuse it so that both the perpetrator and their target are portrayed as mere victims of circumstance.[9] The next section explores how the phenomenon of *narrative complicity* connects to and upholds this community-enabling support for structural gaslighting.

Narrative Complicity

Exploring the relationship between community dynamics and abuse at the interpersonal scale can help provide insight into the role of community collusion in abusive dynamics at the scale of structural oppression. This section looks at the phenomenon I refer to as *narrative complicity*—community participation in the deployment and uptake of public narratives about abuse that control the construction of blame and culpability so as to minimize or diminish the responsibility of the perpetrator. This dynamic is not only integral to the social phenomenon of domestic violence and interpersonal abuse, it is also a key component in the dynamics of structural gaslighting.

Just as gaslighting and abuse can occur at psychological, interpersonal, and sociological scales, narrative complicity plays an enabling role for abuse at multiple scales. An in-depth look at Alisa Bierria's insightful work on community accountability reveals some of the forms that narrative complicity can take. In her (2012) discussion of the public discourse surrounding Rihanna's experience of domestic violence by her then-boyfriend Chris Brown, Bierria offers a powerful inquiry into survivor subjectivity and narratives surrounding survivor accountability. Her piece investigates what happened when a purportedly "private" act of abuse became public after LAPD officers sold their photographs of Rihanna's facial injuries to the gossip blog *TMZ*. Through an analysis of the online discussions that surrounded both the initial incident and Rihanna's later choice to temporarily return to her relationship with Brown, Bierria finds a range of responses. These include overt misogynoir predicated on controlling images of Afro-Caribbean women (e.g., "Caribbean women are crazy, she probably cut him"), extensions of sympathy toward Rihanna that are contingent on her leaving the relationship and retracted upon her returning (e.g., "I'm sorry but I no longer feel sorry for her, because she's going right back to the person who put her in that situation"), and more subtle forms of condemnation projecting a lack of self-love onto Rihanna or holding her responsible for enabling men's violence against women and girls. All of these responses demonstrate narrative complicity with Brown's abuse by offering rhetorical justification, minimization, and exculpation of the perpetrator's actions through positioning Rihanna as sharing culpability for the abuse.

Among the most vicious and overtly misogynoiristic responses was the common assumption that Rihanna must have enacted physical violence against Brown first and that he was merely responding to this purported attack. While many liberal white feminist analyses rejected these responses as episodes of victim blaming, Bierra notes the inadequacy of this framework when it comes to the public narratives that are often constructed around Black women victims of violence. She writes, "Characterizing this dynamic as 'victim-blaming,' which salvages a notion of a 'victim' but contends that the victim enabled the violence, misses a key point. Black women who are victims of violence are not simply accused of bringing it upon themselves, they are dis-positioned as its *perpetrator*" (106). Responses that painted Rihanna as the aggressor rather than the victim of violence are in line with the pattern of Black women and girls (both cis and trans) being treated as instigators of violence when they are in fact defending themselves from violence.[10]

To different degrees and in different ways, each of the themes Bierria uncovers engages in narrative complicity surrounding Rihanna's experience of violence, and they all enable the broader structural gaslighting of Black women victims of violence. The responses range from inverting the perpetrator and target of abuse, justifying the abuse, and holding the target of abuse accountable for other instances of men's violence toward women. These responses engage in narrative complicity with a culture that enables abuse by removing accountability from the perpetrator and placing it elsewhere. The sources of narrative complicity here are myriad and diverse. They include white feminism, toxic self-help culture, Black respectability politics, and misogynoir about Afro-Caribbean women that is rooted in the eroticization of Blackness foundational to the white-dominated industry of colonial tourism (Bierria 2012, 105). Bierria's careful analysis of these instances of narrative complicity reveals the many ways that abuse is enabled by community. Indeed, this is the opening point Bierria makes while identifying the role of public imaginaries in the narrative construction of domestic abuse. She writes:

> Domestic violence, despite its brand, is usually not constrained to a domestic sphere or a zone of privacy. It spills over the tenuous boundaries of an abusive relationship, implicating a public who share a knowing, witness the shadows, or sustain the consequences from the violence. Bound to a situation they cannot control, others often attempt to manage the disquiet of domestic violence by crafting overly confident explanations

> about the relationship and investing in the comfort of a coherent narrative about something that defiantly resists coherence. People who share community with individuals within an abusive relationship tend to provide the most primary and impactful response. Yet their own biases, premises, and needs frequently drive their evaluations and choices, which puts demands on how the principal target of violence and the person responsible for a pattern of violence are defined and narrated. (Bierria 2012, 101)

Even at the interpersonal scale, gaslighting and other forms of abuse have always relied on collusion from the target's and perpetrator's communities. At the structural scale, the dynamics are much the same. Ideological justifications for oppression offer "overly confident explanations" that help people feel okay about systems designed to produce violence at the level of populations. Narrative complicity at the structural scale involves removing responsibility for the population-level harms (including individual instances of said harms) from the structures of oppression that produce them. The conjured idea that the *targets* of violence and oppression are actually their *perpetrators* forms a core part of the webs of narrative complicity in structural gaslighting. We see this particular narrative practice across a wide range of domains, both interpersonal and structural.[11] The notion of structural gaslighting is therefore not simply metaphorical. It is a wide-scale application of the exact tactics that abusers rely on and that bystanders and community members enable through narrative complicity.

Structural gaslighting reflects the power of collusion that structures of oppression offer to perpetrators of abuse—both individual and systemic—to narrativize the abuse in ways that enable it to continue without community intervention. Sources of narrative complicity are wide-ranging and not confined to a specific domain or set of rhetorical practices. In the next section, a powerful source of narrative complicity—scientific theorizing—takes center stage.

SCIENCE AND STRUCTURAL GASLIGHTING

Scientific theorizing and its role in naturalizing and entrenching socially determined inequalities is one of the most prolific producers of structural gaslighting. Structures of oppression depend on authoritative justifications for their continued maintenance, and science often provides such authority. Science's ability to stealthily produce justifying stories that make unjust social structures seem natural, normal, and inevitable is central to understanding its role in upholding oppression through structural gaslighting. As I noted in (Berenstain 2020), structural gaslighting "both draws its power from and simultaneously reinforces structural oppression in an unending positive feedback loop." The mythologies and theoretical justifications of structural oppression are established as "common sense" or "common knowledge." In turn, they provide the background framework that reinforces the plausibility and credibility of structural gaslighting. Science and structural oppression are thus enmeshed in their shared production of "common knowledge."

Why is science particularly well positioned to produce structural gaslighting? Science is a collection of social institutions and processes that are embedded within larger sociocultural contexts, conceptual frameworks, and value systems. Certain ways that social values affect science are widely recognized, such as how research funding distribution is influenced by which questions are seen as culturally and commercially valuable, or how institutional goals determine the way scientific results are applied in practical contexts. But beyond these widely known examples of influence, social values permeate each stage of the scientific method. This is especially true in the social sciences, and it is most significant when an area of science addresses socially contentious issues. Gathering of data, observation reporting, interpretation of data, definitions of variables, operationalization of concepts, and inference drawing all involve numerous decisions that rely on a variety of background assumptions.

Many popular and academic understandings of science are limited in the extent to which they acknowledge it as a socially embedded and constructed process. One consequence of this is that both public and academic imaginaries construe scientific framings of socially contentious issues as more objective and well founded than they actually are. The authority that is rightly earned by certain sectors of science can be illegitimately transferred to other areas, subsectors, or research programs. For instance, while the general theoretical framework of evolutionary biology is quite well supported, the additional background assumptions that inform many of the hypotheses in research on the evolutionary psychology of gender differences are relatively less so (Meynell 2021).[12]

For certain socially embedded concepts, there is no way to define them that does not involve value-based choices and decisions. Value-based assumptions cannot be separated out from methodological choices about how to operationalize, define, and measure concepts such as *race, sex,* or *disability*. But few people are versed in the way that social values influence the *internal* process of science, through operationalization of key concepts and evaluation of background assumptions, for instance. When combined with science's presumed authority and objectivity, these factors make science especially well positioned to be a primary producer of the justifying stories and explanations that exemplify structural gaslighting. Ideologically grounded assumptions often provide the background theoretical frameworks against which data are interpreted and scientific hypotheses are confirmed. This creates a feedback loop of scientific studies confirming ideological frameworks that in turn create more scientific studies that rely on the same ideological frameworks.[13]

Science frequently investigates presumed inherent differences between dominant and subordinated groups (Longino 1990). This is one of the central ways that science engages in narrative complicity by justifying structures of oppression. As Shelley Tremain's characterization of Dorothy Roberts's work on "the old bioscience" indicates, the naturalization playbook is a well-developed method of structural gaslighting that obscures the social production of inequalities by ascribing their causes to the presumed biologically defective features of the bodies of those subordinated:

> First, the old biosocial science approach separates nature from nurture in order to locate the origins of social inequalities in inherent traits rather than imposed societal structures; second the old biosocial science postulates that social inequalities are reproduced in the bodies, especially the wombs, of socially disadvantaged people rather than reinvented through unjust ideologies and institutions; third, the old bioscience identifies problems that stem from social inequality as derived from the threats that oppressed people's biology itself poses to society rather than from structural barriers and state violence imposed upon oppressed people; and fourth, the old bioscience endeavors to intervene and fix perceived biological deficits in the bodies of oppressed people rather than end the structural violence that dehumanizes them and maintains an unjust social order. (Shelley Tremain on Dorothy Roberts, *Foucault and Feminist Philosophy of Disability* [2017, 4])

This theoretical strategy has adherents across many areas of the biosciences, as such tactics pervade research into sex differences (e.g., in hormones, sexual behavior, intelligence) and the relationship between gender and sexuality (especially research that frames transgender experiences in terms of psychiatric disorder). These tactics are foundational both to racial science and to disability bioethics, two interlinked areas that aim to target and often eliminate the presumed intrinsic deficits that are projected onto racialized and disabled populations. I turn next to one of the formidable giants of the "old bioscience," namely, scientific racism.

Scientific Racism

> They are forced to labor, and yet commonly are not even adequately nourished. It is said that they tolerate hunger easily, that they can live for three days on a portion of a European meal; that however little they eat or sleep, they are always equally tough, equally strong, and equally fit for labor. How can men in whom there rests any feeling of humanity adopt such views? How do they presume to attempt to legitimize by such reasoning those oppressions that spring solely from their thirst for gold?[14]
>
> —Georges-Louis Leclerc, Comte de Buffon,
> *Histoire Naturelle*, 1749

The tradition of scientific racism has long been essential to the US project of racecraft. Scientific racism is a complex and multifaceted set of practices, many of which exemplify structural gaslighting. Much scientific racism consists in naturalizing socially produced inequalities among racialized groups by postulating their origins in biological differences among "races." These "scientific" explanations often entail that contingent social hierarchies are in fact necessary and inevitable results of the natural order. They cover over the causes and effects of white supremacy and disappear the role of structural racism in producing inequities like racial health disparities. As I noted in (Berenstain 2020), "Conceptually severing individual instances and broader patterns of discrimination, violence, and oppression from the larger structures that produce them is a linchpin of structural gaslighting." Negative health outcomes for victims of racism become something that follows from their inherent state of being, an inevitable consequence of the natural order of things.

Consider the claims of so-called "slave medicine" and the work its practitioners and ideological proponents did to buttress the institution of slavery. Nineteenth-century enslaver and physician Josiah Nott contended that slavery was morally permissible because craniometry empirically established that forced labor and bondage benefited African and African-descended peoples. He wrote that "the negro attains his greatest perfection, physical and moral, and also greatest longevity, in a state of slavery" (Nott 1847, 281). Dr. Samuel Cartwright also created scientific justifications for racial oppression by purporting to develop empirical methods showing that African-descended peoples achieved optimal health in bondage. After finding differences in lung capacity between white people and enslaved Africans and African-descended people, Cartwright (1851) claimed the differences were innate and referenced them in his arguments against the abolition of slavery. Specifically, he suggested that not subjecting enslaved African and African-descended peoples to forced manual labor would result in inadequate oxygen reaching their brains of because of their innately lower lung capacity. Nott's and Cartwright's work demonstrate the historically tight connection between scientific racism and structural gaslighting. The function of scientific racism has always been to justify socially maintained structures of racist oppression by suggesting they are borne of a natural biological hierarchy.

Purportedly scientific explanations for racial differences rooted in the supposed inferiority of Black bodies have long been a hallmark of scientific racism, and they continue to be found in a variety of its contemporary manifestations.[15] While some of today's proponents of scientific racism are as explicitly white supremacist as Nott and Cartwright, individual researchers need not consciously endorse racism and white supremacy for their work to uphold scientific racism. Their work can still serve to promote and maintain structural racism regardless of their individual beliefs or commitments. Indeed, plenty of "well-intentioned" research aimed at closing racial health gaps traffics in scientific racism. In the next section, a case study of the FDA's approval of BiDil as a race-based drug illustrates how interventions into racial health inequities that purportedly aim to promote Black health can still do the nefarious work of structural gaslighting.

Naturalizing Racist Health Inequities: The Case of BiDil

> At work here is an appropriation of race as reified in the BiDil story to serve larger political agendas aimed at transmuting health disparities, rooted in social and economic inequality, into mere health differences, rooted in biology and genetics.
>
> —Jonathan Kahn (2005)

In her (2011b) article "What's Wrong with Race-Based Medicine?" Dorothy Roberts shows how the FDA's unprecedented approval of BiDil as a race-based drug formed a new chapter in the long legacy of scientific racism. A multitude of factors reflect scientific racism at the heart of the BiDil case. The drug company NitroMed's campaign and the FDA's resulting decision 1) presumed a biological/genetic reality of racial differences without evidence, 2) relied on inadequate science, 3) suggested biology was the cause of social inequality, 4) was motivated by the capitalist pursuit of profit, 5) indicated that results from drug trials done on Black patients could not be universalized to all people, and 6) located the causes of health problems in Black communities within Black bodies rather than within the environment structured by white supremacy. Roberts's analysis of the scientific racism in this decision process reveals the role that structural gaslighting played in both NitroMed's campaign for FDA approval and the FDA's justification for is decision. It also illustrates the positive feedback loop between structural gaslighting and the structures of oppression it relies on and reinforces.

Before 2005, the FDA had never approved a drug for a race-specific use. When BiDil was approved, it was approved not as a *generalized* treatment for congestive heart failure but as a treatment specifically for *African American congestive heart failure*—despite the fact that BiDil had not been *designed* as a race-specific drug. In fact, BiDil was not a newly developed drug at all but merely a combination of two well-known generic drugs that were already widely in use as treatment for heart failure, isosorbide dinitrate and hydralazine hydrochloride. Neither was BiDil a pharmacogenomic drug—a pharmaceutical specifically designed to work with an individual's particular genetic makeup, which could theoretically target a genotype that people with recent African ancestry are statistically more likely to have than those without. One might reasonably presume that a drug approved specifically for African American congestive heart failure would, at the very least, have been shown to be *more effective* in African American populations than in other populations. However, this was not the case; such a hypothesis was never tested. The trial that tested BiDil's efficacy, known as the African American Heart Failure Trial (A-HeFT), included only 1,050 self-identified African American patients. The drug was found to be extremely effective, increasing survival by 43 percent and reducing hospitalizations by 39 percent. But because the efficacy of BiDil was not tested on any non-Black patients, no comparisons could be made about its rate of effectiveness across populations.

Despite the total lack of empirical evidence for different rates of efficacy between racial groups, NitroMed relied on presumptions of biological race differences as its speculative explanation for the drug's efficacy in self-identified Black patients. NitroMed's press release for BiDil stated, "Observed racial disparities in mortality and therapeutic response rates in black patients may be due in part to ethnic differences in the underlying pathophysiology of heart failure" (Roberts 2011b, 4). The company made a statement, unsupported by empirical evidence, that the difference in death rates between Black and non-Black patients with heart failure might be due to differences *in the mechanisms of heart failure itself* between differently racialized groups. In other words, maybe Black people experiencing heart failure die at higher rates than white people experiencing heart failure do because *Black people's hearts work differently than white people's hearts.*

NitroMed's tactic engaged in structural gaslighting by i) obscuring the structural connection between white supremacy and African American heart failure and ii) positing an unfounded "biological" cause for a health disparity that is actually produced by numerous dimensions of anti-Black racism. The company's structural gaslighting further played into the long legacy of scientific racism in a number of ways. For one, NitroMed stood to make an extraordinary profit off of marketing BiDil specifically as a drug for Black populations. NitroMed's patent for the race-neutral version of the drug was set to expire in less than ten years, and an FDA approval for BiDil's race-specific purpose would afford NitroMed an additional thirteen years of patent-protected profits.[16] Relying on inadequate or nonexistent empirical data to confirm presumptions about racial differences produced within a white supremacist society has a long history in the United States—especially to uphold profitable forms of racial oppression such as slavery, the school-to-prison pipeline, and other forms of racial capitalism.[17] The kind of racialized medicine that NitroMed was promoting was simply a repackaged variant of racial capitalism, which would allow white-owned companies to profit economically from a Black underclass, in this case one characterized by their alleged physical inferiority.

The presumed inferiority of Black bodies that NitroMed exploited to win FDA approval for marketing BiDil as a race-based drug reflects the structural gaslighting at the heart of this process. NitroMed argued that since BiDil had been tested only on Black patients, the data licensed its approval only for Black patients. But, as Roberts emphasizes, "This kind of logic had never resulted in a racial indication before. In the past, the FDA has had no problem generalizing clinical trials involving white people to approve drugs for everyone. That is because it believes that white bodies function like human bodies." This is an excellent illustration of the methodological component of structural gaslighting. By affirming the idea that data from trials run only on white patients could be universalized while trials run only on Black patients could not, the FDA licensed different *inferential relations* between data derived from Black bodies and data collected from white ones. Roberts writes, "By approving BiDil only for use in black patients, the FDA emphasized the supposed distinctive, and substandard, quality of black bodies. It sent the message that black people cannot represent all of humanity as well as white people can" (2011b, 3). This two-track inferential system and its bifurcated methodological mandate—a form of what Ruíz (2020, 705) terms *epistemic apartheid*—tacitly promotes a metaphysics of biological deviancy for Black bodies. This metaphysics provides the methodological barrier blocking inferences from data about how a drug works in Black bodies to conclusions about how it works in human bodies generally.

As Roberts argues, in response to NitroMed's empirically baseless campaign of scientific racism, the FDA could have made one of two non-racist decisions: Either they could have rejected NitroMed's request for BiDil's approval altogether, or they could have approved its use as a treatment for congestive heart failure in all populations. This latter option would have made the drug available to the vulnerable populations who were most in need of it without reinforcing the baseless and harmful public perception that racial health disparities are caused by biological racial differences between groups. Instead of taking this route, the FDA chose to legitimize the empirically ungrounded speculation that the higher rates of death from heart failure among Black patients was reflective of an underlying uniqueness in the biology and mechanics of Black heart failure, a move that structurally gaslights Black populations by suggesting that the deleterious health effects they experience as a result of white supremacy and anti-Black racism are actually caused by their own physiological inferiority.

The FDA's endorsement of NitroMed's speculation is emblematic of structural gaslighting. A number of social factors produced by white supremacy contribute to the higher rates of congestive heart failure that Black patients experience. Hypertension is one of the primary predictors of heart failure, and stress is a major contributor to hypertension (Dimsdale 2008). Because of white supremacy, Black populations experience a range of stressors that are more severe than those experienced by white populations. These include, among many others, the stress of racial discrimination (Williams 2018), greater exposure to pollutants due to environmental racism (Cheeseman et al. 2022, Taylor 2014), higher rates of eviction and housing precarity (Bluthenthal 2023), greater vulnerability to sexual violence and a lower chance of legal redress (Armstrong, Gleckman-Krut, and Johnson 2018; Ritchie 2012), a widening racial wealth gap (Aladangady and Forde 2021), and the ongoing trauma of publicly consumed spectacles of Black death (Wright 2018, Mowatt 2018). Black Americans also have more restricted access to quality health care than do white Americans (Dickamn et al. 2022, Rooks et al. 2008). Yet NitroMed's knee-jerk presumption that differential rates of death due to heart failure among Black and white populations must be due to underlying pathophysiological differences in heart function, and the FDA's decision to approve BiDil as a race-specific drug on the basis of this assumption, obscures and deflects from this reality. It suggests that the solution to negative health outcomes brought on or exacerbated by white supremacy need not involve changing white supremacy itself; its effects can simply be treated with individual pharmaceutical prescriptions. As Roberts points out, it also attributes the cause of a socially produced racial health disparity to intrinsic failures of Black bodies. Suggesting that Black people are *preternaturally* more vulnerable to heart failure than non-Black people are is just the sort of sleight of hand that deflects attention from the real causes of racial health disparities—namely, racism—in an impressive feat of racecraft.

That "structural gaslighting is not identified in terms of any specific intention or goal of the perpetrator but by the function of its operation" (Berenstain 2020, 735) is illustrated by the example of Esteban Burchard's work on why Puerto Rican children are especially susceptible to developing asthma. We know that a range of environmental factors related to the presence of allergens and irritants contributes to the likelihood of developing asthma. Exposure to pests, air pollution, and insect droppings are contributing factors. We also know that Black and Puerto Rican children have especially high rates of asthma—13 percent and 19 percent, respectively, compared to only 8 percent of white children. An NYU study that tracked exposure to air pollution using monitors attached to the backpacks of asthmatic schoolchildren living in the South Bronx found that the children "who were twice as likely to attend a school near a highway as children in other parts of the city, were exposed to fine-particle pollution from diesel exhaust (a known asthma trigger) that exceeded EPA standards" (Roberts 2011a, 109). Factors such as environmental racism play a clear role in determining the level of air pollution and environmental toxicity that differently racialized groups are exposed to. A recent study found that race was a much stronger predictor than income for levels of exposure to environmental pollution (Paolella et al 2018). Another found that while people of color are exposed to greater levels of fine particulate matter than white people, white people were *responsible* for creating more air pollution than people of color (Tessum et al 2019).[18] The study found that "white people enjoy a so-called pollution advantage. They bear the burden of 17 percent less air pollution than is generated by their own consumption. Blacks and Hispanics, on the other hand, experience a "pollution burden." They face 56 percent and 63 percent more exposure, respectively, than is caused by their consumption" (Stanley-Becker 2019). The physical landscape sculpted by white supremacy plays an obvious and central role in structurally producing racial disparities in autoimmune conditions such as asthma. Nonetheless, Burchard's research engages in structural gaslighting by attributing racial differences in such conditions to genetic differences, which Burchard postulates account for different rates of asthma among differently racialized groups. Specifically, he conjectures that there must be a "distinctive genetic variant" that Puerto Ricans have, which predisposes them to asthma. He conjectures that this imagined genetic variant derives from their recent African ancestry and thus also explains high asthma rates among African Americans.

To be clear, Burchard does recognize that environmental factors play some role in producing these discrepancies, and he intends for his work to address and remedy these problematic disparities. But regardless of Burchard's intention in pursuing genetic explanations of racial disparities that we know to be caused, at least in part, by environmental racism, his work serves to deflect from the socially produced landscape that benefits white children while harming Black and Puerto Rican children and normalizes Black and Puerto Rican children having heightened rates of asthma. The hypothesis of genetic predisposition to asthma based on recent African ancestry makes higher rates of asthma in such communities appear to be natural, normal, and inevitable. And it averts attention from the role structural oppression plays in creating these disparities. This shows that merely giving lip service to the fact that structural oppression plays *some* role in producing a relevant pattern is not enough to preclude one's proffered explanation of said pattern from producing structural gaslighting.[19]

As this investigation into the relationship between scientific racism and structural gaslighting demonstrates, the practice of naturalizing socially created disparities that trace back to structural oppression is a key tactic of structural gaslighting. Naturalization is an especially central structural gaslighting tactic of ableism, a structure whose roots are deeply intertwined with those of scientific racism (Metzl 2009). I turn now to an investigation of the naturalization and medicalization of disability as a form of structural gaslighting.

Ableism and the Medicalization of Disability

Shelley Tremain's important and insightful conceptualization of *disability as an apparatus of power* reveals how ableist ideologies, including the individualization, naturalization, and medicalization of disability, are forms of structural gaslighting. Tremain rejects the presumption that there are "natural" or prediscursive ontological components to disability, arguing that disability is a "contingent social phenomenon" that is metaphysically inextricable from cultural and historical context and that it is an apparatus of power in which all people are implicated. Her view is thus deeply at odds with those who take disability to be either a biological trait possessed by individuals or a feature of constructed environments that gives social significance to "impairments," which are themselves construed as natural biological traits that exist transculturally and transhistorically. Just as racecraft transforms collective acts and upholding of *racism* into intrinsic features of racialized persons, the apparatus of disability transforms the collective action of *disablement* into the intrinsic biological features of disabled persons.

Tremain contends that the apparatus of disability differentially subjects peoples "to relatively recent forms of power on the basis of constructed perceptions and interpretations of (inter alia) bodily structure, appearance, style and pace of motility, mode of communication, emotional expression, mode of food intake, and cognitive character" (23). All such forms of human diversity are shaped by myriad social factors and cultural understandings of their significance. She writes:

> To understand disability as an apparatus is to conceive of it as a far-reaching and systemic matrix of power that contributes to, is inseparable from, and reinforces other apparatuses of historical force relations. On this understanding, disability is not a metaphysical substrate, a natural, biological category, or a characteristic that only certain individuals embody and possess, but rather is a historically contingent network of force

relations in which everyone is implicated and entangled and in relation to which everyone occupies a position. (2017, 22)

Tremain's account is particularly well suited to capturing the intersectional nature of ableist systems of oppression and their corresponding reliance on structural gaslighting, as it recognizes that the historical force relations that the apparatus of disability comprises are inseparable from the network of force relations that make up settler colonial white supremacist capitalist cis-heteropatriarchy. The apparatus of disability construes disabled people as naturally inferior and defective in numerous ways, most of which have racialized, gendered, and sexualized dimensions.

An important feature of structural gaslighting is that it is defined by the functions it performs within systems of oppression. Another key feature of structural gaslighting is that the mythologies and storytelling that produce it ultimately uphold and justify pervasive and ubiquitous forms of structural violence while simultaneously disappearing said violence from view. Tremain's conceptualization of disability is a radical anti-gaslighting tool in the fight against ableism. Like Fields and Fields's conception of racecraft, Tremain's picture reveals how ableism's sleight of hand transforms the systems created and the actions perpetrated into features of disabled persons themselves, disappearing from view both the apparatus of disability and the non-disabled persons who benefit from it, a paradigmatic act of structural gaslighting.

The function of naturalizing stories of disability, such as those offered by the medical model and the British Social Model (BSM), is to construct disability as an undesirable defect and to license interventions aimed at eliminating both disability and disabled people.[20] Tremain critiques the medical model of disability and the British Social Model (BSM) for naturalizing as "static" the conceptual objects that emerge from them: disability in the former case, and impairment in the latter (86). By naturalizing these conceptual objects while also construing them as inherently defective and undesirable, these models of disability construe disabled people "as a problem to be rectified or eliminated" (Tremain 2020).

The social and political interventions that the ableist structural gaslighting tactic of naturalization licenses are eugenicist and, in many cases, exterminationist forms of structural violence. These include forced institutionalization and incarceration (Appleman 2018); forced sterilization; invasive medically unnecessary surgeries (Smith 2012); physical and sexual abuse (Singer and McMahan 2017); denial of adequate health care and quality of life; work with pay below minimum wage (US Dept of Labor 2021); use of solitary confinement as punishment in public schools (Richards, Cohen, and Chavis 2019); discrimination in education, employment (Robert 2003), and housing; exclusion from community and public life; and state-sponsored and medically promoted death (Parliament of Canada, Bill C-7).

Consider the relationship between the structural gaslighting of ableist ideologies of naturalization and Illinois public schools' use of a carceral punishment system involving placing children who act out in solitary confinement. Though the isolation rooms are purportedly used only as a last resort for physical aggression, a ProPublica report found that they were frequently used for minor nonthreatening disciplinary infractions like disobedience and insubordination. Most of the students isolated in solitary confinement are disabled. While some school districts ban this form of punishment, they often funnel disabled students to schools that do not. The report explains, "A few school districts in Illinois prohibit seclusion, including Chicago Public Schools, which banned it 11 years ago. But these districts often send students with disabilities to schools that do use it, such as those operated by most of Illinois' special-education districts" (Richards, Cohen, and Chavis 2019).

The use of isolation and imprisonment as punishment for disabled students is exactly the sort of abusive practice that we ought to expect within an ableist society that uses structural gaslighting to construe disabled people as biologically inferior and thus less than human. Scott Danforth, a professor at Chapman University who studies the education of disabled children, ascribes the lack of concern about the abusive practice of isolation to the fact that it is primarily disabled children who are the targets of its abuse. "Danforth said seclusion goes unexamined because it largely affects students with disabilities. To put children in time-out rooms, "you really have to believe that you're dealing with people who are deeply defective. And that's what the staff members tell each other. . . . You can do it because of who you're doing it to.'" (Richards, Cohen, and Chavis 2019). In this case, ableist structural gaslighting portrays disabled students as both incapable of responding to and unworthy of compassionate and humane treatment because of being inherently defective. The work of structural gaslighting is apparent when abusive and exploitative treatment is justified by reference to "who you're doing it to." This tactic is evident across patterns of justification of ableist abuse from Goodwill's practice of paying disabled workers pennies an hour to hang clothing at their stores to Applied Behavior Analysis (ABA) practitioners justifying the use of electric shocks on autistic children as a form of "treatment" and "therapy."

Ableism's structural gaslighting is what facilitates the use of harmful treatments, interventions, and even so-called "cures" for autistic children—another manifestation of ableism's eliminationist logic. ABA specifically involves aiming to replace autistic behaviors with socially acceptable ones regardless of whether the autistic behaviors cause harm to the child or others. Many interventions aimed at making autistic children easier to manage are harmful and abusive. ABA is often one of the only autistic "therapies" covered by medical insurance. Some forms of ABA aim at punishing children (with the use of "aversives") for displaying autistic modes of behavior and cognition and rewarding them for suppressing their natural forms of self-expression and emotional regulation, including self-stimulating or "stimming" behaviors such as rocking or hand-flapping. These practices are rooted in structural gaslighting narratives that i) obscure the fact that these are merely behaviors that fall outside the contingent and arbitrary realm of what is deemed socially acceptable in this particular moment, and ii) disconnect the social harms of engaging in autistic behaviors from the ableism that stigmatizes, degrades, and devalues these behaviors.

ABA is rooted in a theoretical framework of radical behaviorism, framing behaviors as produced solely by external stimuli and eliding thoughts and emotions (Sandoval-Norton, Shkedy, and Shkedy 2021). This framework ignores and even denies the existence of specifically autistic subjectivities. Ivar Lovaas, one of the founders of ABA, was known for his belief that autistic people are not really people.[21] In a 1974 interview with *Psychology Today*, Lovaas said, "You have a person in the physical sense—they have hair, a nose and a mouth—but they are not people in the psychological sense" (Chance 1974). The founder of ABA sees autistic people not as human beings but as physical shells inside of which the ABA therapists must do the work of constructing a person where otherwise there is none. This construction often takes place through abuse. ABA interventions have involved forced eye contact, forced compliance and obedience, and forced exposure therapy to stimuli and situations that cause experiences of anxiety and even terror. "Aversives" include the use of slapping, pinching, electric shock, noxious odors, and physical restraints (Dawson 2004). Sessions can last up to eight hours and sometimes involve denying breaks to the autistic child even when they are experiencing sensory or emotional overload.

The practices of and justifications for abusive ABA interventions reveal how the process of structural gaslighting plays out from the ableist degradations of autistic ways of being to the abuses that ableism's violently dehumanizing ideology necessitates. ABA sets autistic children up to accept abuse (Lynch 2019). This is because it teaches compliance and obedience above all, including when experiencing unwanted physical touch and other boundary violations, and it encourages children to ignore and suppress their feelings of discomfort, overstimulation, and pain. As one autistic adult reported about their experience of childhood ABA, "The focus on compliance made it harder for me to say no to people who hurt me later" (McGill and Robinson 2020). This is an example of how ableist structural gaslighting, which is itself abusive, enables further abuse by limiting targets' ability to identify and resist abuse. Others described how ABA "created internalised ableism, self-loathing" and produced long-term PTSD. The parallels between ableism's large-scale structural gaslighting and the kind of gaslighting used to cover abuse at the interpersonal scale are apparent. In each case, the perpetrator explains why the abuse is not only justified but is actually *for the victim's own good*. As emphasized in the discussion on narrative complicity, these reasons are endorsed by the broader public. And, just as in gaslighting at the interpersonal scale, ableist structural gaslighting can encourage its targets' compliance with further abuse.

Philosophy and Ableist Gaslighting

Revealing policies of structural violence as socially imposed and therefore reversible, rather than as natural consequences of biology, is a necessary step in the fight to end ableist structural gaslighting and the widespread harms it causes. As Tremain (2017, 2020) has demonstrated, professional philosophy is deeply complicit in the promotion of ableist ideologies that produce, justify, and disappear from view pervasive violence in the lives of disabled people. This complicity traverses across diverse topics and areas, including political theory, development ethics, and white feminist philosophy. The capability approach to justice and human dignity (Sen 1999, Nussbaum 2003, 2007), for instance, has been critiqued for relying on and promoting various forms of ableism (Kittay 1999, Montgomery 2001). The approach conceives of human welfare in terms of certain objectively construed capabilities to which a person must have access to live a life of flourishing. Since many of these capabilities are ones that are held solely by non-disabled people, the result is often a theory that denies disabled people the possibility of flourishing and produces structural gaslighting by obscuring the role that the apparatus of disability plays in both producing disability and preventing the flourishing of those it disables.

The literature on disability and adaptive preferences, to which the capabilities approach gives rise, is an example of professional philosophy's structural gaslighting of disabled people. A foundational assumption of that literature is that positive or neutral attitudes reflected in the testimony of disabled people about the quality of their lives should be treated as an "adaptive preference" and thus discounted from bearing on the question of whether, all else being equal, disability makes one's life less worth living (Barnes 2009). The suggestion is that disabled people can't be trusted about how disability affects their quality of life, because they can be expected to develop subjective views and preferences that make their undesirable bodies and lives more bearable.

Interestingly, we do not see parallel alternate views considered, such as the idea that disabled people who testify that their lives are worse off and that they wish they had not been disabled might feel that way because of pervasive ableist structural gaslighting, or that expressing a preference for a non-disabled life is an "adaptive preference" to living in a deeply ableist society that labels one irrational for preferring or feeling neutral about a disabled bodymind. Nor do we see the possibility considered that *non-disabled* people's testimony about their quality of life being better than disabled people's might itself be an adaptive preference within an ableist society. The "adaptive preferences" justification for explaining away the testimony of disabled people who reject the idea that their bodyminds make them inherently worse off than non-disabled people structurally gaslights disabled people. It does so by obscuring the relationship between ableism and disabled people's experiences of their lives. This literature paints disabled ways of being as inherently worse off than non-disabled ways in order to locate the cause of disabled people's suffering within their own bodies and minds, rather than within the structures of ableism that produce it. It then goes a step further by telling them that their evaluative judgments of their own lives and experiences simply can't be trusted—gaslighting at its finest.

It is further important to recognize that the harms of philosophy's ableist structural gaslighting go beyond the epistemic to include, for instance, the promotion of physical and sexual violence against disabled people. In 2017, Peter Singer, one of the world's most famous philosophers, joined forces with Jeff McMahan in the *New York Times* to defend a white woman's repeated rape of a disabled Black man. Justifying grievous violence against disabled people wasn't new territory for Singer, who is well-known for arguing that killing disabled infants is morally permissible as long as they count as "severely" disabled on his arbitrarily determined personal scale.[22] For this reason, Singer is considered by many disability justice activists to be a proponent of genocide against disabled people (McBryde Johnson 2003). In their pro-rape op-ed, Singer and McMahan (2017) argue for a view that permits sexual abuse of intellectually disabled people who cannot articulate the harms done to them through rape.

The essay engages with the conviction of Anna Stubblefield, former chair of the Rutgers-Newark Philosophy Department, for sexual assault. Stubblefield, a white woman, performed "facilitated communication" with a disabled, nonverbal Black man with cerebral palsy who was the older brother of one of Stubblefield's students. Facilitated communication is a pseudoscientific practice by which a verbal person "determines" (i.e., either decides or unconsciously projects) what a nonverbal person is attempting to communicate by stabilizing the disabled person's wrist or hovering the disabled person's finger over a keyboard to infer which letters they are trying to point to (Lilienfeld et al. 2014).[23] Even if facilitated communication were a scientifically grounded therapy, it should be fairly obvious that such an enormous power disparity would not allow for the possibility of sexual consent between the disabled person and their facilitated communicator. This would follow from the fact that the facilitated communicator would be the *sole link* between the disabled person's inner thoughts and their ability to express themselves to the outside world, creating an unmitigated level of power over the disabled person that is not only ripe for abuse but that would *attract* abusers to the "profession."[24] Nonetheless, Stubblefield claimed that her client, through facilitated communication, expressed a desire for sexual intimacy with her and later said that he was in love with her. Stubblefield proceeded to repeatedly sexually assault him, including during a time in which she kept his family unaware of his whereabouts.[25]

Singer and McMahan defend Stubblefield's "innocence" and frame her repeated sexual assaults as genuine acts of love.[26] They also deny the possibility that the person she victimized could have experienced harm from her assaults or that the assaults could have resulted in anything other than pleasure for him. They write, "On the assumption that he is profoundly cognitively impaired, therefore, it seems that if Stubblefield wronged or harmed him, it must have been in a way that he is incapable of understanding and that *affected his experience only pleasurably*" (emphasis added). The article indulges in numerous grotesque rape myths (e.g., he probably enjoyed it; he would have resisted if it were really rape since "he was capable of struggling to resist"; "he surely would have found a way to express his hostility to Stubblefield on that occasion or subsequently," etc.) that likely would not have passed muster with the editorial review board had they been applied to a case involving anyone but a white woman rapist and a disabled person of color as the target of sexual abuse.[27]

Interestingly, Singer and McMahan are so deeply committed to dehumanizing disabled people of color that they fail to notice that their view *also* commits them to the moral permissibility of sexually abusing infants and other young children who cannot readily articulate the harms of abuse and may even experience pleasure from it. It is striking (though not surprising) that when given the choice between i) not providing cover for child sexual abusers and ii) promoting sexual violence against disabled people, Singer and McMahan choose the latter. The article's title, "Who Is the Victim in the Anna Stubblefield Case?," is supremely fitting for a work emblematic of gaslighting, as one of its most common tactics involves reversing the victim and the abuser to frame the abuser as the *real* victim. Singer and McMahan engage in structural gaslighting by arguing that certain groups of disabled people simply can't be sexually assaulted. Further, they place the locus of this impossibility in disabled people's purportedly inferior bodyminds, covering over the ableist structures and their beneficiaries that in fact place disabled people, particularly disabled people of color, among those who are the *most vulnerable* to sexual assault—especially by those who are trusted with their care, as is exemplified by the Stubblefield case. The narrative complicity of the *New York Times* is evident in the fact that it was more plausible to their editorial board that disabled people of color deserve dehumanization and abuse than that the newspaper should decline to publish such racist, poorly reasoned rape apology.

While Singer and McMahan's rape apology treatise is an extreme example of the violent ableism and white supremacy that philosophers promote through structural gaslighting, less explicitly violent instances of structural gaslighting in ableist philosophy also promote structural violence against disabled people. Much academic philosophy suggests disabled people cannot truly have lives worth living and encourages the discounting of disabled voices from philosophical discussions. In an ableist society in which eugenicist policies continue to thrive, such rhetoric serves only to further entrench the justifications for disability discrimination and elimination that are already present within mainstream liberal and conservative political movements and the promotion of structural violence and exterminationist practices against disabled people.

Disableization and Dispossession

> To analyze disability as an event, that is, would involve determination of the process of (what we might call) "disableization," whereby the apparatus of disability variously incorporates a growing number of people's lives, through a multiplying number of means and techniques, in order to distinguish certain subjects from others, identify them, improve them, render them more productive, eliminate them, and govern them in a host of other ways.
>
> —Shelley Tremain (2017, 96)

On Tremain's account, subjects *are made* disabled and impaired by the apparatus of disability, which includes "an accelerating array of social policies, administrative decisions, medical and scientific classifications and examinations, techniques of surveillance and registration, cultural representations, aesthetic practices, and academic research" (2017, 96). Tremain's apparatus conception of disability involves analyzing the processes that produce subjects *as disabled* and *impaired* rather than construing disability and impairment as something subjects "have." Her concept of *disableization* helps illuminate the role that the production of disability plays in facilitating forms of structural violence such as mass incarceration and settler colonial land theft.[28] Structural gaslighting occurs through both the process of disableization as well as through the coverup of said process through the naturalization of disability and the ascription of disability to biological features of people's bodyminds.

Incarceration has long been a central strategy of managing disabled populations in settler colonial societies, as has disableizing racialized and Indigenous populations so as to manage them and remove them from their land. In 1898, Congress passed a bill licensing funding for the creation of the Canton Indian Insane Asylum in North Dakota. Also called the Hiawatha Insane Asylum, the institution forcibly committed and imprisoned more than 350 Native Americans, at least 121 of whom died or were killed at the facility. Ella Callow, director of the Office of Disability Access and Compliance at UC-Berkeley, incisively summarizes the relationship between the US government's disableization of Native Americans and its foundational projects of settler capitalist land dispossession—a relationship obscured through structural gaslighting. She explains,

> My family comes out of Indian country and, you know, for us, it's always kind of like, it's always a money grab. They're always trying to make money off of Indians. That's what it always is. It's take the land, take the water, get whatever you can get. And just one more thing that can be gotten is bodies—literal bodies that people make money off of. You label them, you call them something, put them somewhere, and you can make money from them.
>
> Every time Indigenous people get taken off their land, removed from their community and put away, there is a chance that that's one less person making it back, having a family who will have treaty rights they can enforce, who will have descendants who have treaty rights they can enforce, who can hold the government to its obligations to Native people. (Brice 2020)

Callow reveals the intentional and purposive nature of the settler administrative systems that trade in disability and mental-illness narratives so as to eliminate Native peoples in order to eliminate their claims to land. In 1913, one Lakota man was sent to St. Elizabeth's Hospital, another federally funded psychiatric institution, after he was accused of stealing horses, which he denied, and diagnosed with "horse-stealing mania." He was later transferred to Hiawatha, which had a policy requiring the forced sterilization of those imprisoned there. The intertwining of settler colonialism and ableist structural gaslighting provides justification for eugenicist projects of eliminating "problem" populations, such as those who either require community care that the settler government does not want to provide or who have claims to land that the settler government does not want to honor. The forced institutionalization of Native people also provided an economic lifeline to the white settler population in Canton, who sued to keep the institution open after it was finally closed in 1933 following extensive documentation of the facility's abusive and inhumane conditions.

The production of disability for Native populations to facilitate their violent displacement and dispossession through incarceration is also evident in the history of residential boarding schools in the United States and Canada. These institutions were not places of learning and education so much as they were carceral spaces for abuse, punishment, and the promotion of cultural genocide through forced assimilation. The legacy of kidnapping and removal for the purposes of assimilation persists today in the contemporary practice of removing Native children from their homes because of a parent's purported "mental illness" and placing them in non-Native homes. In South Dakota, for instance, a Native child is eleven times more likely to be placed within the foster system than is a white child. Despite the Indian Act's recognition that Native children in the foster system should be placed with Native families, Callow notes that when the child-welfare issue is framed in terms of a Native parent's disability or mental illness, that tends to be treated as superseding the rights of the child to be raised in a home that is in line with their tribal or cultural identity (Brice 2020). That Native children are often placed in non-Native (and especially white) homes when Native foster homes are available reflects that a continuation of the legacy of forced removal for the purposes of eliminating a people through the attempted elimination of their culture. The structural gaslighting here is multidimensional. It inheres both in the apparatus that disableizes Native parents and in the naturalizing narratives that obscure the non-accidental connection between settler colonialism and the production of disability for Native populations.

The apparatus of disability within settler colonial societies thus cannot be disentangled from the settler colonial project of Indigenous land dispossession that requires the elimination of Native peoples for its completion, both of which require structural gaslighting to accomplish. The settler logic of elimination underwrites the desire to extinguish a range of diverse lifeways and forms of disabled existence. Extinguishing non-neurotypical behaviors often takes the form of coercing, abusing, and incarcerating the people who engage in them. The effort to extinguish autistic lifeways, for instance, to make an autistic person become "indistinguishable" from a neurotypical person is rooted in much the same logic as General Richard Pratt's call to "Kill the Indian, Save the Man." This admonition was the motto of the residential Carlisle School, where Native children were punished with abuse for speaking their language and were taught white Christian ways of being to replace their own, as they were forced to cut their hair and wear clothing styles consonant with settler aesthetics. Residential schools formed a backbone of the cultural assimilationist tactics that underwrite settler colonial genocide. In a range of cases, forced compliance and incarceration underlie the effort to replace ways of being that threaten settler colonial ableist white supremacist cis-heteropatriarchy with those that do not.

Concluding Remarks

Structural gaslighting occupies of range of rhetorical styles, domains, narratives, practices, and strategies. It can be explicit and blatant or subtle and stealth. It can come from widely accessible popular discourse or from within the protected walls of the ivory tower. What should be clear from the range of cases considered here, however, is that structural gaslighting is not metaphorical, and neither are its harms. The epistemic rarely remains solely epistemic. It reaches into every aspect of our lives. It underlies the ideologies that many of us are so steeped in that we don't even realize they are there. It constructs our systems of violence, and it disappears them from view just as quickly as it builds them. Structural gaslighting facilitates and covers up real material abuse in people's lives, including sexual violence, incarceration, forced sterilization, land theft, and state-sponsored death. Those concerned with disrupting the material harms caused by structural oppression ought not ignore the essential role that stealth epistemic tactics like structural gaslighting play in upholding the systems that produce them.

Notes

1. The goal of the structural gaslighting surrounding Israel's current US-backed genocide of the Palestinian people, for instance, does not lie in convincing Palestinians that they deserve unmitigated cruelty, dehumanization, torture, sexual violence, starvation, and mass execution. Rather, it lies in convincing *those who have the power to stop the genocide* that such heinous atrocities and crimes against humanity are not only justified and deserved but necessary for the preservation of "Western civilization."

2. For the account of structural violence on which I am relying, see Ruíz (2024).

3. As I previously emphasized, "Individuals, institutions, political systems, and social groups engage in structural gaslighting, regardless of whether they intend to do so, when they invoke oppressive ideologies, disappear or obscure the actual causes and mechanisms of oppression, and conceptually sever acts of oppression from the structures that produce them" (Berenstain 2020).

4. For a further unpacking of this idea, see Dotson's "Bad Magic" in (Berenstain, Dotson, Paredes, Ruíz, and Silva 2022).

5. For one of the most vivid origins of the "Matriarch" image, see Daniel Patrick Moynihan's 1965 report by the Office of Planning and Policy, US Department of Labor—"The Negro Family: A Case for National Action." The report offers many examples of structural gaslighting via misogynoiristic controlling images.

6. Christina Cross's (2020) research on educational attainment among extended family households similarly analyzes the various rationales offered for racial disparities in educational and socioeconomic status between white children and children of color. She shows how the figure that "57 per cent of Black and 35 per cent of Hispanic children ever live in an extended family, compared with 20 per cent of White children" is used to elide the structural disadvantages produced by intersecting oppressions for children of color.

7. See Ruíz (2024) for an incisive account of the construction and preservation of what she terms "white dynastic formations."

8. Racecraft is a constructed "mental terrain" with "topographical features that Americans regularly navigate," and which "we cannot readily stop traversing" (Fields and Fields 2014, 19). This landscape crafted by collective imaginings influences and structures a wide range of actions. Fields and Fields theorize racecraft as originating in the magical thinking necessary to force human populations into the organizational taxonomy of "race" that categorizes humans on the basis of presumed inborn traits, distinguishes groups from one another, and structures them into a naturally hierarchical ranking of value. They write, "Fitting actual humans to any such grid immediately calls forth the busy repertoire of strange maneuvering that is part of what we call *racecraft*" (16). In these "strange maneuverings" are exemplary illustrations of the mechanics of structural gaslighting.

9. It is worth emphasizing that structural gaslighting need not involve promoting false claims, though it often does. It can also involve wielding *true* claims to achieve deflection, manipulate attention, imply relevance, create epistemic exploitation, etc. A lesson from Dotson (2018) is that salience and relevance norms are often more important than truth when it comes to producing (and undermining) epistemic oppression. The same is true for structural gaslighting.

10. Marissa Alexander, CeCe McDonald, and Cyntoia Brown have all served time in prison for defending themselves from physical and sexual violence. McDonald, a trans woman, was forced to serve her time in a men's prison.

11. Cis men who physically and sexually assault trans women, for instance, often portray their victims as having perpetrated a sexual violation against them (Bettcher 2007).

12. Lloyd (2001) is an excellent example of using the well-supported theoretical and methodological frameworks of evolutionary biology to debunk the purported empirical evidence for the evolutionary psychological hypothesis that rape behavior

is a biological adaptation. Buss and Schmitt (2015) also serves as an extensive repertoire of undersupported evolutionary psychological hypotheses of sex differences.

13. See Fine's (2010) *Delusions of Gender* for compelling examples from neuroscience.

14. The motivation and function of theories of scientific racism was to protect white wealth by legitimizing the brutality of enslavement by way of "empirically" confirming both the *sub-* and *super-*human-ness of African and African-descended peoples. It is notable that even a white European count in the eighteenth century could see these justifications for what they were.

15. However, it should also be noted that anti-Black racism is by no means the only form of racism for which science has produced theoretical justifications.

16. See Kahn (2004) for an extensive accounting of the commercial motivations for classifying BiDil as a race-specific drug.

17. White settler capitalists were not interested in blocking the abolition of slavery *solely* because they wanted to maintain their racial power. They also wanted to protect the profits they accrued from the system of racial capitalism (Robinson 1983).

18. This latter comparison of racial differences in *responsibility* for pollution is one that is rarely studied. The lack of focus on disparities in culpability has the same sleight-of-hand effect that Fields and Fields identify by hiding the role that white people play in creating and maintaining racist systems.

19. For further illustration that mere lip-service attention to structural factors is inadequate for preventing structural gaslighting, see the extended critique of Fricker's analysis of hermeneutical injustice and sexual harassment in Berenstain (2020).

20. The medical model of disability conceives of disability as an intrinsic biological deficiency or deficit of the individual and rejects the social construction of disability. The BSM acknowledges that the social environment plays a role in producing disability, for instance, by being constructed primarily for sighted people and people who do not use wheelchairs. However, it takes disability to be constructed from a substrate of *impairment*, which is conceived of as a negatively valenced intrinsic biological property of the individual, much the same way that the medical model conceives disability, as Tremain (2017) points out.

21. Lovaas was also a pioneer of gay conversion therapy—now recognized as abuse by the American Psychological Association.

22. Singer, for instance, counts disabilities as diverse as spina bifida, Down syndrome, and hemophilia as "severe" enough to license the killing of infants who have them (1979).

23. Facilitated communication differs from Augmentative and Alternative Communication (AAC), which uses technology to unlock the voices of otherwise nonverbal persons.

24. The client of the facilitated communicator would, for instance, have no way of expressing to anyone else that they *did not* consent to a sexual relationship with the facilitated communicator.

25. It is also noteworthy that Stubblefield decided to *give him a new name* and call him only by that name, echoing the practice of white enslavers and slave mistresses renaming the Black people they enslaved as an expression of ownership and domination (Engber 2016).

26. The first of many signs of their extraordinary ignorance about the phenomenon of sexual violence is their assumption that acts of sexual assault are incompatible with the perpetrator feeling genuine love for their victim.

27. The gendered racist controlling image that portrays Black men as inherently sexually aggressive and predatory (especially toward white women) likely contributed to Singer and McMahan's refusal to see a Black man as a victim of sexual violence, just as the presumed innocence and fragility of white femininity likely contributed to their refusal to see a white woman as a perpetrator of sexual violence.

28. While Tremain's notion of disableization is valuable for interrupting the production of ableist force relations, it is also important to recognize that Indigenous conceptions of ableism and their corresponding concerns cannot be subsumed under non-Indigenous ontologies of ableism. For a discussion of how Indigenous interventions into the ontologies of ableism found in disability studies might attend to the disablement of land wrought by settler colonialism, see Jaffee and John (2018).

Works Cited

Abu-Laban, Yasmeen, and Abigail B. Bakan. 2022. "Anti-Palestinian Racism and Racial Gaslighting." *Political Quarterly* 93 (3): 508–16.

Appleman, Laura. 2018. "Deviancy, Dependency, and Disability: The Forgotten History of Eugenics and Mass Incarceration." *Duke Law Journal* 68 (3): 417–478.

Aladangady, Aditya, and Akila Forde. 2021. "Wealth Inequality and the Racial Wealth Gap." *FEDS Notes*, federalreserve.gov. https://doi.org/10.17016/2380-7172.2861.

Armstrong, Elizabeth A., Miriam Gleckman-Krut, and Lanora Johnson. "Silence, Power, and Inequality: An Intersectional Approach to Sexual Violence." *Annual Review of Sociology* 44: 99–122.

Barnes, Elizabeth. 2009. "Disability and Adaptive Preference." *Philosophical Perspectives* 23 (1): 1–22.

Berenstain, Nora. 2020. "White Feminist Gaslighting." *Hypatia* 35 (4): 733–58.

———, Kristie Dotson, Julieta Paredes, Elena Ruíz, and Noenoe K. Silva. 2022. "Epistemic Oppression, Resistance, and Resurgence." *Contemporary Political Theory* 21: 283–314.

Bierria, Alisa. 2012. "'Where Them Bloggers At?': Reflections on Rihanna, Accountability, and Survivor Subjectivity." *Social Justice* 37 (4): 101–24.

Bluthenthal, Cleo. 2023. "The Disproportionate Burden of Eviction on Black Women." *Center for American Progress*. https://www.americanprogress.org/article/the-disproportionate-burden-of-eviction-on-black-women/.

Brice, Anne. 2020. "How the U.S. Government Created an 'Insane Asylum' to Imprison Native Americans." *Berkeley News*. https://news.berkeley.edu/2020/11/19/using-disability-to-imprison-native-americans/.

Brice, Anne. 2020. "How State Courts Use Disability to Remove Native Children From Their Homes." *Berkeley News*. https://news.berkeley.edu/2020/11/24/podcast-how-state-courts-use-disability-to-remove-native-children-from-their-homes/.

Buss, David, and David Schmitt. 2011. "Evolutionary Psychology and Feminism." *Sex Roles* 64: 768–87.

Cartwright, Samuel. 1851. "Report on the Diseases and Physical Peculiarities of the Negro Race." *New Orleans Medical Surgery Journal* 7: 691–715.

Chance, Paul. 1974. "After You Hit a Child, You Can't Just Get Up and Leave Him; You Are Hooked to That Kid. (O. Ivar Lovaas Interview)." *Psychology Today* 7 (8): 76–84.

Cheeseman, M. J., B. Ford, S. C. Anenberg, M. J. Cooper, E. V. Fischer, M. S. Hammer, et al. (2022). "Disparities in Air Pollutants Across Racial, Ethnic, and Poverty Groups at US Public Schools." *GeoHealth* 6: e2022GH000672.

Collins, Patricia Hill. 2000. *Black Feminist Thought: Knowledge, Consciousness, and the Politics of Empowerment.* New York: Routledge.

Cowing, Jessica. 2020. "Settler States of Ability: Assimilation, Incarceration, and Native Women's Crip Interventions." Dissertations, Theses, and Masters Projects, William & Mary. Paper 1616444427. http://dx.doi.org/10.21220/s2-j31a-n741.

Cross, Christina J. 2020. "Racial/Ethnic Differences in the Association Between Family Structure and Children's Education." *Journal of Marriage and Family* 82 (2): 691–712.

Davis, Angelique M., and Rose Ernst. 2020. "Racial Gaslighting." In *The Politics of Protest: Readings on the Black Lives Matter Movement*, edited by Nadia E. Brown, Ray Block Jr., and Christopher T. Stout, 47–60. New York: Routledge.

Dawson, Michelle. 2004. *The Misbehavior of Behaviorists: Ethical Challenges to the Autism-ABA Industry.* https://www.sentex.ca/~nexus23/naa_aba.html

Dickman, Samuel L., Adam Gaffney, Alecia McGregor, David U. Himmelstein, Danny McCormick, David H. Bor, and Steffie Woolhandler. 2022.

"Trends in Health Care Use Among Black and White Persons in the US, 1963–2019." *JAMA Network Open* 5 (6): e2217383. https://doi.org/10.1001/jamanetworkopen.2022.17383.

Dimsdale, Joel E. 2008. "Psychological Stress and Cardiovascular Disease." *Journal of the American College of Cardiology* 51 (13): 1237–46.

Dorceta, Taylor. 2014. *Toxic Communities: Environmental Racism, Industrial Pollution, and Residential Mobility.* New York: NYU Press.

Dotson, Kristie. 2018. "Accumulating Epistemic Power." *Philosophical Topics* 46 (1): 129–54.

Engber, Daniel. 2016. "What Anna Stubblefield Believed She was Doing." *New York Times Magazine.* https://www.nytimes.com/2016/02/03/magazine/what-anna-stubblefield-believed-she-was-doing.html.

Fears, Darryl. 2020. "Shingle Mountain: How a Pile of Toxic Waste Was Dumped in a Community of Color." *Washington Post.*

Fields, Karen E. and Barbara J. Fields. 2014. *Racecraft: The Soul of Inequality in American Life.* London: Verso Books.

Fine, Cordelia. 2010. *Delusions of Gender: How Our Minds, Society, and Neurosexism Create Difference.* New York: W.W. Norton.

Finn, K., E. Gajda, T. Perin, and C. Fredericks. 2017. "Responsible Resource Development and Prevention of Sex Trafficking: Safeguarding Native Women and Children on the Fort Berthold Reservation." *Harvard Women's Law Journal* 40: 1.

First Peoples Worldwide. 2020. "Violence from Extractive Industry 'Man Camps' Endangers Indigenous Women and Children." University of Colorado Boulder. January 29, 2020. https://www.colorado.edu/program/fpw/2020/01/29/violence-extractive-industry-man-camps-endangers-indigenous-women-and-children.

Jaffee, L., and John, K., 2018. "Disabling Bodies of/and Land: Reframing Disability Justice in Conversation with Indigenous Theory and Activism." *Disability and the Global South* 5 (2): 1407–29.

Hatch, Anthony R. 2022. "The Data Will Not Save Us: Afropessimism and Racial Antimatter in the COVID-19 Pandemic." *Big Data & Society* 9 (1): 20539517211067948.

Kahn, Jonathan. 2005. "Misreading Race and Genomics after BiDil." *Nature Genetics* 37: 655–56. https://doi.org/10.1038/ng0705-655.

Kahn, Jonathan. 2004. "How a Drug Becomes "Ethnic": Law, Commerce, and the Production of Racial Categories in Medicine." *Yale Journal of Health Policy, Law, and Ethics* 4 (1): 1–46.

Kittay, Eva Feder. 1999. *Love's Labor: Essays on Women, Equality and Dependency.* Abingdon, UK: Taylor and Francis.

Scott O. Lilienfeld, Julia Marshall, James T. Todd & Howard C. Shane. 2014. "The Persistence of Fad Interventions in the Face of Negative Scientific Evidence:

Facilitated Communication for Autism as a Case Example." *Evidence-Based Communication Assessment and Intervention* 8 (2): 62–101. https://doi.org/10.1080/17489539.2014.976332.

Lloyd, Elisabeth. 2001. "Science Gone Astray: Evolution and Rape." *Michigan Law Review* 99 (6): 1536–59.

Longino, Helen. 1990. *Science as Social Knowledge: Values and Objectivity in Scientific Inquiry*. Princeton, NJ: Princeton University Press.

Lowe, Lisa. 2015. *The Intimacies of Four Continents*. Durham, NC: Duke University Press.

Lynch, C. L. 2019. "Invisible Abuse: ABA and the Things Only Autistic People Can See." *Neuroclastic*. https://neuroclastic.com/invisible-abuse-aba-and-the-things-only-autistic-people-can-see/.

McBryde Johnson, Harriet. 2003. "Unspeakable Conversations." *New York Times*, February 16., 2023. https://www.nytimes.com/2003/02/16/magazine/unspeakable-conversations.html.

McGill, Owen, and Ann Robinson. 2020. "'Recalling Hidden Harms': Autistic Experiences of Childhood Applied Behavioural Analysis (ABA)." *Advances in Autism* 7 (4): 269–82.

McMahan, Jeff, and Peter Singer. 2017. "Who Is the Victim in the Anna Stubblefield Case?" *New York Times*, April 3, 2017. https://www.nytimes.com/2017/04/03/opinion/who-is-the-victim-in-the-anna-stubblefield-case.html.

Metzl, Jonathan. 2009. *The Protest Psychosis: How Schizophrenia Became a Black Disease*. Boston: Beacon Press.

Meynell, Letitia. 2021. "What's Wrong with (Narrow) Evolutionary Psychology." In *The Routledge Handbook of Feminist Philosophy of Science*, edited by Sharon Crasnow and Kristen Intemann, 303–15. New York: Routledge.

Montgomery, Cal. 2001. "Critic of the Dawn." *Ragged Edge Online*. http://www.raggededgemagazine.com/0501/0501cov.htm.

Morin, Brandi. 2020. "Pipelines, Man Camps, and Murdered Indigenous Women in Canada." *Al Jazeera*, May 5, 2020. https://www.aljazeera.com/features/2020/5/5/pipelines-man-camps-and-murdered-indigenous-women-in-canada.

Morris, Monique. 2016. *Pushout: The Criminalization of Black Girls in Schools*. New York: The New Press.

Mowatt, R. A. 2018. "Black Lives as Snuff: The Silent Complicity in Viewing Black Death." *Biography* 41 (4): 777–806.

Nussbaum, Martha. 2003. "Capabilities as Fundamental Entitlements: Sen and Social Justice." *Feminist Economics* 9 (2–3): 33–59.

———. 2007. *Frontiers of Justice: Disability, Nationality, Species Membership*. Cambridge, MA: Harvard University Press.

Paolella, David A., Christopher W. Tessum, Peter J. Adams, Joshua S. Apte, Sarah Chambliss, Jason Hill, Nicholas Z. Muller, and Julian D. Marshall. 2018. "Effect of Model Spatial Resolution on Estimates of Fine Particulate Matter

Exposure and Exposure Disparities in the United States." *Environmental Science & Technology Letters* 5 (7): 436–41. https://doi.org/10.1021/acs.estlett.8b00279.

Parliament of Canada. 2021. "Statutes of Canada 2021, An Act to Amend the Criminal Code (Medical Assistance in Dying)." https://parl.ca/DocumentViewer/en/43-2/bill/C-7/royal-assent.

Richards, Jennifer Smith, Jodi S. Cohen, and Lakeidra Chavis. 2019. "The Quiet Rooms." *ProPublica.* https://features.propublica.org/illinois-seclusion-rooms/school-students-put-in-isolated-timeouts/.

Richie, Beth E. 2012. *Arrested Justice: Black Women, Violence, and America's Prison Nation.* New York: NYU Press.

Robert, Pamela. 2003. "Disability Oppression in the Contemporary U.S. Capitalist Workplace." *Science & Society* 67 (2): 136–59.

Roberts, Dorothy, 2002. *Shattered Bonds: The Color of Child Welfare.* London: Civitas Books.

———. 2011a. *Fatal Invention: How Science, Politics, and Big Business Re-Create Race in the Twenty-First Century.* New York: The New Press.

———. 2011b. "What's Wrong with Race-Based Medicine?: Genes, Drugs, and Health Disparities." *Minnesota Journal of Law, Science, and Technology* 12 (1): 1–21.

Rooks, Ronica N., Eleanor M. Simonsick, Lisa M. Klesges, Anne B. Newman, Hilsa N. Ayonayon, and Tamara B. Harris. 2008. "Racial Disparities in Health Care Access and Cardiovascular Disease Indicators in Black and White Older Adults in the Health ABC Study." *Journal of Aging and Health* 20 (6): 599–614.

Ruíz, Elena. 2020. "Cultural Gaslighting." *Hypatia* 35 (4): 687–713.

———. 2024. *Structural Violence: The Makings of Settler Colonial Impunity.* Oxford: Oxford University Press.

Ruíz, Elena, and Nora Berenstain. 2018. "Gender-Based Administrative Violence as Colonial Strategy." *Philosophical Topics* 46 (2): 209–27.

Sandoval-Norton, Aileen, Gary Shkedy, and Dalia Shkedy. 2021. "Long-term ABA Therapy Is Abusive: A Response to Gorycki, Ruppel, and Zane." *Advances in Neurodevelopmental Disorders* 5: 126–34.

Seamster, Louise. 2016. "Race, Power and Economic Extraction in Benton Harbor, MI." PhD diss., Duke University. https://doi.org/10.31235/osf.io/6qx9j.

Sen, Amartya. 1999. *Development as Freedom.* Oxford: Oxford University Press.

Simpson, Leanne Betasamosake. 2017. *As We Have Always Done.* Minneapolis: University of Minnesota Press.

Smith, S. E. 2012. "Is the Ashley Treatment Right? Ask Yourself if Disabled People Are Human." *Guardian.* https://www.theguardian.com/commentisfree/2012/mar/16/ashley-treatment-disabled-people.

Stanley-Becker, Isaac. 2019. "Whites Are Mainly to Blame for Air Pollution, but Blacks and Hispanics Bear the Burden, Says a New Study." *Washington Post*. https://www.washingtonpost.com/nation/2019/03/12/whites-are-mainly-blame-air-pollution-blacks-hispanics-bear-burden-says-new-study/.

Tessum, Christopher W., Joshua S. Apte, Andrew L. Goodkind, Nicholas Z. Muller, Kimberley A. Mullins, David A. Paolella, Stephen Polasky, Nathaniel P. Springer, Sumil K. Thakrar, Julian D. Marshall, and Jason D. Hill. 2019. "Inequity in Consumption of Goods and Services Adds to Racial-Ethnic Disparities in Air Pollution Exposure." *Proceedings of the National Academy of Sciences* 116 (13): 6001–6. https://doi.org/10.1073/pnas.1818859116.

Tremain, Shelley. 2017. *Foucault and Feminist Philosophy of Disability*. Ann Arbor: University of Michigan Press.

———. 2021. "Philosophy of Disability, Conceptual Engineering, and the Nursing Home-Industrial-Complex in Canada." *International Journal of Critical Diversity Studies* 4 (1): 10–33.

United States Department of Labor. 2021. "Subminimum Wage." https://www.dol.gov/agencies/whd/special-employment.

Weiss, Jonathan A., and Michelle A. Fardella. 2018. "Victimization and Perpetration Experiences of Adults with Autism." *Frontiers in Psychiatry* 9: 203.

Williams, David. R. 2018. "Stress and the Mental Health of Populations of Color: Advancing Our Understanding of Race-related Stressors." *Journal of Health and Social Behavior* 59 (4): 466–85. https://doi.org/10.1177/0022146518814251.

Wright, Willie Jamaal. 2018. "As Above, So Below: Anti-Black Violence as Environmental Racism." *Antipode* 1–19.

2

Theorizing Structural Gaslighting as Gaslighting

Holly Longair

In recent years, the term "gaslighting" has become increasingly common in popular discourse. It has been used to identify a set of strategies that seem meant to undermine, dismiss, manipulate, and otherwise cause psychological, epistemic, and social harm to people across a wide range of contexts. However, the exact meaning and parameters of the term have remained somewhat unclear among its various uses. As a result, there is a growing body of academic literature dedicated to analyzing and theorizing the phenomenon.

The majority of that literature, tracing back to psychoanalytic work in the 1980s, has focused on gaslighting as a phenomenon that occurs between individuals in the context of close personal relationships. Several different kinds of gaslighting at the individual level have been identified, including *epistemic gaslighting* and *manipulative gaslighting*. More recently, increasing attention has been paid to the ways in which gaslighting does not only happen on the individual, interpersonal level. Starting with the identification and theorization of phenomena such as racial gaslighting (Davis and Ernst 2017) and developed further through the publication of a cluster of papers by Gaile Pohlhaus Jr., Elena Ruíz, and Nora Berenstain in *Hypatia* (2020), attention has turned to what has been named "structural gaslighting." These theorists have been integral to showing the wide variety of ways in which gaslighting can occur at a structural level. However, they have remained focused on cases of epistemic gaslighting. There has not been discussion of whether other kinds of interpersonal gaslighting, particularly manipulative gaslighting, can have a structural form. Furthermore, although these discussions have been productive in elucidating cases of structural gaslighting and its harms, they often do not make clear why the described phenomena are cases of gaslighting rather than a related structural form of injustice.

In this chapter, I propose a theory of what makes these structural cases a kind of gaslighting rather than something else. I take structural gaslighting to be a phenomenon that meets all of the necessary conditions for gaslighting as it is defined in theories of interpersonal gaslighting, but where there is no particular agent as the perpetrator. To determine the necessary conditions for gaslighting, I discuss three of the early philosophical theories of gaslighting: Kate Abramson's general account of gaslighting, Veronica Ivy [Rachel McKinnon]'s epistemic gaslighting, and Cynthia Stark's manipulative gaslighting. My goal is to provide a more general theorization of the connections between transactional and structural gaslighting, making clear how something can be a structural phenomenon yet still gaslighting.[1] I then discuss how the work of Gaile Pohlhaus Jr., Elena Ruíz, and Nora Berenstain informs a shift from thinking about epistemic gaslighting on the level of interpersonal transactions to thinking structurally. I draw on Elizabeth Anderson's discussion of structural epistemic injustices to provide a theoretical framework for shifting from thinking about gaslighting on the level of interpersonal transactions to thinking structurally. Finally, I use this framework and the criteria I outline to examine several examples (specifically Charles Mills's account of white ignorance, the epistemic violence described by Ruíz, and Kate Manne's account of misogyny), with the aim of clarifying why these structural phenomena are in fact cases of gaslighting rather than a related kind of injustice or other harm.

Theories of Transactional Gaslighting

Abramson's Gaslighting

Kate Abramson presents the earliest philosophical theorization of gaslighting in her 2014 paper "Turning up the Lights on Gaslighting."[2] She generally defines gaslighting as "a form of emotional manipulation in which the gaslighter tries (consciously or not) to induce in someone the sense that her reactions, perception, memories and/or beliefs are not just mistaken, but utterly without grounds" (2014, 2). To achieve this effect, there are usually multiple incidents accumulating over time, with either more than one gaslighter or a gaslighter and accomplices, and the increasing isolation of the target of the gaslighting (Abramson 2014, 2). The gaslighter usually tells their target that the target is "crazy, paranoid, hysterical" and other language meant to indicate a lack of capacity for rationality (Abramson 2014, 2).

Abramson argues that the unique feature of gaslighting is evident in this characteristic language. The gaslighter wants to discredit their target as a source of genuine disagreement, not just to onlookers but also to the target themselves (Abramson 2014, 10). Abramson argues that gaslighting is a tactic used by perpetrators who are not able to "tolerate even the possibility of challenge" from their target (Abramson 2014, 9) to such an extent that they seek to eliminate the independent moral and epistemic standing from which the target could issue such challenges (Abramson 2014, 10). They are trying to put their own worldview beyond dispute. In doing so, the gaslighter creates conditions where, if the gaslighting is successful, their target is not simply wrong or mistaken, but not even able to judge for themselves whether they are wrong or mistaken (Abramson 2014, 8).

The result is that a gaslighter's interactions with their target are characterized by "an interpersonal need for assent, intolerance for challenge or even the possibility of being challenged, and the manipulative destruction of the gaslightee's standing to issue challenge" (Abramson 2014, 12). Abramson argues that this is brought about in a four-step process, which constitutes the basic structure of gaslighting:

> First, the target is framed in the mind of the gaslighter as crazy, paranoid, overreacting or oversensitive—framed in such a way, that is, that she cannot be the source of genuine disagreement. Then the gaslighter tells her this is how he sees her, in the form of a proclamation . . . Then s/he insists on the dismissive framing in their interactions; re-entrenching or using other terms of dismissal if she resists. And finally (though often this is going on throughout), the gaslighter manipulates his target. (Abramson 2014, 14)

One of the most insidious features of gaslighting is that through this process, the target of the gaslighting will often become complicit in their own destruction (Abramson 2014, 16). This is because the forms of manipulation that are employed play off of key aspects of the target's moral life and relationships, perverting them so that the individual contributes to their own gaslighting in order to fulfill other important aspects of their life and identity (Abramson 2014, 22).[3]

Abramson also argues that the gaslighter often will not even be aware of the motive behind their actions. They will have a specific, primary aim with regard to their actions toward their target, but it will not consciously be to eliminate them as an independent source of challenge. The gaslighter will also have several secondary, basic desires that may be benign by themselves, but can contribute to the gaslighting (Abramson 2014, 8).[4] However, successful gaslighting will often create conditions that relieve deep anxieties in the gaslighter (Abramson 2014, 6), and it is that unconscious motivation that Abramson indicates as the feature that makes gaslighting a distinct phenomenon from other forms of dismissal or domination.

Gaslighting is closely related to several other phenomena that have been more thoroughly analyzed by philosophers. Abramson argues that gaslighting contains elements of "manipulation, failure of recognition respect, torture, epistemic injustice, and silencing" (Abramson 2014, 18).[5] However, she argues that none of these other forms of wrongdoing fully captures the immorality of gaslighting. Each provides only a piece of the picture. I now focus on two further attempts to theorize kinds of gaslighting that take as their starting point these related phenomena: Ivy's account of epistemic gaslighting and Cynthia Stark's account of manipulative gaslighting.

Ivy's Epistemic Gaslighting

Veronica Ivy identifies two kinds of gaslighting. The first is the kind of psychological abuse modeled in the 1944 film *Gaslight* (Ivy [McKinnon] 2017, 168). The second is an epistemic injustice, specifically a kind of testimonial injustice (Ivy [McKinnon] 2017, 167).[6] Other scholars have named this *epistemic gaslighting* (Stark 2019, 221). Cases of epistemic gaslighting are characterized by the gaslighter raising doubts about whether their target has reliably perceived the events that their testimony is about (Ivy [McKinnon] 2017, 168), particularly with regard to a harm or injustice the target has experienced. The gaslighter expresses doubts that events "really happened as the speaker claims" (Ivy [McKinnon] 2017, 168), with the doubt resulting from an identity prejudice against the speaker (Ivy [McKinnon] 2017, 169).

This sounds like a paradigmatic case of testimonial injustice and aligns with Abramson's claim that gaslighting includes elements of epistemic injustice. However, Abramson also emphasizes that there is more to gaslighting than testimonial injustice. In Ivy's analysis, what seems to be the feature that makes epistemic gaslighting conceptually distinct from testimonial injustice is that the target's testimony is dismissed as a misperception of events (Ivy [McKinnon] 2017, 169). The content of the testimony is specifically about the target's experience, and the gaslighter's dismissal of that testimony is denial that some event happened the way the target claims it happened. If repeated often enough, this kind of testimonial injustice would quite likely have the effect that Abramson argues is the motivation for gaslighting: it not only discredits the target as wrong or mistaken, but also throws doubt on their ability to judge for themselves whether they are wrong or mistaken (Abramson 2014, 8).

Another core feature of Abramson's account of gaslighting is that the gaslighter not only attempts to convince any onlookers that the target misperceived what they claim to have experienced, but they also try to convince the target. It is this attempt to convince the target that their own perceptions are unreliable that makes this a case of epistemic gaslighting rather than a close cousin in the same family of dismissive interactions (Abramson 2014, 10). It is not entirely clear from the examples used by Ivy whether she thinks that the recruitment of the target into the gaslighting is a necessary feature of epistemic gaslighting. However, the language used in the hypothetical conversation between Susan (gaslighter) and Victoria (target) in Ivy's central example of a transwoman being mispronouned by a colleague shows a clear case of a gaslighter trying to convince her target that the target did not experience what she thought she experienced (Ivy [McKinnon] 2017, 168). In trying to convince Victoria that the incident didn't happen, Susan is trying to make Victoria complicit in her own gaslighting.

Ivy identifies the wrong of epistemic gaslighting as "a failure to afford the first person (epistemic) authority of disadvantaged speakers their appropriate epistemic weight" (Ivy [McKinnon] 2017, 170). The result is that the target is degraded as a knower (Stark 2019, 222), the same primary harm that Miranda Fricker identifies as occurring in epistemic injustice. However, gaslighting has an additional harm because it occurs in a context that should imply trust. Ivy's key example focuses on how gaslighting violates the trust that a trans woman should be able to have in someone who claims to be an "ally" (Ivy [McKinnon] 2017, 171). This results in a loss of epistemic and moral support, often leading to the isolation and exclusion of already vulnerable individuals (Ivy [McKinnon] 2017, 171). This requirement is more generally applicable, however, as a similar violation of trust that results in betrayal, exclusion, and isolation can be seen in other paradigmatic cases of gaslighting, such as domestic abuse.

Stark's Manipulative Gaslighting

Cynthia Stark identifies an important social phenomenon that epistemic gaslighting does not capture, but that is closely related (Stark 2019, 221). She names this phenomenon *manipulative gaslighting* and defines it as occurring when "a person (the 'gaslighter') manipulates another (the 'target') in order to make her suppress or doubt her justifiable judgments about facts or values" (Stark 2019, 223). She provides four criteria that must be met for a case to count as manipulative gaslighting rather than a related phenomenon: "the target's judgments are justifiable" (Stark 2019, 224), "the gaslighter's judgments are unjustified" (Stark 2019, 224), "the gaslighter sidesteps challenges to his judgment that would expose it as unjustified" (Stark 2019, 225), and "the gaslighter displaces, that is, he attributes a flaw to the target to 'explain' her judgment and thereby prove it not credible" (Stark 2019, 225). These last two criteria are particularly important, as they are the primary methods that manipulative gaslighters use on their targets to deny their credibility and independent standing.

Stark emphasizes several ways in which manipulative gaslighting differs from epistemic gaslighting. The wrong of manipulative gaslighting is the manipulation, which results in the target "losing confidence in oneself both as a knower and as a moral equal" (Stark 2019, 222). Epistemic gaslighting is more concerned with degradation of the target as a knower (Stark 2019, 222). Manipulative gaslighting does not require an identity prejudicial credibility deficit and is not primarily concerned with testimony, while epistemic gaslighting is (Stark 2019, 222). Both require some kind of inequity in power to be at play; however, epistemic gaslighting requires a difference in social power, while manipulative gaslighting can result from any power differential that provides the gaslighter with leverage against their target (Stark 2019, 223). Last, and more important for Stark, epistemic gaslighting is unintentional (because epistemic injustice is unintentional), while manipulative gaslighting is always intentional. Manipulation always has an aim, even if the manipulator is unaware of it, and manipulative gaslighting is no different (Stark 2019, 223). That is the key different between the two: in manipulative gaslighting there is always an aim and intent, while in epistemic gaslighting there is not (Stark 2019, 223).

The Necessary Conditions for Gaslighting

From the examination of these different theories of interpersonal gaslighting, the following three common features become evident:

1. Gaslighting always involves an attempt to discredit, undermine, isolate, and/or destroy the target through some kind of *distortion* of the target's reality.

2. All cases of gaslighting involve an attempt by the gaslighter to obtain the *complicity* of the target, to in some sense get the target to either accept or contribute to the distortion of their own reality.

3. All cases of gaslighting require some kind of *power differential* that contributes to the gaslighter's ability to distort reality and gain their target's complicity.

I take these three features to constitute the necessary conditions for a case to count as one that should be labeled "gaslighting," whether transactional or structural.

From the Transactional to the Structural

As stated previously, all three of the theories of gaslighting explored above focus primarily on gaslighting as a phenomenon that occurs in individual interactions. All three also recognize that those individual gaslighting interactions are often part of overarching systems of oppressive behavior (Abramson 2014, 5), such as misogyny in Stark (2019, 229) or prejudice against trans women in Ivy (2017, 167). However, despite this recognition, their theorization of gaslighting is always put in terms of interactions between gaslighter and target, hearer and speaker, perpetrator and victim.

Gaile Pohlhaus Jr., Elena Ruíz, and Nora Berenstain challenge this focus, each elaborating on a conception of structural gaslighting. Pohlhaus defines structural gaslighting as "both the structural aspects that enable epistemic gaslighting by individuals, and how those structural aspects can function to gaslight on their own, independent of any particular perpetrator" (Pohlhaus 2020, 678), while Berenstain focuses on the conceptual work occurring behind structures of oppression (Berenstain 2020, 734). In both cases, there is not an identifiable agent who is the gaslighter, but instead a system holding in place the conditions that gaslight the members of particular groups. As a result, their analyses make clear how structural gaslighting is structural. However, they do not make it as clear how structural gaslighting is gaslighting.

In fact, Ruíz critiques the focus on the interpersonal kind of gaslighting that originated the term, arguing that "the greatest success of the gaslighting paradigm is that it provides cover for the structural dimensions of gaslighting" and "there is nothing accidental about the popularization of the narrowed psychological understanding of gaslighting as interpersonal, emotional abuse" (Ruíz 2020, 688), as it "diverts critical attention away from structural oppressions that continue to underwrite the colonial project" (Ruíz 2020, 689). Ruíz successfully highlights the importance of the structural aspects of colonialism in the cases she points to. However, her analysis does not justify why the structural phenomenon she describes is a kind of gaslighting, rather than another kind of epistemic violence and oppression.

Because the term "gaslighting" did develop first in the psychological context, if the term is to be used to identify the pressing situation that Ruíz describes, some attention must be paid to making the conceptual connection clear between gaslighting as an interpersonal transaction and as a structural feature of colonial societies. In the remainder of this chapter, I propose a way of theorizing why structural gaslighting, as a structural phenomenon that cannot be traced to any individual perpetrator because it is caused instead by the structures of society and the systems they uphold, should still be considered a kind of gaslighting.

From Transactional to Structural Injustice

Elizabeth Anderson's discussion of transactional and structural epistemic injustices (2012) provides a useful model for discussing transactional and structural gaslighting. To demonstrate the importance of theorizing structural epistemic injustices, Anderson draws a parallel to theorizing justice in political philosophy. She argues that theories of distributive justice can be understood as either transactional or structural. Transactional theories look at particular exchanges between individuals to determine the criteria of justice and whether or not they are fulfilled (Anderson 2012, 163–64). Structural theories, on the other hand, look at "global properties of a system of rules that govern transactions" to determine what constraints need to put in place to ensure that the cumulative effects of innocent-seeming individual transactions do not result in large-scale injustices (Anderson 2012, 164). Transactional theories work on the individual level, while structural theories look at the entire system rather than at particular wrongdoers and victims. Both kinds of theories are important for getting at features of distributive justice because transactional theories by themselves are not able to account for all of the ways in which the system of rules at play in a society can unfairly disadvantage particular groups and individuals.

Like distributive justice, epistemic injustice needs both a transactional and structural theory (Anderson 2012, 164). Anderson argues that theories of epistemic injustice need to pay attention not just to how single or even recurring transactions between speakers and hearers can harm individuals in their capacities as knowers, but also to "the cumulative effects of how our epistemic system elicits, evaluates, and connects countless individual communicative acts can be unjust, even if no injustice has been committed in any particular epistemic transaction" (Anderson 2012, 164–65). The two kinds of theory are clearly evident in Miranda Fricker's discussion of epistemic injustice. Testimonial injustice, as described by Fricker, is clearly a transactional injustice "because a fault can be traced to an identifiable agent" (Anderson 2012, 165). However, hermeneutical injustice is a structural injustice. Anderson argues that an injustice is structural when "institutions are set up to exclude people without anyone having to decide to do so" (Anderson 2012, 166), with no particular actor or group of actors being identifiable as the cause of the injustice. Fricker is explicit that this lack of an identifiable actor is the case with hermeneutical injustice (Fricker 2007, 159).[7]

Anderson provides only minimal theorization of what exactly a structural epistemic injustice entails beyond hermeneutical injustice. However, the key characteristic that differentiates structural from transaction injustices is that feature where, in structural cases, there is no particular agent who can be identified as the perpetrator of the injustice. Instead, the cause of the injustice is embedded in the institutions, norms, laws, and other components of the society in which it takes place, reflecting systemic flaws that lead to oppression and domination. To get at all of the features of injustice, both transactional and structural theories are important.

Epistemic Structural Gaslighting

Drawing a similar parallel, Anderson's argument can now be used to understand how epistemic gaslighting can also be both transactional and structural. Since Ivy and those drawing on her work frame epistemic gaslighting as an instance of epistemic injustice, Anderson's argument can be applied directly to this understanding of epistemic gaslighting. Ivy focuses on epistemic gaslighting as a kind of testimonial injustice, making it explicitly a transactional injustice between individuals. However, as mentioned above, there are other kinds of epistemic injustice that are clearly structural, and the characteristics that make something a case of epistemic gaslighting specifically rather than an epistemic injustice in general could also be present in these cases. The gaps in the collective interpretive resources available to the dominant group that cause hermeneutical injustice can create similar reality-distorting effects as those that characterize gaslighting, particularly when paired with a power differential between the dominant group and victim of the hermeneutical injustice. The victims of hermeneutical injustice can also be made complicit in their own marginalization and the creation of such gaps. However, under the three previously mentioned theories of gaslighting (from Abramson, Ivy, and Stark), such cases could not be considered instances of gaslighting because there is no identifiable gaslighter present. Hermeneutical injustice is a structural injustice, the result of the background conditions of the society in question, and it cannot be attributed to any specific perpetrator. Yet the harms inflicted when the necessary conditions for gaslighting are present in a case of hermeneutical injustice need to be recognized as part of the phenomenon of gaslighting. Such cases should be understood as cases of *structural epistemic gaslighting*.

For the purposes of demonstrating how these cases are both structural and instances of gaslighting, I turn my attention to an example of structural epistemic gaslighting that is discussed in brief by both Pohlhaus and Berenstain: Charles Mills's account of *white ignorance*.[8] White ignorance is the epistemological contract that is one component of what Mills calls the racial contract, the foundation of the contemporary political system of white supremacy (Mills 1997, 2-3). Mills argues that to be "granted full cognitive standing in the polity, the official epistemic community" (Mills 1997, 18) that is established by the racial contract, one must "learn to see the world wrongly, but with the assurance that this set of mistaken perceptions will be validated by white epistemic authority" (Mills 1997, 18). This requires agreeing "to misinterpret the world" through a pattern of cognitive dysfunctions that produce "the ironic outcome that whites will in general be unable to understand the world they themselves have made" (Mills 1997, 18).

Angelique Davis and Rose Ernst have already provided an in-depth analysis of how racial gaslighting names "the political, social, economic and cultural process that perpetuates and normalizes a white supremacist reality through pathologizing those who resist" (Davis and Ernst 2017, 3). However, the focus of their account on specific legal cases still lends itself to an emphasis on transactional interactions between individuals that manifest the background structural processes. In focusing on Mills's account of white ignorance, it can be made clearer how structural epistemic gaslighting is present even when no such interactions are taking place and no perpetrators can be identified.[9]

White ignorance entails all three of the necessary conditions for gaslighting that were described earlier. It clearly involves a distortion of reality, since those who experience white ignorance live in "an invented delusional world, a racial fantasyland, a 'consensual hallucination'" (Mills 1997, 18). It may be less clear how this distortion discredits, undermines, isolates, or otherwise destroys the target as a source of independent moral and epistemic standing. However, Mill argues that membership in "the official epistemic community" and the political community as a whole is contingent on accepting the delusion that white ignorance offers. As a result, white ignorance reflects the same aim that characterizes Abramson's account of gaslighting. White ignorance is how white supremacy eliminates the possibility of an independent epistemic perspective and worldview from which the political system could be challenged. In doing so, it meets the first necessary condition for a case of gaslighting.

There is also a clear sense in which white ignorance involves complicity on the part of those who experience it. Mills talks about this phenomenon in terms of "an agreement to misinterpret the world" and "a consensual hallucination" (Mills 1997, 18). Furthermore, white ignorance is described explicitly as an epistemological racial contract. By its very nature, a contract has to involve agreement. If white ignorance is a consensual agreement, then those who are party to it are complicit in the wrongs and harms that it causes. One might object that those who agree to the epistemological contract of white ignorance are primarily white people, while the harms and wrongs fall on people of color, and so the question of complicity does not have the same insidious effects that characterize gaslighting. However, Mills argues that white ignorance is not only experienced by white people. Someone can be black and still accept the invented delusion of white ignorance to gain admittance into the epistemic and political community (Mills 2013, 38–39). Such cases would most closely fit the descriptions of gaslighting provided earlier. In addition, white ignorance causes harm (although clearly a different kind and severity of harm) to the white people who embrace it. It distorts the way that white people understand both the world and their selves. The fact that they agree to the delusion meets the second condition for a case of gaslighting.

The power inequity necessary for gaslighting is also present in white ignorance. Mills argues that accepting the worldview posed by the epistemic racial contract is required for someone to be considered a member of the epistemic community within the white supremacist political system. It is also a requirement for "achieving Whiteness" and being considered a person and a political actor (Mills 1997, 18). To have any power within the system that the racial contract puts in place, one must accept the delusion that white ignorance prescribes. However, additional structural inequalities will mean that various social groups are impacted in different ways by the distortion of reality that white ignorance causes. Although white people are epistemically harmed by white ignorance because it interferes with their ability to understand the world and themselves, the privileged position of power that whiteness is given within the political system prevents them from facing the harms that people of color face, such as marginalization and oppression. As a result, there are several sets of power inequities at play in white ignorance. At one level, there is the power held by those who agree to the racial contract over those who do not. At another, there is the power of white people over those who are not white. In both cases, the power differential provides the context in which the first two conditions for gaslighting take hold, fulfilling the third condition for a case of gaslighting.

White ignorance, then, fits all of the necessary conditions for gaslighting that were distilled from the three earlier theories. However, in cases of white ignorance, there is no clear gaslighter. White ignorance is a component of the larger racial contract, a system of domination that is embedded in the formal and informal structures of society. As a result, it creates a structural rather than transactional injustice. Several scholars have argued that white ignorance should be considered a kind of hermeneutical injustice (Mason 2011, 303; Medina 2012a, 214; Pohlhaus Jr. 2012, 722), making it a structural injustice in Anderson's account. I agree with this analysis. However, I add that white ignorance should be considered an instance of structural epistemic gaslighting, both a kind hermeneutical injustice and a kind of gaslighting. Such an account allows theorists to recognize that white ignorance manifests all of the necessary conditions for counting as a case of gaslighting, while also recognizing the structural nature of the kind of oppressive system of which it is a part.

The example of structural gaslighting presented by Elena Ruíz also fulfills the three necessary conditions for cases of gaslighting that I have identified. Ruíz's account of cultural gaslighting describes "the effort of one *culture* to undermine another *culture*'s confidence and stability by causing the *victimized collective* to doubt [its] own sense and beliefs" (Ruíz 2020, 689). This is clearly a structural account, as there is no identifiable individual who is the gaslighter and gaslightee. Furthermore, as discussed previously, Ruíz argues that focusing on interpersonal transactions when discussing gaslighting serves to obscure what is actually happening (Ruíz 2020, 689).

Her description of how the current paradigm of gaslighting as interpersonal and psychological actually facilitates structural gaslighting is the first indication that the distortion necessary for a case of gaslighting is present in Ruíz's description of cultural gaslighting. She goes on to describe how cultural gaslighting in settler colonial society has a "world-building epistemological function . . . to produce totalizing and abusive ambients . . . that work to destroy resistance to settler cultural authority as natural claims to Indigenous land" (Ruíz 2020, 696). It is reinforced by settler moves to ignorance, which involve strategies that keep in place those in positions of power or privilege while relieving their feelings of guilt or responsibility (Ruíz 2020, 696 discussing Tuck and Yang 2012, 9). Distortion of reality in the service of discrediting, undermining, isolating, and destroying the colonized is further extended through epistemic exploitation, which involves "the disappearing of violences," "the ruling out of Indigenous knowledges as knowledge," and the use of what Kristie Dotson calls "legitimating narratives" (Ruíz 2020, 698–99). All of this serves to support the project of dispossession that the continued settler colonial presence seeks to maintain in an ongoing process of hermeneutical violence that arose in conjunction with colonization and eased its path (Ruíz 2020, 701). The distortion and usurpation of reality is a key component of the system of structural phenomena that Ruíz describes and a key part of gaslighting.

The second necessary condition that I identified, the attempt of the gaslighter to obtain the complicity of the target, is not explicitly discussed in Ruíz's account. However, anyone familiar with the history of Indigenous people in various settler colonial states can see the ways in which forced complicity with what Ruíz describes as "techniques of settler colonial dispossession" (Ruíz 2020, 696) has been (and continues to be) present. For example, the residential school system imposed on Indigenous peoples in Canada was a process of forcefully ensuring that generations of children would contribute to distorting the realities of colonization imposed on their communities. Forcing those children on pain of punishment to stop using their own languages, eventually leading to the complete destruction of those languages and the understandings of reality that they helped to facilitate, was just one piece in the processes of hermeneutical violence that Ruíz describes. It was further replicated when many of those children became parents and made the decision not to teach their own children about their languages and cultures. This kind of coerced complicity, through various means extending from threat of violence to economic incentives, has been present throughout settler colonial societies past and present.

The power differential in Ruíz's account between the settler colonial culture and those it is imposed on is obvious and fulfills the final condition for gaslighting. Although there are several places where it is explicitly identified as being used as a tactic of gaslighting, such as in discussing the medical dimensions of cultural gaslighting (Ruíz 2020, 690) and settler moves to ignorance (Ruíz 2020, 696), the entire account is premised on that difference in power. In fact, cultural gaslighting is primarily about the acquisition and consolidation of power by colonizers and the overthrow of previous power structures among Indigenous peoples (Ruíz 2020, 701–2).

All three of the necessary conditions that I have identified in previous interpersonal accounts are present in Ruíz's description of cultural gaslighting. Furthermore, it is clear that the epistemic kind of gaslighting is one of the central mechanisms of this element of settler colonial consolidation. However, Ruíz's account goes further than that, suggesting that an account not only of structural epistemic gaslighting but also of structural manipulative gaslighting is needed to draw out a full understanding of what is happening in cultural gaslighting.

Manipulative Structural Gaslighting

It should now be clear how structural epistemic gaslighting is clearly a kind of gaslighting. However, it is less clear whether a link can be made between structural injustice and Stark's account of manipulative gaslighting, and little work has been done to develop the concept. Furthermore, manipulative gaslighting is neither a distributive nor an epistemic injustice, and so Anderson's account has nothing to say about it directly. More challenging still, Stark's account emphasizes several characteristics that seem to be necessarily transactional.

The main component that differentiates manipulative from epistemic gaslighting is that the gaslighter has a particular aim in the former but not the latter (Stark 2019, 223). As stated previously, Stark argues that the manipulation is always intentional because "the gaslighter always has an aim even if they are unaware of it" (Stark 2019, 223). Since structural gaslighting has no identifiable gaslighter, there is a question of whether a theory of structural manipulative gaslighting is sound. The answer seems to rest on whether manipulation can happen without an identifiable manipulator acting on a particular intention. If it is possible for manipulation to occur with an aim but no conscious intention, requiring instead a more general goal or purpose of some kind, it seems possible to make the claim that there can be an aim to manipulative gaslighting without a gaslighter. However, it is not clear to me that this is the kind of aim Stark has in mind, and so it remains a possible challenge.

Another problem for an account of a structural version of this kind of gaslighting is Stark's second criteria. She argues that in a case of manipulative gaslighting, "the gaslighter's judgments are unjustified" (Stark 2019, 224). This requirement ensures that her account leaves room for people to disagree about their judgments without gaslighting each other (Stark 2019, 225). However, if there is no gaslighter in a particular case, then there's no way to say the gaslighter's judgments are justified or not, and so it would seem that it cannot be a case of manipulative gaslighting. Although an account of structural manipulative gaslighting could leave out this criterion, there would then be no grounds on which to distinguish legitimate disagreement from manipulative gaslighting. To try to maintain this distinction while also giving a structural account, I suggest that coercion can be used in the place of justifiability to determine whether a case is one of legitimate disagreement or structural manipulative gaslighting. If coercion based on a power differential is present, and an attempt is made to undermine or dismiss a target whose judgment is justifiable, then the first and second criteria of manipulative gaslighting would be met in the structural case.

The third and fourth criteria for manipulative gaslighting may also pose a problem for a structural account. Both identify particular actions by the gaslighter that would seem impossible to fulfill if there is no identifiable gaslighter in a particular case. Sidestepping and displacement are criteria that appear to require a particular actor acting in specific, transactional ways. However, it is likely that structural manipulative gaslighting would simply require different tactics that transactional manipulative gaslighting. The two tactics Stark describes are employed by the manipulative gaslighter to first avoid the evidence that their judgment is unjustified and then attribute a defect to the target to undermine their credibility (Stark 2019, 224). If structural coercion replaces the gaslighter's unjustifiable judgment as the second criteria in the structural account, then other methods for sidestepping and then displacing accusations of coercion could replace the third and fourth criteria of structural manipulative gaslighting.

Further evidence for the theoretical soundness of an account of structural manipulative gaslighting can be found within Stark's own work. To illustrate the harmful effects of manipulative gaslighting, she draws on an example that she explicitly describes as a structural phenomenon: Kate Manne's account of misogyny. She uses Manne's account to show how gaslighting is used in the service of that social system as a tool of the structures of misogyny (Stark 2019, 227). However, I argue that she actually demonstrates how manipulative gaslighting can itself be a structural phenomenon. Gaslighting is not just a tool of misogyny, but rather misogyny is a form of structural manipulative gaslighting.

Drawing on Manne, Stark describes misogyny as "a property of social systems wherein noncompliant women are subjected to various kinds of hostility, the purpose of which is to enforce certain patriarchal norms, in particular the demand that women, graciously and amenably, serve men" (Stark 2019, 226). Misogyny is characterized as a collective phenomenon, because "it is delivered through a collection of ordinary actions" that have a collective aim achieved through collective actions (Stark 2019, 230). Although it only targets women who are seen as noncompliant, it serves as a threat to all women, delivered "through a collection of ordinary actions" whose collective aim may be distinct "from the aims of the individuals engaging in those actions" but nevertheless achieved through them (Stark 2019, 230).

She then argues that gaslighting is part of the structure of misogyny, "punish[ing] women . . . whose actions challenge a legitimizing ideology that portrays such conduct [of misogyny] as rare or benign" (Stark 2019, 229). Misogynistic gaslighting is also a collective phenomenon (Stark 2019, 229), embedded in the unwitting everyday practices of the culture, and "induc[ing] women to suppress or doubt their judgments in the domain of gender relations" (Stark 2019, 230). It is experienced by women regardless of whether they are "personally involved in gaslighting relationships," and it is most effectively enacted publicly (Stark 2019, 30).

These characterizations seem more structural than transactional. Stark does point out individual perpetrators, such as "a public figure, or by an agent in whom the public has placed its trust, or by ordinary people operating in the public domain" (Stark 2019, 230). However, the characterization of misogynistic gaslighting as collective, impacting even those at whom it is not aimed through a collection of ordinary actions, makes the identification of a particular, individual gaslighter increasingly doubtful. If almost everyone's actions contribute to misogynistic gaslighting, it seems unlikely that a particular target could point to a particular perpetrator or even a long series of interactions with numerous perpetrators like Abramson describes (Abramson 2014, 5). The distortions and manipulations that are characteristic of misogynistic gaslighting and not misogyny more generally are so pervasive in our culture that they are part of its very structure. As a result, a structural account of manipulative gaslighting is necessary for the true extent and nature of cases like misogynistic gaslighting to be understood.

Although Ruíz describes cultural gaslighting as a kind of epistemic gaslighting, her account suggests that it actually has all of the features of structural manipulative gaslighting as well. She explicitly describes how intent is present, specifically what she calls *cultural intent*, in the history and present existence of settler colonial violence toward Indigenous peoples (Ruíz 202, 695). The dispossession that has occurred and continues to be maintained is described as a "long-term strategic process," and a strategic process always has an aim. In this case, that aim is specifically the case for "white Anglo-European settlers to irrevocably take possession of Native Amerindian lands" (Ruíz 2020, 696). Ruíz describes how this kind of cultural project requires "foresight into counter revolutionary strategy and cooptation of resistant cultural narratives, providing clear instances of manipulation" (Ruíz 2020, 696). She argues that the "cultural narrative of presumed unintentionality [of European colonizers imposing their worldview on Native Amerindians] has enabled settler interpretative resources to accumulate epistemic power" (Ruíz 2020, 701). The denial of intent, then, serves to facilitate structural gaslighting. This feature, in addition to cultural gaslighting meeting all of the necessary conditions for gaslighting as described earlier, makes it clear that structural manipulative gaslighting is central to Ruíz understanding of gaslighting as a whole. It also makes it clear that this is indeed gaslighting.

Conclusion

"Gaslighting" has become a buzzword, to such an extent that it may risk people beginning to doubt its theoretical or even popular usefulness. However, the concept has also helped many people identify a particularly harmful phenomenon they have experienced but been unable to name. This is particularly true when it comes to the structural ways in which experiences of those who are oppressed are distorted and denied. To retain the power that being able to identify the phenomenon gives to victims of gaslighting, work should be done to bring the varied accounts of gaslighting into conversation with each other to identify not only their commonalities but also the gaps between them. This is the case even where there are doubts about the utility of some of those concepts. This chapter has been an attempt to identify and conceptualize one such gap, clarifying why those structural phenomena are in fact cases of gaslighting, in the hopes that doing so will elucidate another piece of the puzzle that forms our social lives.

Notes

1. Those aware of Elena Ruíz's critique of these interpersonal accounts may question the efficacy of starting with the interpersonal accounts. However, the term "gaslighting" did originate from the context of psychology. As a result, I feel that it is necessary to start with those accounts to provide a theoretical explanation of why the structural phenomena that Bailey, Pohlhaus, Ruíz, Berenstain, and others identify and conceptualize should be labeled structural *gaslighting* rather than something else.

2. Elena Ruíz discusses gaslighting in her own 2014 article but does not provide a theoretical analysis of the concept.

3. Abramson identifies five of the most common tools used to provide leverage for this manipulation: love, empathy, practical consequences such as job loss, the authority or purported authority of the gaslighter or audience, and the self-doubt that the structure of sexism inculcates in women (Abramson 2014,

20–22). All are most effective against a background of power inequities, whether structural or personal (Abramson 2014, 19).

4. For example, a gaslighter who denies someone's claims of discrimination may be motivated by a desire to keep the peace in a work environment. The motive of wanting a collegial work atmosphere is not itself morally problematic if it is treated in complete isolation from the other elements of the situation at hand.

5. Abramson describes a failure of recognition respect as the grounds for a Kantian account that what is wrong with manipulation is that it is "causing me to act for reasons which I cannot rationally endorse" (Abramson 2014, 15). An epistemic injustice is a wrong done to someone in their capacities as a knower (Fricker 2007, 1). Rae Langton describes silencing as occurring either when someone is prevented from speaking or when someone's speech is prevented from "counting as the action it was intended to be" (Langton 1993, 299).

6. Testimonial injustice "occurs when prejudice causes a hearer to give a deflated level of credibility to a speaker's word" (Fricker 2007, 1).

7. Hermeneutical injustice "occurs at a prior stage, when a gap in collective interpretive resources puts someone at an unfair disadvantage when it comes to making sense of their social experiences" (Fricker 2007, 1). It is important to note here that Berenstain identifies Fricker's discussion of hermeneutical injustice as a paradigm example of structural gaslighting (Berenstain 2020, 734). I think using Anderson's discussion of the concept in this context is still useful, with Berenstain's critique in mind, as it models the shift from the transactional to the structural in a way that is productive for understanding transaction and structural accounts of gaslighting. I continue to use the concept of hermeneutical injustice in what follows, as that is what Anderson uses, but see Berenstain (2020) for a detailed critique of Fricker, and Ruíz for an alternative concept of hermeneutical violence (Ruíz 2020, 701–2).

8. It is important to note that there has been some debate over whether or not white ignorance should be considered a hermeneutical injustice (for example, see the exchange between José Medina, Miranda Fricker, and Charles Mills in the *Social Epistemology Review and Reply Collective* 2013 3 [1]). However, I think that regardless of whether white ignorance is considered a hermeneutical injustice or not, there is something useful in understand the phenomenon through the lens I present here. Thinking about white ignorance in terms of gaslighting helps to highlight some of the features that Mills emphasizes, particularly with regard to how people of color who buy into white ignorance are affected.

9. Ruíz and Berenstain also each present examples of structural gaslighting. Ruíz (2020) provides a powerful account of how the treatment of women of color in settler nations such as the United States and Canada exemplifies structural epistemic gaslighting, including cultural gaslighting. Berenstain's (2020) discuss of feminist social epistemology in general and Miranda Fricker's discussion of hermeneutical injustice in particular illustrate clear cases within academia. Although

both of these examples provide rich and complex discussions of these structural phenomena, I have chosen not to analyze them here. In both cases, the question of victim complicity as a feature of gaslighting is particularly complicated and is not discussed. For the purposes of the analysis in this chapter, I have chosen to focus on white ignorance instead. It is a phenomenon that these theorists agree is a case of epistemic structural gaslighting, while at the same time it also clearly demonstrates all three of the necessary conditions for gaslighting I have identified. A deeper analysis of these conditions in the context of Ruíz and Berenstain's examples will have to be left to future work.

Works Cited

Abramson, Kate. 2014. "Turning Up the Lights on Gaslighting." *Philosophical Perspectives* 28: 1–30.

Anderson, Elizabeth. 2012. "Epistemic Justice as a Virtue of Social Institutions." *Social Epistemology* 26 (2): 163–73.

Bailey, Alison. 2020. "On Gaslighting and Epistemic Injustice: Editor's Introduction." *Hypatia* 35: 667–73.

Berenstain, Nora. 2020. "White Feminist Gaslighting." *Hypatia* 35: 733–58.

Davis, Angelique M., and Rose Ernst. 2017. "Racial Gaslighting." *Politics, Groups and Identities* 7 (4): 761–74.

Fricker, Miranda. 2007. *Epistemic Injustice: Power and the Ethics of Knowing.* Oxford: Oxford University Press.

Ivy, Veronica [McKinnon, Rachel]. 2017. "Allies Behaving Badly: Gaslighting as Epistemic Injustice." In *The Routledge Handbook of Epistemic Injustice*, edited by Ian James Kidd, José Medina, and Gaile Pohlhaus Jr., 167–74. New York: Routledge.

Langton, Rae. 1993. "Speech Acts and Unspeakable Acts." *Philosophy & Public Affairs* 22 (4): 293–330.

Mason, Rebecca. 2011. "Two Kinds of Unknowing." *Hypatia* 26 (2): 294–307.

Medina, José. 2012. "Hermeneutical Injustice and Polyphonic Contextualism: Social Silences and Shared Hermeneutical Responsibilities." *Social Epistemology* 26 (2): 201–20.

Mills, Charles. 1997. *The Racial Contract.* Ithaca, NY: Cornell University Press.

———. 2013. "White Ignorance and Hermeneutical Injustice: A Comment on Medina and Fricker." *Social Epistemology Review and Reply Collective* 3 (1): 38–43.

Pohlhaus, Gaile, Jr. 2012. "Relational Knowing and Epistemic Injustice: Toward a Theory of Willful Hermeneutical Ignorance." *Hypatia* 27 (4): 715–35.

———. 2020. "Gaslighting and Echoing, or Why Collective Epistemic Resistance Is Not a 'Witch Hunt.'" *Hypatia* 35: 674–86.

Ruíz, Elena. 2014. "Musing: Spectral Phenomenologies: Dwelling Poetically in Professional Philosophy." *Hypatia* 29 (1): 196–204.
———. 2020. "Cultural Gaslighting." *Hypatia* 35: 687–713.
Stark, Cynthia A. 2019. "Gaslighting, Misogyny, and Psychological Oppression." *Monist* 102: 221–35.
Tuck, Eve, and K. Wayne Yang. 2012. "Decolonization Is Not a Metaphor." *Decolonization: Indigeneity, Education and Society* 1 (1): 1–40.

3

Gaslighting and Social Power

Mills, Medina, and Moi on
Knowledge and the Social Imaginary

Sabrina L. Hom

Gaslighting is a form of manipulation that leads the target to distrust her own affects, perceptions, memories, and beliefs, usually by means of repetitive and sustained acts of undermining, questioning, or contradicting the target.[1] It is a form of epistemic injustice because, by definition, gaslighting harms people in their epistemic capacity by undermining their confidence as epistemic agents. Furthermore, this harm is often distributed along lines that reflect other social injustices; in this chapter, I focus on its relation to race and gender. Recognizing the full dimension of gaslighting as an epistemic injustice, however, requires a conception of epistemic injustice that expands Fricker's conception of injustice from one that targets individuals on the basis of their identity to one that acts on whole communities along structural and systematic lines. Gaslighting, especially on a large scale, is not only an epistemic injustice, but one that consolidates social power by securing the contested limits of knowledge and imagination.

In her groundbreaking account of epistemic injustice, Fricker uses the example of a woman of color professor who, accused of misconduct by a graduate student, spends more than a year consumed with self-doubt; neither she nor her colleagues fully accept her own version of the events at stake until it emerges that the student has engaged in a pattern of false accusations (48). Fricker treats this deep self-doubt as at most a "secondary effect" of testimonial injustice (the injustice the professor endured when her account was not, at first, believed) rather than a central case of epistemic injustice in itself because, as she points out, such self-doubt can result from a skepticism that is not, in and of itself, unjust. Unlike Fricker's example of the professor, the gaslighting I describe fits the description of epistemic injustice in and of itself both because it is a distinct form of epistemic harm and because it results from systematic efforts not only to stifle specific types of claims, but to overwhelm the claimants with self-doubt.

For Fricker, testimonial injustice is paradigmatically a result of a deficit of "identity power." People are deemed credible or in-credible on the basis of various judgments, including stereotypes about which sorts of people can be believed. When these stereotypes are grounded in pernicious social prejudice—related, for example, to gender or race—then they result in an unjust credibility deficit. This credibility deficit is a function of the knower's identity—for example, as a woman of color who is stereotyped as irrational or biased—and therefore of a piece with larger systems of racial and gendered oppression. It is this connection to identity-based prejudice that marks testimonial injustice as such, for mistakes about credibility that are not related to such prejudice are, to Fricker, accidents as opposed to injustices.

While the outlines of Fricker's account of testimonial injustice are foundational for an account of gaslighting, Fricker's strict, identity-based definition of testimonial injustice hampers a complete account. As Dotson points out (2012), Fricker's insistence on a closed system—in which anything not described in her tightly defined taxonomy of epistemic injustice is not epistemic injustice at all—threatens to reproduce epistemic injustice by silencing discussion of related epistemic phenomena. Indeed, Berenstain (2020) argues that omitting an analysis of structural oppression in Fricker's system itself amounts to gaslighting. By defining epistemic injustice solely as a function of *individual* prejudice, Fricker neglects forms of epistemic injustice that are grounded in *systemic* racism and other forms of prejudice. Instead of relying on Fricker's closed system, I situate my account in Medina's "epistemology of resistance," which builds off of Fricker's conception of epistemic injustice and situates epistemic injustice in the context of a "social imaginary" in which certain "affects and relations"—and claims and judgments—"have been rendered *incredible* (in fact, almost unintelligible)" (67). While Medina uses the concept of the social imaginary to elaborate Fricker's concept of hermeneutical injustice (70), it is equally apt to testimonial injustice; the limits of the social imaginary will render competing of testimony incredible, not because of the identity of the speaker, but because of the content of her claims.

In Fricker's definition, people whose accurate testimony is dismissed because of its implausible content instead of their identity would not be reckoned as victims of testimonial injustice at all: instead, the knowers who suffered from a credibility deficit in this particular instance would be considered to be merely the victims of bad epistemic luck. But to reduce this systematic stifling to "bad luck" would be to neglect an important—and in my argument, paradigmatic—example of testimonial injustice. First, many of the claims that are most incredible or unintelligible within any given social imaginary will be those that challenge the existing structures of political, economic, and symbolic power, such that stifling these claims will likely entrench existing patterns of injustice. Secondly, to paraphrase Collins, these knowledges are most likely to come from the "outside" (1986), so such a silencing will disproportionately impact members of otherwise marginalized groups; this mental violence is elaborated by Ruíz (2020). And finally, as I will argue, the social-imaginary model of testimonial injustice describes the dynamics of real-life examples in a more accurate and fine-grained way than does the identity-based version.

Of course, accounts of testimonial injustice based on identity power and on the social imaginary are not irreconcilable. First, accounts of identity-based epistemic injustice often focuses on instances where the *content* of the claim is contentious because it is in these instances that the claimant's credibility will be most in question. Second, while I argue that testimony that goes against the social imaginary may be stifled regardless of who utters it, the process of discrediting women and people of color often plays on identity-based stereotypes. Third, those discrediting stereotypes are not indifferent to content, as many prejudices exist that discredit specific types of knowers particularly when they speak on certain content (for example, the stereotypes that women tend to lie about consent in sexual encounters, or Black people tend to "play the race card" by ascribing neutral encounters to racism.) Still, it is a significant distinction whether the primary function of epistemic injustice attaches to individual identities by way of stereotype, or whether it functions also on the level of a limit to the "social imaginary" that renders some types of testimony—and broader patterns of experience—unspeakable. In the former case, epistemic injustice would best be addressed by combating stereotypes about, for example, women and people of color; indeed, Fricker emphasizes the "anti-prejudicial virtue" of a hearer who can neutralize her stereotyped prejudgments. In the latter case, we might emphasize, instead, the epistemic virtues of embracing the friction and discomfort of competing views (Medina 2013, 75) or critically questioning the assumptions, values, and beliefs that predominate in one's social milieu.

If centering the social imaginary suggests different cures for epistemic injustice, it also sheds new light on the phenomenon of gaslighting. This focus illuminates the struggle over the very bounds of the imaginable that takes place between the victims and perpetrators of gaslighting. It emphasizes the ways in which larger social patterns, such as a general silence and skepticism toward claims of abuse, enable acts of individualized gaslighting. Further, it opens up analysis of large-scale instances of gaslighting: the ways in which large groups of people—including the most privileged and powerful—may come to distrust their own observations or judgments in very specific contexts. When this large-scale gaslighting serves to sustain a system that exploits or represses certain groups, we can and should call this an epistemic injustice—not (or not primarily) against those privileged persons who have doubted their own observations, but certainly against those people whose oppression is enabled by this forgetting.

The Social Imaginary

Fricker's conception of the social imagination is primarily as a repository of stereotypes and prejudices that apply to various groups of people—sometimes justly, sometimes not. This minimal conception of the social imaginary does not capture many of the salient ways in which it shapes the credibility economy. I argue for a more expansive conception of the social imaginary, drawn from the work of psychoanalytic feminists, social theorists, and race theorists. Of the various terms that are used to describe this general idea, I have chosen this one in part because it is the one used by Lorraine Code when she made a similar critique of Fricker's work in an early review (2008). The social imaginary is a pervasive set of interconnected values, beliefs, and methods that together conduce to a certain way of being in the world—generally, the prevailing social order. While the social imaginary may have a certain elasticity—not every member of a society will share precisely the same values or beliefs, and some communities will resist aspects of the dominant imaginary (Medina 2013)—it delimits a generally acceptable set of values and beliefs (a set of beliefs that includes, but does not reduce to, prejudices about identity groups). Some of the values and beliefs that ground a way of being will be relatively apolitical; Origgi gives the example of her ingrained belief as an Italian in the superior healthfulness of olive oil (230). Others will have serious moral and political dimensions: for example, beliefs about what sorts of lives are to be valued and what sort are to be labeled as deviant. In other words, the social imaginary ensconces certain value judgments and claims about reality as authoritative, and others as all but unimaginable. To follow Foucault, these boundaries may be more reflective of power than of the truth or defensibility of claims. I do not mean to shift into what Fricker describes as a postmodern relativism here, but rather to point out that power structures within a society may elevate certain claims as authoritative, and others as implausible, independently of whether those claims are true.

To understand how the social imaginary works to delimit the bounds of credible claims and to buttress extant social power, we have only to note a few cognitive habits. Social psychologists describe the "just world fallacy": people have a cognitive bias toward believing that the world they live in is just, that the privileged and dispossessed are deserving of their status, and that the institutions and habits of their community are justified (see Lerner 1980). As a result of this bias, claims of unfairness and injustice tend be treated as improbable or exceptional. Such a bias obviously benefits those who happen to be in power, since it suggests that existing power relations and practices must have prior justification.

More specifically, in his work on the racial contract and "white ignorance," Charles Mills has demonstrated the enormous cognitive effort undertaken to establish the narrative of white settlers as civilized, enlightened persons whose sovereignty is justified by their commitment to universal rights and freedoms. This counterfactual worldview makes use of certain stereotypes—for example, myths of foolish Native Americans who sold their land for a pittance or of enslaved Africans too childlike for freedom—but far exceeds them, not least by deliberately suppressing historical knowledge that would contradict it. The racial contract that grounds a white settler state is, for Mills, in part an epistemic contract precisely because it delimits the sorts of claims that can and cannot be made about race and history, freedom, and so-called "civilization." Once this worldview has established itself, Mills points out, it is sustained by another cognitive bias, "confirmation bias": "seemingly disconfirming, or at least problematic, perceptions are filtered out or marginalized. In other words, one will tend to find the confirmation in the world whether it is there or not" (2007, 25). We can see how the habits embedded in this social imaginary will function to discredit or fully suppress claims about, for example, racial injustice in the United States, which would contradict both the just-world hypothesis in general and the specific, local justificatory narrative that the United States is a free and enlightened country. Mills names this "white ignorance," a stubborn denial and forgetting of racism and colonialism. As in this case, the limits of the social imaginary will often function to silence members of marginalized groups and to support institutions and practices that benefit the existing racial, class, and gender hierarchy.

The language of the social imaginary as foreclosing, or rendering unintelligible, certain types of claims may produce the impression that what is at stake here is hermeneutical, rather than testimonial, injustice: that claims are rendered unintelligible because we lack the conceptual tools to articulate them. No doubt the limits of the social imaginary, with its ability to smother whole areas of inquiry and categories of knower, also serves to limit the types of concepts available in any given society. But in the above example, in which a sanitized national self-concept serves to stifle accounts of racial injustice, this stifling is not for any lack of conceptual resources. American people, after all, have a robust conceptual vocabulary for freedom and bondage, oppression and self-determination, civilization and savagery; for example, these concepts figure centrally in the national origin story of brave freedom fighters revolting against an oppressive government. When the familiar concepts of oppression and savagery are used to describe the foundations of the United States as a white settler state—as in the case of the *1619 Project*, which argues that the brutal institution of slavery, and the vicious racial prejudices used to justify it, are central to US history—we see the mechanisms of suppression mobilize *against the specific claims made*. This repression does not result from the lack of relevant concepts, but from organized and entrenched resistance to claims that challenge the national mythos.

An account of testimonial injustice rooted in a more expansive conception of the social imaginary serves—like Fricker's more limited conception—to highlight the ways in which epistemic injustice correlates to other forms of injustice. As is clear from the examples above, the limitations of the social imaginary often correlate closely to the interests and self-conception of privileged classes within that society, and, furthermore, these limitations tend to support and justify the existing order of racial, class, or gendered hierarchy. Contrary to the identity-based model, however, these injustices occur as a result of systematic and societal forces, rather than the existence of individual prejudice. The social-imaginary model of epistemic injustice fits well with contemporary accounts of racism and oppression, which hold that individual prejudices are only one piece of a larger, systematic, and institutional apparatus.

As an example of the way that the limits of the social imaginary, rather than identity prejudice per se, shape testimonial credibility, I draw a comparison between two related types of cases in nineteenth-century American courts: rape cases and illegitimacy cases. Nineteenth-century American rape cases generally show precisely the pattern one might expect from a contemporary analysis of rape culture: victims are often treated with extreme skepticism, shamed for their past sexual history, and forced to publicly describe their assaults in vivid detail (Block 2006). Women of color and poor or marginalized women of all races were especially likely to be not only disbelieved, but personally humiliated in rape proceedings (Sommerville 2005). These cases cohere neatly to the interpretation that women are silenced because of their identity as women, particularly in realms related to sexuality. Illegitimacy cases were similar insofar as they are proceedings in which women made claims about their sexual experiences, asking a jury to hold men liable for the financial support of illegitimate children. In illegitimacy cases, however, the epistemic biases of rape cases were reversed: women of all classes were treated with an overwhelming presumption of truthfulness; discussion of their sexual histories, and even other partners at the time of conception, was excluded; and explicit testimony regarding the sexual act was rarely required (Grossberg 1988, 217). Paternity trials were civil, not criminal matters, so the standard of proof was "a preponderance of evidence" as opposed to the stricter standard in a criminal trial, but the standards of proof in illegitimacy cases were exceptional even by civil-court standards. As a North Carolina judge instructed a putative father in 1814, "you may, if you please, submit the question of your guilt to a jury, but the burden of showing your innocence shall be on you" (Grossberg 1988, 216). The contrast between these two courtroom settings—one in which women were readily believed on the subject of sex, and one in which women were treated with extreme skepticism—demonstrates that epistemic oppression is not simply a function of one's identity or even the subject matter (for example, we cannot simply say that women are not believed *when they talk about sex*).

Why were women's claims about sex treated with the utmost skepticism in a rape trial and with the utmost credibility in an illegitimacy trial? Whatever stereotypes regarding the credibility of women held within their society, they held for women involved in both types of trial, so identity power per se cannot account for the distinction. Instead, we can account for the difference by looking at how each type of case fits into the social imaginary—that is to say, with how believing and disbelieving specific types of claims affects the economic, political, and symbolic order of the society. A driving interest in illegitimacy cases was economic: as Grossberg puts it, a primary goal of bastardy law was to "prevent the public from being saddled with the costs of rearing children born outside of wedlock" (1988, 197). While local authorities had a responsibility to support indigent "bastards," the costs would be transferred to the child's father if he could be identified. Disbelieving women about paternity quite literally cost money to the local government, and by extension local taxpayers. In contrast, finding a man guilty of rape would have no economic benefit and would likely create expenses (in the case of a prominent or wealthy man, there would be obvious economic disruptions; for the less prosperous, perhaps the convict's own family would become dependent on the local government). An economic motivation also appears in Sommerville's nuanced and detailed history of rape cases in the antebellum Southern United States. In contrast to the brutal and paranoid reactions of postbellum white Southerners to accusations of rape by white women against Black men, Sommerville details several instances in which enslaved Black men accused of rape by white women met with exceptional leniency, often as a result of pressure from the local white community (2005, 19ff.). Members of the white community at times argued that the (inevitably poor and marginalized) white women in these cases were promiscuous and untrustworthy, while the enslaved men were trusty and hardworking. These pleas for leniency should be seen in context: while enslaved people were subject to extensive physical and emotional brutality, the execution of an enslaved man in his prime would be a significant economic loss to his enslaver.[2] If the dynamics of trust in nineteenth-century courtrooms did not always reduce to stereotypes of racial of gender identity per se, they mapped very neatly to the economic interests of the ascendant class of men.

While economic interests were a driving force, especially in laws around illegitimacy, there are also political and symbolic interests at stake in shaping which women's claims were believed, and when. Nineteenth-century American bastardy law resulted from a series of reforms to English common law, which held the bastard to be "filius nullius," a child with no family at all; such children had no rights of inheritance and were severely marginalized. American reforms to situate illegitimate children within families, including by publicly attaching them to fathers, were seen as humane and enlightened, a move that underlined the distinction between the Americans and the "feudal, aristocratic, and undemocratic" English policy (Grossberg 1988, 211). In contrast, recognizing cases of rape would force communities to acknowledge violence and "savagery" within their own communities. As Mills argues, the epistemic racial contract calls for the forgetting of the savagery of colonists and enslavers toward Black and Indigenous people and the elevation of a myth of civilized and worthy white settlers. The enforcement of this contract can be seen in both bastardy and rape trials, which systematically doubted women's claims about violence within white settler communities while bolstering a narrative of enlightenment and egalitarianism toward illegitimate children and their mothers.

The contrast between nineteenth-century rape and illegitimacy trials demonstrates the power of the social imaginary in delimiting what sorts of testimony are granted credibility; in this instance, otherwise similar women making claims about their sexual experiences were treated as highly suspect in one context and authoritative in another. The example also demonstrates the mundanity of the social imaginary, which—bound up with the economic and social interests of powerful classes—serves to bolster penny-pinching local bureaucrats at the same time that it entrenches patriarchal and white supremacist hierarchies.

Hysteria, Power, and Collective Gaslighting

Psychoanalytic feminism has been fixated on epistemic issues of silencing and ignorance since long before the current emphasis on epistemic injustice. It was Freud who hypothesized that the physical symptoms of his "hysterical" female patients were rooted in deeply repressed fantasies and unspeakable desire and that these symptoms could be cured if the analyst excavated the hidden truths behind the patient's illness. Feminist theorists such as Irigaray reinterpret Freud's theory not as an objective description of the universal structure of the hysteria-prone female psyche, but as a description of a typical structure of female experience within a society structured around male experience, male desire, and male power: that is to say, as a reaction to erasure and silencing (Cixous 1986; Irigaray 1985). The effort of repression takes its toll, leading to physical and psychical suffering as well as the characteristic emotional turbulence and verbal confusion associated with hysterics. Importantly, hysterics don't know what it is that they are hiding in order to create this misery and confusion. They find their experiences, desires, and affects are so inconceivable within the social imaginary as to be unintelligible even to themselves. In the feminist interpretation, hysterics are the victims of a silencing so thorough that it destabilizes their own epistemic agency—in other words, they are victims of gaslighting. Hysteria, then, is intimately connected to gaslighting—not only because the victims of gaslighting are often dismissed, in gendered terms, as "hysterical" in the vernacular sense, but because it is a reaction to gaslighting and silencing. Feminist psychoanalysts interpret hysteria not merely as a pathology but also as a reminder of the force that maintains male dominance and represses desires or experiences that would challenge its social imaginary. Their analysis emphasizes the relationship between gaslighting—both at the individual and, as I discuss shortly, the collective level—and existing relations of social power.

To elaborate on the connection of gaslighting to hysteria, and on what contemporary feminist epistemology can gain from it, I draw out points related to Freud's famous case study of "Dora" in *Fragments of an Analysis of a Case of Hysteria*. Dora, whose real name was Ida Bauer, was brought to Freud for psychoanalysis by her father. While Dora suffered from a number of symptoms, including a persistent cough, her analysis was precipitated when she accused her father's friend "Herr K" of propositioning her. Dora alleged that her father meant to arrange a liaison between herself and Herr K to reciprocate for his own affair with Herr K's wife. Freud did not accept Dora's account, not least because he thought that a healthy girl of her age ought to have responded to the older man's proposition with desire;[3] instead, he posited that Dora suffered from hidden but powerful desires that led to both hysterical symptoms and to what he considered a pathological lack of normative heterosexual desire. Freud variously imagined that the real object of Dora's desire was her own father, then Herr K, and finally Frau K, his wife.

The dynamic between Dora and Freud emphasizes the collective and social aspect of gaslighting. Dora's claims—which Freud attempted to repress and reinterpret—were claims of abuse: a sexual assault by Herr K, who grabbed her and tried to kiss her, and the machinations of her father, who hoped to exploit his daughter sexually to enable his own affair with

Frau K. Freud dismissed these claims as hysterical fantasy. In fact, so many of Freud's hysterical patients made such claims that he had once—prior to the mature theory he articulates in relation to Dora—considered hysteria to be the result of childhood sexual abuse. Within the limits of the social imaginary, of course, the idea that large numbers of prominent and respected men had sexually abused their daughters was deeply implausible. These accounts of abuse were explained away not only by Freud, but also by a social imaginary that was (and often, still is) hostile to accounts of non-heteronormative desire and deeply skeptical of abuse survivors. Indeed, in instances where gaslighting is a form of individualized abuse—part of the arsenal, perhaps, of a controlling spouse—the social imaginary is nonetheless complicit. Adkins describes this phenomenon as "gaslighting by crowd" (2019). For example, let us imagine a woman whose husband flies into inexplicable rages and engages in vicious emotional abuse. After the fact, he behaves in a loving manner and insists that she misinterpreted the events—that he had legitimate reasons for being angry with her, that marital tiffs are normal, and that the way he behaved really wasn't so bad. If he is successful at gaslighting, she will come to believe that this abuse is normal and deserved. If she is persuaded, this will likely be abetted by any number of inadvertent co-conspirators: friends who respond to her descriptions of abuse with skepticism, saying things like "oh, is it really that bad?" or "he seems so sweet to me"; the producers of artistic works that normalize manipulative and volatile behavior in relationships; anyone who wonders what she might have done to set her husband off. In this example as in many others, gaslighting is not merely an individual act of abuse, but an act enabled by a social imaginary that treats claims of abuse as inherently suspect. (I would suggest that this reluctance is not unconnected to the reluctance to believe accusations of rape described above.)

In her account of the Dora case study, Toril Moi emphasizes that the psychoanalytic scene is an epistemic power struggle, one in which the analyst works to assert the authority to reinterpret the words and gestures, desires, and experiences of the analysand. Because Freud's analysands were often female, this struggle is often a gendered one; since exploring the "dark continent" of female sexuality is one of his fixations, the struggle is often over the truth about women's desire.[4] Freud's goal was for his patients to accept his interpretation of their true and hidden desires and hence recover from their hysterical repression. In the case of Dora, he believed at first that accusations toward Herr K hid a jealous desire for her own father—a man of similar age and station to Freud himself. Moi, like Lacan and Irigaray before her, points out the significant of countertransference here (Moi 1981, 65), emphasizing Freud's unconscious interest in and desire for his own desirability. As he immortalizes Dora as hysterical fantasist, Freud attempts to impose his own interpretation—a heteronormative one that affirms that older men such as himself are highly desirable to young women—on Dora. The status of analysis as a "struggle for the possession of knowledge" (70) is laid bare precisely because she refuses to comply with this interpretation: Dora quits analysis abruptly and only returns, a year later, to report that she had confronted the K's and extracted a full confession. Significantly, Freud is fighting here not for epistemic agency itself, but for "total, absolute knowledge . . . a finished, closed whole," possession of which is continuous with social power (70). As Abramson points out in her analysis of gaslighting, "[t]he central desire or aim of the gaslighter, to put it sharply, is to destroy even the possibility of disagreement—to have his sense of the world not merely confirmed, but placed beyond dispute" (2014, 10). We should read gaslighting, both at the individual and collective levels, as an assertion of power, and specifically as an assertion of the exclusive power to define and delimit the social imaginary.

I have argued, by way of feminist psychoanalytic theory, that gaslighting can be seen as a power struggle over the limits of social imaginary—that is, over the commonly accepted beliefs of what sorts of things can and cannot be believed. The example of Dora demonstrates some of the ways in which both individuals and society as a whole work to discourage individual agents from speaking or believing things that fall outside the social imaginary. But the social imaginary itself, of course, is preserved as such not only because a few individuals accept it, but also because the mainstream of society itself is committed to it. Presumably this sort of epistemic consensus is sometimes possible because the limits of the social imaginary match well with the perceptions and experiences of community members, but community members often have diverse experiences, and the bounds of the social imaginary are not necessarily a close match to reality. In the latter instances, the bounds of the social imaginary itself are in question, and large-scale gaslighting is a strategy to defuse such conflict.

The concept of collective gaslighting rose in prominence during the Trump era, when citizens were all too often asked to ignore misdeeds that occurred, to paraphrase Richard Pryor, before their "lying eyes." In an early instance, in the runup to the 2016 presidential election, Jamelle

Bouie describes then–vice presidential candidate Mike Pence's debate performance as "national gaslighting" (Bouie 2016). During the debate, rival candidate Tim Kaine read off a series of racist and sexist statements that had been made by Pence's running mate, Donald Trump, in highly public settings—generally, during nationally televised speeches or on Twitter. How could Pence defend such statements, Kaine asked? Pence didn't: instead, he accused Kaine of campaigning dirty by launching an "avalanche of insults" at Donald Trump. Pence didn't just deny that Trump had said such things; he argued that to disparage Trump *with his own words* was a terrible insult. Pence confidently asserted an alternate vision of reality that contradicted events that had been witnessed by millions of people, including many of the debate viewers.

Significantly, the act of collective gaslighting described by Bouie depends on the very limits of the social imaginary described by Mills. The statements Kaine read included Trump's fearmongering and xenophobic description of Mexicans as "murderers and rapists," his claim that a judge was unqualified to preside over a case because of his Mexican heritage, and a series of incidents in which he disparaged women as "pigs" and "dogs." Mills's account of the racial contract, of course, is that it requires participants to ignore or forget evidence of racialized abuse and cruelty—even when they witness it themselves. Maintaining this studied ignorance of racism, and the myth of a fundamentally free and equal state, requires that participants dispel their own memories of the American presidential candidate openly and obviously expressing racist and xenophobic animus. Of course, not every American acted as a "signatory" or participant in the racial contract in this instance: many insisted on what they had seen. It is no coincidence that the author who called out this gaslighting, Jamelle Bouie, is an African American man and a longtime commentator on racial politics; as Medina argues, pockets of epistemic resistance exist against a dominant social imaginary, and Black "counter-memory" is one example (2012, 233). Many Americans, however, were all too ready to be gaslit—to deny their own observations in the interest of a racially innocent vision of their country—while others found themselves confused and caught between the competing narratives.

Similarly, the overwhelming resistance to believing accusations of sexual assault and abuse makes it all too easy—at least, in some circles—to ignore Trump's public degradation of women, the many accusations against him, and his own taped admission of serial sexual assault. Once again, I want to emphasize that these acts of forgetting or eliding abuse are not simply a matter of doubting the victims—a more straightforward example of testimonial injustice. Instead, because of the highly public nature of Trump's misdeeds and admissions, it requires gaslighting: participants must put aside *their own* observations of reality and adopt an alternate account.

I have described instances in which agents discredit or repress their own perceptions in a seemingly willing and voluntary way: in Mills's terms, they are "signatories" and participants in the racial contract. I have also described people, such as Bouie himself, who strenuously resist such gaslighting. But the reality is more complicated. In recent years, many Americans have found themselves destabilized by what some have called a political "war on reality" (for example, Bookman 2016; Robertson 2017; Sargent 2020). Can it really be so bad to ask a foreign government for help in an election, they wonder, if it is done brazenly, in a nationally televised interview? Was the January 6 riot at the Capitol really so bad if so many people are downplaying it? Are the innocent victims of videotaped police violence really innocent if local police and reporters can dig up a history of minor misdeeds? I do not mean to suggest that these doubts are exculpatory, but rather that collective gaslighting can undermine agents' epistemic confidence and trust in their own judgment, even if they are not fully persuaded to disavow their observations. In the process, objective statements of demonstrable facts are reduced to the level of controversial and partisan political opinions. Such a process undermines the epistemic agency of those who are gaslit while also hindering their moral and political agency in relation to events taking place in their society.

In this chapter, I have argued that gaslighting is a form of epistemic violence, but, unlike the forms of epistemic violence Fricker describes, one that is 1) frequently collective and 2) dependent not on identity power but on the limits of the social imaginary. Contrary to Fricker's identity-based account of epistemic injustice, credibility often has less to do with identity and more to do with how specific claims fit into the economic, political, and symbolic interests of a dominant class. The social imaginary delimits the set of beliefs and perceptions that are considered plausible within a community, and it is often constructed in alignment with raced, classed, and gender interests. Gaslighting occurs when an agent comes to question her own credibility, at least in part because her observations and experiences fall outside the limits of the social imaginary. This gaslighting often occurs as a result of the social imaginary's skepticism toward claims of racism, abuse, and sexual assault. While gaslighting can occur as a form of individualized abuse, it also occurs on the collective scale, leading agents to doubt their own observations in charged areas such as racism, misogyny, and abuse.

Notes

1. This definition is paraphrased from Abramson 2014, 3.

2. This point is emphasized by Angela Davis, who points out that lynching as a system of racial terrorism did not take hold until after emancipation, since it was in the economic interest of enslavers to use alternate forms of social control, such as beatings and rape, which did not destroy valuable property. See Davis 1973, 183.

3. The uninvited embrace of the much older Herr K "was surely just the situation to call up distinct feelings of sexual excitement in a girl of fourteen," Freud remarked notoriously (1997, 21).

4. Freud's fixation with, and frustration over, the "mystery" of feminine desire is discussed at length in Irigaray 1985; see 19ff.

Works Cited

Abramson, Kate. 2014. "Turning Up the Lights on Gaslighting." *Philosophical Perspectives* 28: 1–30.
Adkins, Karen C. 2019. "Gaslighting by Crowd." *Social Philosophy Today* 35: 75–87.
Berenstain, Nora. 2020. "White Feminist Gaslighting." *Hypatia* 35 (4): 733–58.
Block, Sharon. 2006. *Rape and Sexual Power in Early America*. Chapel Hill: University of North Carolina Press.
Bookman, Jay. 2016. "Why Trump Cannot Be Allowed to Win His War on Reality." *Atlanta Journal-Constitution*. https://www.ajc.com/blog/jay-bookman/why-trump-cannot-allowed-win-his-war-reality/tgYpmNiF1RBMcqlKii81UK/.
Bouie, Jamelle. 2016. "This Wasn't a Debate. This Was a National Gaslighting." *Slate*. https://slate.com/news-and-politics/2016/10/mike-pence-won-because-he-was-shameless-about-denying-reality.html.
Cixous, Hélène. 1986. *The Newly Born Woman*. Vol. 24 of *Theory and History of Literature*. London: Tauris.
Code, Lorraine. 2008. "Epistemic Injustice: Power and the Ethics of Knowing." *Notre Dame Philosophical Reviews* 3.
Collins, Patricia Hill. 1986. "Learning From the Outsider Within: The Sociological Significance of Black Feminist Thought." *Social Problems* 33 (6): 14–32.
Davis, Angela Y. 1983. *Women, Race, and Class*. New York: Vintage.
———. 2012. "A Cautionary Tale: On Limiting Epistemic Oppression." *Frontiers: A Journal of Women Studies* 33 (1): 24–47.

———. 2014. "Conceptualizing Epistemic Oppression." *Social Epistemology* 28 (2): 115–38.
Dotson, Kristie. 2011. "Tracking Epistemic Violence, Tracking Practices of Silencing." *Hypatia* 26 (2): 236–57.
Freud, Sigmund. 1997. *Dora: An Analysis of a Case of Hysteria*. New York: Simon and Schuster.
Fricker, Miranda. 2007. *Epistemic Injustice: Power and the Ethics of Knowing*. Oxford: Oxford University Press.
Grossberg, Michael. 1988. *Governing The Hearth: Law and the Family in Nineteenth-Century America*. Chapel Hill: University of North Carolina Press.
Irigaray, Luce. 1985. *Speculum of the Other Woman*. Ithaca, NY: Cornell University Press.
Lerner, Melvin J. 1980. *The Belief in a Just World*. Boston: Springer.
Medina, José. 2013. *The Epistemology of Resistance: Gender and Racial Oppression, Epistemic Injustice, and the Social Imagination*. Oxford: Oxford University Press.
Mills, Charles. 2007. "White Ignorance." In *Race and Epistemologies of Ignorance*, edited by Nancy Tuana and Shannon Sullivan, 26–31. Albany: State University of New York Press.
———. 2014. *The Racial Contract*. Ithaca, NY: Cornell University Press.
———. 2017. *Black Rights/White Wrongs: The Critique of Racial Liberalism*. Oxford: Oxford University Press.
Moi, Toril. 1981. "Representation of Patriarchy: Sexuality and Epistemology in Freud's Dora." *Feminist Review* 9 (1): 60–74.
Origgi, Gloria. 2012. "Epistemic Injustice and Epistemic Trust." *Social Epistemology* 26 (2): 221–35.
Robertson, Nic. 2017. "Trump's War on Reality Is Truly Baffling." *CNN.com*. https://www.cnn.com/2017/03/03/opinions/why-does-trump-attack-media-nic-robertson-opinion/index.html.
Sargent, Greg. 2020. "Trump's War on Reality Just Got a Lot More Dangerous." *Washington Post*. https://www.washingtonpost.com/opinions/2020/05/26/trumps-war-reality-just-got-lot-more-dangerous/.
Ruíz, Elena. 2012. "Cultural Gaslighting." *Hypatia* 35 (4): 687–713.
Sommerville, Diane Miller. 2005. *Rape and Race in the Nineteenth-Century South*. Chapel Hill: University of North Carolina Press.

4

Moral Gaslighting

KATE MANNE

Victims' testimony about what was done to them—and by whom—is a powerful weapon in the fight against injustice. Women testifying to the reality of sexual assault and harassment galvanized the world in 2017, following the popularization of Tarana Burke's #MeToo movement. The testimony of people of color has similarly played a crucial role in greater (if still highly imperfect) social awareness of the realities of racism. But sometimes a person who has been subject to one injustice is then subject to another: the deprivation of her ability to tell her tale, and even her own sense of its validity.

Gaslighting is one of the ways this happens, and this is one of the reasons I am interested in it. There are other reasons too. I am interested in gaslighting not only as a mask for misogyny (among other forms of injustice) but also because, as we will see, misogyny can serve as a tool or technique of gaslighting. Thus, for someone trying to make sense of the logic of misogyny, gaslighting demands and rewards close examination.

And gaslighting is also an inherently puzzling phenomenon that deserves study in itself. Somehow, some agents manage to induce others not to believe the evidence of their senses—along with testimonial evidence, the evidence provided by their memories, and other generally reliable belief-forming methods. How does this work? How could it? And could it operate purely structurally, as well as interpersonally, in some cases?

Philosophers have turned their attention to gaslighting only recently and have made considerable progress in analyzing its characteristic aims and harms. I am less convinced, however, that we have fully understood its nature. I argue in this chapter that philosophers and others interested in the phenomenon have largely overlooked a phenomenon I call moral gaslighting, in which someone is made to feel morally defective—for example, cruelly unforgiving or overly suspicious—for harboring some mental state to which she is entitled. If I am right about this possibility, and that it deserves to be called gaslighting, then gaslighting is a far more prevalent and everyday phenomenon than previously has been credited.

~

Various definitions of gaslighting have been proposed in the literature, typically in passing. Neal A. Kline defines gaslighting as "the effort of one person to undermine another person's confidence and stability by causing the victim to doubt [their] own senses and beliefs" (2006, 1148). Veronica Ivy [Rachel McKinnon] writes that gaslighting occurs "when a hearer tells a speaker that the speaker's claim isn't that serious, or they're overreacting, or they're being too sensitive, or they're not interpreting events properly" (2017, abstract). Paige L. Sweet characterizes gaslighting as "a type of psychological abuse aimed at making victims seem or feel 'crazy,' creating a 'surreal' interpersonal environment" (2019, 851), which, as a substantive matter of fact, often "[relies] on the association of femininity with irrationality" (2019, 855). And Kate Abramson writes: "Very roughly, the phenomenon that's come to be picked out with [the term 'gaslighting'] is a form of emotional manipulation in which the gaslighter tries (consciously or not) to induce in someone the sense that her reactions, perceptions, memories and/or beliefs are not just mistaken, but utterly without grounds—paradigmatically, so unfounded as to qualify as crazy" (Abramson 2014, 2). These definitions are similar to one another inasmuch as they focus on the ways gaslighters try to depict their victims as, or actually make them feel, "crazy,"[1] insane, mentally unstable, irrational, hysterical, paranoid, and so on—broadly rational defects. The *Oxford English Dictionary*'s current definition of gaslighting is similar too: it holds that gaslighting is "the action or process of manipulating a person by psychological means into questioning his or her own sanity" (OED 2016).

Although these definitions doubtless capture something important, I believe they leave out a lot as well.[2] In my view, gaslighting can weaponize morality as well as rationality against its targets and victims. And once we have recognized this, we can make better sense of the possibility of purely structural cases of gaslighting, which the above authors find little room for (with both Sweet and Abramson rejecting it). I think such gaslighting is a real phenomenon, and the moral form of gaslighting explains how it is possible, and indeed not uncommon.

∼

It will help to begin with the original case of gaslighting, which is responsible for the introduction of the term to the English language. In the 1938 play *Gas Light*, performed on Broadway as *Angel Street* (Hamilton 1942), Mr. Manningham is a cruel and abusive husband who torments his wife, Bella, in a variety of ways. He hides household objects around their home and accuses her of stealing them; he implies that she is sick, feeble, and mentally unstable; and he accuses her, most painfully of all, of deliberately hurting their pet dog, whom Bella loves dearly.

Why does Mr. Manningham do all this? As emerges late in the play's first act, he is actually the diabolical Sydney Power, who murdered the previous resident of the home, Alice Barlow, to steal her rubies. Power then slit Barlow's throat to silence her, we learn from the play's resident detective, Detective Rough, who comes to visit Bella to tell her this sordid tale. Some fifteen years on, Mr. Manningham has married Bella (under this false name) to persuade her to use her inheritance to buy the Barlow residence, where he can look for the rubies he never located all those years ago. He searches for the rubies every night up in the attic, having told Bella he is going out for the evening.

This is where the flickering of the gaslights comes in. Their telltale ebbing has allowed Bella to infer where her husband is going every night (though not why he is going, or what he is doing, up there). For, every night, ten minutes after her husband ostensibly leaves the house, the gaslight ebbs; and then, ten minutes before he returns, it reverts to its former, full flame. This means that a light must have been switched on, then off again, somewhere else in the house, since the gas pressure from one light being turned on siphons off gas pressure from another. And the only plausible candidate location is the attic, which is shut up and off-limits to everyone in the house (bar, it turns out, its master).

The following exchange between Detective Rough and Bella brings out that Bella knew all along, at least deep down, that her husband was creeping about in the attic each night:

MRS. MANNINGHAM: It all sounds so incredible [but] . . . when I'm alone at night[,] I get the idea that—somebody's walking about up there—[Looking up.] Up there—At night, when my husband's out—I hear noises, from my bedroom, but I'm too afraid to go up—

ROUGH: Have you told your husband about this?

MRS. MANNINGHAM: No. I'm afraid to. He gets angry. He says I imagine things which don't exist—

ROUGH: It never struck you, did it, that it might be your own husband walking about up there?

MRS. MANNINGHAM: Yes—that is what I thought—but I thought I must be mad. Tell me how you know.

ROUGH: Why not tell me first how you knew, Mrs Manningham.

MRS. MANNINGHAM: It's true, then! It's true. I knew it. I knew it! (Hamilton 1938, Act One)

Though Bella is triumphant in her extant knowledge in that moment, she has suffered terrible epistemic losses: her husband has made her so doubtful of herself that she doesn't dare to question his movements, let alone his motives.[3] And this, presumably, is partly why he is doing it—to discredit her in advance of her potentially discovering and acting on the truth about his misdeeds. There is also the undoubted pleasure he takes in his cruelty. (The cruelty is partly the point for him, to borrow a phrase from Adam Serwer [2018].)

Notice that, even in this example, where Mr. Manningham does depict his wife as mentally unstable—and arguably tries to make her so—there are also moral elements to his gaslighting behavior. His accusations toward her of stealing objects and hurting their pet dog are straightforwardly moral complaints and seem designed to impugn her moral character, rather than her rationality, sanity, or similar. To establish the role this plays in destabilizing her, and many other victims of such gaslighting, let us turn to another case that sheds further light on the matter.

Moral Gaslighting | 107

∾

The possibility that gaslighting can proceed by weaponizing moral norms comes out even more clearly in a case drawn from the recent hit podcast *Dirty John*—which also has the benefit of showing that there are real-life cases of gaslighting scarcely less extreme than the foregoing, fictional one.

In this case, Debra Newell, a woman in her late fifties, falls in love with and marries a con artist named John Meehan. He pretended to be an anesthesiologist (dressing up in scrubs on their dates), while in reality he was a nurse anesthetist who had been fired for stealing drugs intended for patients (some of whom were on the operating table at the time and thus would have been left in agony). He had a long history of addiction to prescription pain medication and had stalked many women. He boasted of raping at least one of them. He had been repeatedly arrested, served with restraining orders, and when he met Debra, unbeknownst to her, he had just come out of prison a day or two earlier for felony drug theft. "Just the most devious, deceptive person" was how one hardened career cop described John Meehan—hence his eponymous moniker. Some people also called him "filthy."

Debra's children had strong suspicions about John and worried about their mother. Eventually she found incontrovertible evidence of his myriad deceptions—arrest warrants, prison records—and moved out of their shared home in Newport Beach, California. Meanwhile, John was in the hospital following back surgery and ensuing complications. When Debra withdrew from him, he began to threaten her and depicted her as the wrongdoer: accusing her of stealing from him, hitting him, and other supposed misdeeds she had never committed. This was a go-to move for John: painting himself as the victim with no basis in fact whatsoever. Debra hid from John in hotels on the advice of a police detective whose help she had appealed to.

Nonetheless, somehow, despite all this, Debra not only forgave John but was persuaded by him that it was all a big misunderstanding—she bought his demonstrable, dangerous lies all over again. It's not altogether clear from the podcast whether John gaslit, or merely lied to Debra, originally. But it is clear that, whatever the case, Debra was subsequently (re)gaslit. Here's *LA Times* journalist Christopher Goffard interviewing Debra in a dialogue that provides important insights into how John managed to achieve this:

DEBRA: So twenty-three days go by [while he's in the hospital] and I just want to look him straight in the face and ask him why he did this. So I went in there and he said that those stories are wrong, that he was set up. He was trying to tell me so many times that he was set up and had to go to jail. Please forgive him. He just knew that I wouldn't understand until he had all the evidence in front of him.

CHRISTOPHER: All a big misunderstanding?

DEBRA: All a big misunderstanding and he had an answer for everything; and it was so convincing that I thought, Okay. He, literally, had convinced me, at this point, that he is not this person.

CHRISTOPHER: Despite all of the paperwork?

DEBRA: Yes. All the facts were right there in front of me and he is that convincing that I would say that . . . I was also in love with him. It's so hard, when you're in love, to listen. You're listening to your heart, not your head.

CHRISTOPHER: Did you ask about his nickname, Dirty John?

DEBRA: He said it wasn't true. He said, "I don't know where you got that from." It was as if everything . . . He was able to convince me. He was so good at it, it could be a cold day out and he could convince me that it's 95 degrees, that's how good he was. To where you questioned yourself.

CHRISTOPHER: It's almost like he convinced you that all the facts about his life were some kind of hallucination on your part?

DEBRA: Yes, he made me out to be the one . . . That he was this great guy and that everyone else had done him wrong, is what he had said . . . [H]e always, again, he always had a story. He told me that he had lied because he thought he'd lose me, that he feels so lucky that I'm such a forgiving person who, hell, I'm the love of his life, that I've made him a better person. Just all this kind of stuff . . . I felt guilty, to some degree, that

I'd married him and that he's in the hospital, but at the same time, I feared . . .

CHRISTOPHER: Explain that to me. Guilty why?

DEBRA: Because I made a commitment. I made a commitment to marriage—for better, for worse.[4]

Intuitively, and given the language often used to describe this case in the media, I take this to be a clear case of gaslighting.[5] But notice that, importantly, John never alleged that Debra was crazy, or impugned her rationality in any way—and though she questioned her own perceptions and beliefs (as in many though not all cases of gaslighting, as I eventually argue), she never questioned her very sanity. Rather, John made Debra out to be a bad person when she challenged or withdrew from him, and a good one for believing him. He operated with both a moral stick—the prospect of his condemning Debra—and a moral carrot—the prospect of his celebrating her as a wonderful wife, forgiving person, the love of his life, and so on. His bait for swallowing his story was primarily moral—and affective. It was the prospect of seeming bad or mean, not mad or insane, that made Debra afraid to continue to think ill of John. And that is what allowed him to gaslight her so effectively.

This possibility is not surprising, upon reflection. One of the basic lessons of Miranda Fricker's concept of testimonial injustice (Fricker 2007) and Kristie Dotson's related notion of testimonial quieting (Dotson 2011) is that there are plausibly moral as well as rational defects that wrongly make us disbelieve some people's stories. It is wrong, as well as unreasonable, to doubt a woman's testimony because she is a woman and one implicitly believes women to be incompetent or liars—these being sexist and misogynistic stereotypes. Imagine, then, if John had said to Debra that she was refusing to believe him because of her unjust stereotypes about convicted felons—stereotypes that undoubtedly exist, and that she may have even harbored (like many, if not most, Americans). One can imagine this giving a morally conscientious person grave pause: in failing to believe my partner, am I committing a testimonial injustice against him? Or (as was the case here) am I merely putting two and two together and ceasing to be (too) credulous?

Of course, John did not invoke these technical philosophical notions in gaslighting Debra. Rather, he used more common and ready-to-hand moral norms—such as being a loving and forgiving wife as opposed to a cold and untrusting one—to manipulate her. But the point here is just that there are sometimes moral grounds, as well as rational ones, for second-guessing our initial disbelief in the testimony of certain people.[6] Gaslighters may invoke the specter of these norms to illicitly convince people to buy their narrative—or sob story—even if it is not only false but radically implausible.

Moreover, there are reasons to think that this phenomenon, which I dub "moral gaslighting," may be easier and more effective than impugning a target's rationality to gaslight her.[7] To put it crudely, sanity is a relatively low bar: even speaking as an agent who lives with some history of mental illness (in the form of depression and anxiety), I don't often doubt that I am basically in touch with reality, not prone to hallucination, delusions, and so on. It would be relatively difficult for an agent to convince me otherwise. Whereas I, like any morally conscientious agent, frequently worry that I am getting things wrong epistemically because of some moral failure of mine. Perhaps I am not forgiving enough, or am too cynical about some people's purported moral transformations, or am harboring unjust stereotypes, to give just a few examples. By exploiting these garden-variety worries about the ways in which my imperfect adherence to moral norms may infect my epistemic state—for instance, by making me too skeptical of some people's testimony—I could quite easily become a victim of what I've called moral gaslighting. Arguably these considerations apply more readily to women, which jibes with the observation that women are particularly vulnerable to gaslighting, as Abramson and Sweet both rightly argue (and of which more follows).[8] But I invite all but the most morally confident (overconfident?) readers to generalize to their own case, as applicable.

For morality is a high bar. We do, and should, have worries about our moral imperfections making us worse agents, epistemically (as well as, of course, morally). By amplifying and exploiting these worries, moral gaslighters may target us, and will sometimes be effective.[9]

∼

It helps to pause at this juncture to say something about the characteristic aim of agents who gaslight, with the aid of Kate Abramson's illuminating account of the matter. This allows me to begin to locate my views with respect to hers, and also to say where I think she goes wrong, in characterizing gaslighting more strongly and narrowly than is warranted. After that, in the following section, I am in a position to show how the view I defend about what gaslighting is can accommodate a phenomenon she implicitly denies: structural gaslighting.

According to Abramson, gaslighters are characteristically motivated by a desire to avoid being challenged, or disagreed with, by their victim. "What makes the difference between the fellow who ignores or dismisses evidence . . . and the one who gaslights, is the inability to tolerate even the possibility of challenge," she writes (Abramson 2014, 9). Before going on to give an account of the moral wrong of gaslighting, Abramson writes that "the gaslighter's characteristic desire is to destroy the possibility of disagreement, where the only sure path to that is destroying the source of possible disagreement—the independent, separate, deliberative perspective from which disagreement might arise" (2014, 10). The "successfully" gaslit person is thus so radically undermined that "she has nowhere left to stand from which to disagree, no standpoint from which her words might constitute genuine disagreement." Not only has she been made to feel that she has lost her mind; she actually has. And, on Abramson's view, gaslighters both believe their victims to be, and aim to drive them, crazy.

It's not clear, however, that gaslighters need to take a sure path to achieving their aim, pace Abramson. And, given their other aims, it may be better that they do not. For, as Abramson acknowledges, gaslighters don't solely want to destroy the possibility of disagreement with their interlocutor—if that were all they wanted, then they could pursue many alternative strategies that would be an equally, if not more, certain means to that end. They could, for example, avoid conflict and behave in a submissive fashion themselves; they could avoid their victim entirely; and, as Abramson herself points out, they could even kill their victims, if they had no compunction about murder (as at least some gaslighters do not, including the two men in the foregoing case studies).[10,11]

What some of the most dastardly gaslighters want, I think, is to preserve the appearance of disagreement, or potential disagreement, but to avoid the concomitant risk of actually losing ensuing arguments. He can "win" by stacking the decks heavily in favor of his prevailing, having made her a much more tentative and deferential interlocutor than she would be otherwise. Or he can avoid the ignominy of losing by forestalling conflict in the first place, having heavily incentivized her perpetual, predictable acquiescence to his viewpoint. He thus may dominate her by means of his gaslighting tactics (rather than by dint of physical coercion, emotional blackmail, financial control, or similar—though these tactics may also be used against her concurrently). In view of this, it seems to me that such a gaslighter need not aim to destroy the victim's rational perspective tout court. Indeed, given his aim of preserving an apparent potential disputant, while enjoying the (admittedly hollow) victory of having his perspective at least typically prevail over hers, it seems better not to destroy her perspective whole cloth.[12] Rather, he can proceed by making her afraid to disagree with him, as with Mrs. Manningham, or feel obligated to buy his story, as with Debra Newell, among other possibilities.

So even if we accept Abramson's view that gaslighters characteristically want to avoid disagreement or challenge, as I am inclined to, there is no need to accept her view that gaslighters typically aim to destroy the independent rational perspectives of their victims. Although achieving this would indeed guarantee that this aim would be satisfied, it would conflict with other of the gaslighter's aims, since domination requires preserving a rational agent to subjugate, control, and disempower.[13] Moreover, there are easier ways to satisfy the aim of achieving such domination: making a victim feel fearful or ashamed to mentally "go there," that is, to disagree with or challenge the gaslighter, will often achieve the same end without destroying her mind in the process. This has the further advantage of preserving for the gaslighter the apparent interlocutor he often wants (and wants to preserve, to dominate).

Abramson is sensitive to the criticism that her account may be judged "too sharp by half," and as problematically ruling out less extreme, more everyday cases of gaslighting (2014, 11). But to my mind, her response to this objection—essentially, that a look at long-term iterations of the everyday cases will reveal them to indeed have the above structure—is not fully satisfactory. In my view, gaslighting can aim to skew someone's deliberative perspective without completely destroying it. And gaslighters may pull this off by making a victim feel various negative first-personal moral emotions—guilt and shame, for example—rather than by impugning her rational capacities. It may also make the victim anticipate some positive moral status that incentivizes her to accede to the gaslighter's preferred narrative.

One of my informants was gaslit in this way. Once upon a time, she was romantically involved with an alcoholic. He decided to give up drinking and managed to do so for a time. Then, like many people who live with this disease, he relapsed. When she aired her suspicions that he was regularly inebriated and offered to try to get him help, he vigorously denied that he was drinking again. And he attributed the sure signs—slurred speech, an eerie spaciness, oddly inconsiderate behavior, and mean-spirited comments markedly contrary to his usual character—to a history of trauma and subsequent dissociation. He insinuated, furthermore, that she was undermining his recovery by not being more trusting.

> If you don't believe me, I really will relapse . . . , he said to her on more than one occasion. . . . I need you to trust me . . . , he further insisted, implying that her mistrust emanated from a morally defective trait of hers—roughly, of being too suspicious. This is a real vice, notably, and one she believes that she is prone to. But not on this occasion, as he eventually admitted, after months of making her doubt herself, her judgments, and her moral character. This was, I think, gaslighting, and will be widely agreed to be so.

The case illustrates several points. First, it reiterates the point that the victims of gaslighting need not be made to doubt the rationality, as opposed to the morality, of their belief-forming mechanisms. Second, unlike the previous two cases, gaslighting need not be performed by Machiavellian characters intent on undermining or even destroying their victims. Third, and relatedly, it need not even be malicious. Here, it emanated from a place of shame (though it was not necessarily any less wrong or harmful to its target and victim for that reason).[14] Finally, it targeted a very specific set of beliefs of hers, and not her whole mental life, certainly not aiming to destroy her independent perspective, pace Abramson. But it did, as she holds, try to make disagreement in this specific domain difficult, since morally verboten.[15]

We can also now see how misogyny—and the associated ideals of femininity—can be weaponized against the targets and victims of gaslighting. Misogyny can be a tool or technique of gaslighting, in other words, as well as gaslighting being used to conceal and obscure misogyny. For trust is something particularly expected of women with respect to our male partners. We are meant to be loving, supportive, and . . . cool . . . wives and girlfriends. We are meant to believe in him, and hence to buy his story. If we fail to do this, we may be criticized and punished. If we somehow manage to, there may be rewards and benefits. Misogyny's carrots and sticks operate epistemically too, and this is a social fact that gaslighters may use.

As we have now seen, gaslighting comes in such a wide variety of forms as to initially seem bewildering. It may be intentional or not, Machiavellian or not, malicious or not, more or less domain specific, and it may proceed via weaponizing moral as well as rational norms against a target or victim.

To make matters still worse from a theoretical perspective, this last raises further questions about whether gaslighting must be restricted just to eroding or undermining a person's beliefs, perceptions, and other such cognitive states, or whether it can also work to dislodge her desires, feelings, emotions, and reactive attitudes, among other broadly affective mental states.

I believe it can. Take the following example, from the hit TV show *Succession*. The father, Logan Roy, has committed numerous shady and downright wrongful acts—both ethically and legally—in the course of building his media empire. And he has behaved unforgivably, in myriad ways, toward his four variously feckless and unsatisfactory children. Rather than trying to gaslight them out of the belief that he has indeed acted in these ways, he tries to gaslight them out of feeling negative reactive attitudes toward him—contempt, resentment, and moral disgust, for starters—on this basis. He does so partly by saying, at a family therapy session, "Everything I've done, I've done for my children."[16] This is deeply, and obviously, false. But he thereby tries to manipulate—and, I would say, gaslight—his children into feeling gratitude and love, rather than anything negative, toward him. Given his power, wealth, and gravitas, and his position as the head of the family, this even goes some way toward working (though it is not fully successful). And it is as powerful a portrait of a patriarch weaponizing moral norms of loyalty and fealty against his children as we have seen since King Lear.

What is the common thread, if any, running through this example and all of the above ones? I suggest it lies, roughly, in the fact that gaslit people are made to feel defective in certain fundamental ways—either morally or rationally—for harboring mental states to which they are entitled. These include warranted beliefs and perceptions, valid desires and intentions, fitting feelings and attitudes, and so on.[17] The target or victim is thus gaslit out of occupying cognitive and affective territory that ought to be hers but is ceded to the gaslighter—rendering her not merely dominated but effectively colonized. He does not, and perhaps cannot, tell her what to want, think, and feel; rather, he harnesses her own internal mechanisms—and indeed, often the best parts of herself—to control her mental states in line with his objectives. She becomes mentally unfree, and often less in touch with reality, by dint of her own capacities for morality and reason. She second-guesses herself out of beliefs that might have been knowledge, desires to which she has every right, and feelings that are in fact appropriate to her social and moral situation.

As well as this autonomy-compromising form of mind control, which is obviously damaging and insidious, gaslighting may also damage a person's self-conception. A gaslit person is often caught between a rock and a hard place: either bring your mental states into line with those the gaslighter would have you have or face the prospect of being written off as crazy, irrational, hysterical, disloyal, callous, or otherwise defective by a person to whom you are in thrall. Bella Manningham was thus gaslit out of her incipient belief that her husband was creeping about in the attic by the prospect of being written off as delusional and crazy; Debra Newell was gaslit out of her previous belief that her husband was a con man by the prospect of being written off as cold, hard, and unforgiving; my informant was gaslit out of her belief that her partner was drinking by the prospect of being written off as mistrustful and unsupportive. The idea of "Don't even go there (mentally)!" captures something of the feeling of being caught between one's incipient, rightful mental state and the threat of being punished for fully inhabiting it or acting on this basis.

These examples suggest, fairly obviously, that gaslighting must invoke norms relevant to the mental state in question. The prospect of being judged ugly, say, typically will not work to dislodge certain beliefs in us because beliefs do not—and generally are understood not to—go wrong because we are somehow aesthetically lacking. (Or at least not directly.) Slightly less obviously, the criticism must also have real bite: it is hard to credit the possibility that someone might be gaslit by the prospect of being envisaged (it does not seem right to say . . . written off . . .) as a little bit silly, just slightly ungenerous, or a tad overcautious. This is why I say that gaslighting invokes defects that are fundamental in some way.[18]

These examples also help underscore the point, emphasized by several of the foregoing authors, that gaslighting typically works best ("best") in interpersonal contexts when we are in the grip of another agent's overall domination. If the prospect of being written off by them represents no real threat to us, then it will at least be more difficult for them to gaslight us effectively. This is why gaslighting proliferates in intimate relationships, and also in families, where power may take the form of being able to dictate a family's accepted narratives, scripts, and schema. This power may be held not only by an individual who possesses more power than others in these arrangements, but also in the aggregate, via multiple people acting in concert.

Take the case of Rob, a successful (and otherwise privileged) actor who was gaslit by his family to doubt his extant belief that he had broken his arm as a child. His mother exclaimed: "You never broke your arm. I'm a nurse, I would remember!" His father ridiculed him by presenting Rob with photos of himself sans cast from later on that summer: "Did your arm magically heal overnight?," he ribbed him. Other family members also played a role, with Rob's sister designating herself "the keeper of family memories" and saying she didn't recall it ever happening, with the insinuation being that if it had happened, she wouldn't have forgotten. Rob's brother added, "Oh boy, here we go, another 'I broke my arm, I broke my arm' story. Look, I'm the broken arm guy, that's my role." (Rob's brother indeed broke his arm twice as a child.) Rob was thereby made to feel guilty—like an attention-seeking malingerer who was stealing Rob's brother's thunder—as well as unreliable for insisting that it had happened.

But Rob had broken his arm, just as he remembered, as hospital records eventually revealed. His family members had all somehow forgotten this—their gaslighting was not intentional—and the incident thus had been written out of the official familial narrative. Notably, it took a lengthy investigation by a well-known podcaster and journalist to excavate a truth that otherwise would have been lost—ceded—to family lore via gaslighting.[19]

~

Suppose gaslighting can be defined, as I suggested in the above section, as the process of making someone feel defective in some of the most fundamental ways (for example, morally or rationally) for having (or for that matter lacking) mental states that she is in fact entitled to have (or lack). By the lights of this definition, there is obviously no technical need for it to be an agent (or small group of agents) performing the gaslighting within an intimate setting, as with all of the above examples and the vast majority in the literature. But are there realistic, compelling cases of gaslighting that do not fit this description, and operate on a broader scale?[20]

I believe so. Donald Trump, for example, was accused of gaslighting the United States, both in the well-known podcast *Gaslit Nation*, hosted by Sarah Kendzior and Andrea Chalupa, and in Lauren Duca's viral article "Donald Trump is Gaslighting America" (Duca 2016). For, as they pointed out, Trump employed a wide range of tactics—including brazen lying, decrying reliable news sources as "fake," dismissing opponents with cheap epithets, raging at political enemies, drumming up rousing sentiments during his many rallies, and making false promises ("There will be so much winning. You'll get sick of winning")—which worked to induce a false sense of reality among many of his supporters. The idea was also that Trump's usage of these tactics was far more systematic and insidious than that of any of his American precedents.

Another putative example of non-interpersonal gaslighting comes from the philosophical literature. In a recent article, Elena Ruíz mounts a compelling argument that white settler colonialism in North America does its oppressive work partly by gaslighting Black and Indigenous populations—particularly its female members. She defines "cultural gaslighting" in general as "the social and historical infrastructural support mechanisms that disproportionately produce abusive mental ambients in settler colonial cultures in order to further the ends of cultural genocide and dispossession"—for example, the "systemic patterns of mental abuse against women of color and Indigenous women" in North America, which "distribute, reproduce, and automate social inequalities" in favor of white settler populations (Ruíz 2020, 687).

In a somewhat similar vein, the political scientists Angelique M. Davis and Rose Ernst define "racial gaslighting" as follows: "The political, social, economic and cultural process that perpetuates and normalizes a white supremacist reality through pathologizing those who resist" (David and Ernst 2019, 761). I think these phenomena are real and important. But the possibility of such gaslighting remains controversial. Some of the aforementioned authors believe that gaslighting is, predominantly or necessarily, an interpersonal phenomenon. Kate Abramson writes that the "characteristic aim of gaslighting is *interpersonal* in the sense that it is a need gaslighters have of and directed towards particular persons" (2014, 10, her italics). And Paige L. Sweet argues that "analyses that suggest Trump is gaslighting America go too far," since "Gaslighting occurs in power-laden *intimate* relationships, precisely because trust and coercive interpersonal strategies bind the victim to the perpetrator. The public has too much collective power to experience gaslighting, such that we can fact-check and push counter-narratives into the public sphere" (Sweet 2019, 870, her italics). The point that the public can resist putative cases of gaslighting does not seem sufficient to discredit the possibility of political gaslighting, on the face of it, since some individual agents also successfully resist their abuser's attempts to gaslight them. But it is indeed hard to see how whole groups of people could be made to experience a "surreal environment," which functions to make them feel crazy for having certain beliefs (recalling, from §4.1, Sweet's working definition of gaslighting), at least outside the context of an intimate, cult-like setting.[21] But the possibility of moral gaslighting comes into its own here, showing how political gaslighting can nevertheless be real, and indeed not uncommon. For groups of agents can be made to feel guilty or ashamed for their beliefs with relative ease: if you inspire loyalty in a group, then a savvy political operator can weaponize that loyalty to make its members strongly inclined to stick to the party line, echo the claims of their leader, defend the leader, and so on. These people would then feel guilty and ashamed for not believing or at least accepting the lies of a Donald Trump, for instance.[22] It is moral values, not rational ones, that are the primary means of such political-epistemic manipulation.

Similar observations apply to the categories of cultural and racial gaslighting. One way white supremacy in general, and white settler colonialism in particular, often works is by shaming an oppressed group of people for deviant—say, supposedly ungrateful or excessively angry—attitudes. And sometimes this shaming works. The incipient shame experienced by members of this group can be weaponized to make its members much more reluctant than they otherwise would be to challenge the prevailing narratives about, say, the beneficence of white people's motives or the extent of the harms of racism. Patriarchy can work in a similar fashion: many women have long felt ashamed to come forward to testify to our experiences of sexual assault and harassment or even to admit to ourselves their seriousness and prevalence. It is this collective sense of shame that Tarana Burke's #MeToo movement, popularized in 2017, helped to push back against. In this way, it addressed a silence that was plausibly the result of structural gaslighting wrought by the patriarchy. Notably, such gaslighting has the potential to silence victims' testimony again, even after they have come forward. As I have argued elsewhere, victims eating their words is a common, pernicious effect of the gaslighting that often serves to mask and thereby perpetuates misogyny.[23]

Gaslighting can thus make us witnesses against ourselves. It makes us buy the stories of our abusers and feel good and reasonable for so doing. It makes us not just unreliable, but also treacherous, as narrators. And it can operate on a large scale, even purely structurally, in some cases.

∽

On my proposed definition of gaslighting, it is a considerably broader phenomenon than previous authors have credited. I have suggested, in brief, that the unifying feature common to cases that intuitively count as gaslighting is that agents are made to feel fundamentally defective—bad, mad, or similar—for harboring a mental state to which they are entitled. We can thus talk productively about what agents are gaslit out of: and on my account, this includes not only beliefs, but also desires, intentions, feelings, emotions, reactive attitudes, and so on.

But while broader than is traditional by design, this account is not overly broad either. It does not allow mere denial or disagreement to count as gaslighting, in ways that help to push back against spurious claims that someone is being gaslit when they are merely being challenged. Indeed, the central insight adapted from Kate Abramson suggests that more or less the opposite is true at a social level: a space in which robust, reasonable disagreement proliferates is an antidote to gaslighting. Perhaps, as its best, philosophy can be like this.

On the other hand, this is not to underestimate the ways in which denial and disagreement may play a role in gaslighting in certain social contexts. In the context of broader power dynamics and moral-social structures, a less powerful agent will often be made to feel morally defective—and so guilty or ashamed—for harboring some warranted yet unflattering belief about a more powerful agent.[24] Let's say, for example, that you believe, truly and fairly, that a more prominent philosopher is a transphobic bully who is using his expertise to obscure the fact that he is denying the entitlements, and very existence, of trans women. Others around you, and he himself, splutter in denial: "He's just interested in the truth!," "He's a free thinker!," "He's doing feminist philosophy!," "You're interpreting him so uncharitably!" And, of course, "He's a good guy!" Together these denials conspire to make you feel ashamed of questioning the motives and moral character of someone who is indeed, let's imagine, unjustly targeting trans women and others who violate the bounds of gender. And as a result of these collective efforts, concerted or not, your warranted belief wavers and fizzles; it fails to be knowledge, at least of a sort that you can rely and then act on.

Such gaslighting does not aim to make anyone feel "crazy" or otherwise irrational. Rather, it weaponizes other important norms—moral norms of charitable interpretation, in this case, among others—to rob us of incipient or extant knowledge and warranted reactive attitudes, among other things. In the aggregate, it can rob us of our minds by enlisting the best, most conscientious parts of ourselves against ourselves. Rationality and morality become weapons to make us less ourselves, less in touch with reality, less rational, and less moral.

This is insidious. It is scary. And, if I am right, such gaslighting is endemic in social and moral life as we know it—including in philosophy.

Notes

1. I use this term, which is certainly ableist, with circumspection. But it would be too difficult to do justice to the extant views on gaslighting in the literature without employing it on occasion, at least in scare quotes. I touch on the ways gaslighting often relies on ableist tropes in Manne (2020, ch. 8) (where I also discuss the two main cases that follow). Thanks to Barbara Cohn for useful discussion on this point and others here.

2. To be clear, this is not necessarily harmful to these authors' main projects, which include Abramson's project of identifying the moral wrong of gaslighting, Ivy's project of depicting gaslighting as a type of testimonial injustice, and Sweet's project of theorizing the sociology of gaslighting in general and its gendered dimensions in particular. I think each of these authors has done much to illuminate their respective topics, as is clear from what follows.

3. The setup is thus subtler in the play than in the film, where Paula questions her husband, Gregory, about the gaslights dimming and he denies this is happening—a denial that is arguably too implausible to be credited. Here she doesn't dare to raise the issue in the first place and doesn't doubt these perceptions so much as their significance. (Though Bella does say, above, that her husband dismisses other of her perceptions as delusions or fabrications, and in an angry manner.)

4. I take this dialogue, and the foregoing details, from the podcast *Dirty John*, produced by Christopher Goffard, October 1, 2017, https://www.latimes.com/projects/la-me-dirty-john/.

5. For a representative discussion of the latter kind, see Pilossoph (2019).

6. I put this point carefully, since a commitment to the reality of testimonial injustice—wherein, roughly, people wrongly disbelieve an agent because of broadly moral failures—clearly doesn't imply a commitment to moral reasons for belief per se. But it is nevertheless telling in this connection that the classic case of non-epistemic reasons for belief in the literature, due to John Heil, is that of a wife who decides to trust her husband and overlook the evidence that he is having an affair—a long blond hair on his coat, a lipstick-stained handkerchief, and a matchbook from a romantic French restaurant where she has never been with him (Heil 1983, 752). This wife chooses to believe that her husband is

faithful for "practical" (presumably moral and prudential) reasons. Whether or not one agrees with Heil that this may be the rational course of belief, all things considered, or that there can ever be cases like this, these ostensible non-epistemic reasons for belief can plausibly be weaponized and used to gaslight some people. Similarly, Fricker's point that broadly moral failures may lead us to make genuine mistakes about the credibility of certain people can be weaponized against us for the purposes of gaslighting us, according to my argument in the main text.

7. To avoid the risk of confusion here, note that what I call moral gaslighting need not have a moral (or otherwise normative) proposition as the content of the relevant belief state when beliefs are in question. We'll see an example in due course where someone is subject to moral gaslighting that targets their (straightforwardly empirical) belief that their partner is drinking. Conversely, it's not controversial that what I distinguish here as rational gaslighting can target someone's moral beliefs either. Under the pressure of gaslighting, Bella Manningham's sense of herself as increasingly "mad" leads her to second-guess her doubts about her husband's character, for example. So moral gaslighting is about the content of the incipient criticisms (or praise) used to gaslight someone, not the content of the resulting beliefs or other mental states, as per the above discussion.

8. For the relevant insightful discussions, see Abramson (2014, 3) and Sweet (2019, 854–56).

9. Further evidence of the reality of moral gaslighting comes from Sweet's empirical work, where she interviewed forty-three domestic violence victims who were also the victims of gaslighting. (Sweet had originally hoped to contrast domestic violence victims who had been gaslit with those who had not but, strikingly, found that all of her interview subjects, recruited through a shelter, had in fact been gaslit.) Although Sweet's definition of gaslighting (see §i) meant that she likely wasn't looking for specific evidence of what I call moral gaslighting, she seemingly found it anyway, as many of the women she interviewed had been morally condemned and written off in the course of their (in all but one case male) abuser's gaslighting behavior. What Sweet was looking for here were ways in which women's sexuality is weaponized against them during gaslighting, which explains the particular cast of these examples, but they all still count as moral gaslighting for my purposes:

- Simone was accused of adultery and not being a good enough mother.
- Nevaeh was also accused of being a bad mother.
- Carla was accused of being a "prostitute" and that she too would make a bad mother (while pregnant).
- Rosa, Mariposa, and Adriana were accused of cheating on their partners.

- Jaylene was called a "ho" and a "slut" by her boyfriend.

- Fabiola was called "nasty" and "sick" by her partner after sex, leading to her sense that she was "bad."

- Margaret was accused of deliberately attracting too much sexual attention.

- Maria S. was told she was too sexually forward by her husband (after he propositioned her).

- Rubi was said to be a "witch," trapping her husband in the marriage.

- Rosalyn and Luisa were portrayed by their abusers as the "real" abusers, leading to Rosalyn being arrested.

Sweet thus writes that "crazy bitch" is the classic refrain—the "literal discourse"—of the gaslighter. Here, I am in effect arguing that the second epithet is just as important as the first one (Sweet 2019, 861–65).

10. For a fuller discussion of the "Dirty John" case, including John Meehan's homicidal tendencies, see Manne (2020, ch. 8), which I draw on in describing the cases in the two previous sections.

11. Abramson writes, pithily, "If, for instance, someone kills me, I no longer have an independent perspective from which disagreement with that person might arise. That's not what gaslighters do. Rather, they behave in distinctive ways, ways crudely characterized as forms of emotional manipulation, as the means by which they try to destroy another's independent perspective and moral standing. To that extent, the question of precisely what's wrong with the aims of gaslighting is inseparable from the question of how gaslighters try to satisfy those aims (2014, 13).

12. Abramson says something similar about a particular case of hers: "Satisfaction of his gaslighting desire to destroy de Beauvoir's independent standing, both would and would not support this more specific aim. On the one hand, the more de Beauvoir's own sense of her philosophical abilities is undermined, the more likely she is to sit in awe of Sartre at his feet. On the other hand, if she really came to consistently doubt whether she can 'think at all,' De Beauvoir would be so undermined that she wouldn't have enough sense of her own acumen left to be in awe of Sartre's abilities" (2014, 11).

13. Abramson holds that gaslighters are conflicted in something like this way in discussing the case in the previous footnote. She acknowledges that it may be suggested that "the gaslighter typically wants to undermine his target not to the point where she loses the ability to challenge altogether, but just to the point where he gets other things he wants," before rejecting this proposal in favor of what she calls "the conflicted picture" of the gaslighter (2014, 11–12). In effect, I am arguing that the gaslighter wants to undermine his target to the point

where she appears to be, but is not, capable of posing an effective challenge to his arguments, so that he gets the satisfaction of ostensibly winning without the associated risk of losing. Although this is a tricky tightrope to walk, it is possible, at least in theory, and it contrasts with Abramson's aforementioned conflicted picture of the gaslighter.

14. I say "target and/or victim" here and at various other junctures throughout to reflect the fact that I don't take "gaslighting" to be a "success term" (to use a somewhat unfortunate philosophical term of art here for terms that imply that some process has been carried through to completion). Someone can be targeted by gaslighting, then, without becoming a victim of it (in which case they would have been gaslit successfully—or, perhaps better, "successfully," given its wrongful nature).

15. One possibility is that Abramson and I disagree over the phenomena and that she would deny that the examples of moral gaslighting I moot here and elsewhere count as gaslighting at all. I doubt this is the issue though, since some of her own examples also invoke this possibility. Take, for instance, her case of a junior female academic who rightly complains about being slapped on the butt by a senior male colleague. Another senior colleague responds, "Oh, he's just an old guy. Have some sympathy! It's not that big a deal" (Abramson 2014, 4). This colleague is effectively hinting at punishment if she presses on with the complaint, and rewards (in the form of approval) if she withdraws it and adopts a more sympathetic attitude toward him. Despite this and a few other examples with moral elements, though, Abramson emphasizes rational techniques of gaslighting much more than moral ones in theorizing the phenomenon. And although she does write, at times, about a gaslit agent lacking "independent perspective *and* moral standing" (my italics), it's clear from her discussion that she envisages the latter as occurring because the person has "gone crazy," "lost their minds," or similar because of a long, steady process of rational undermining. The distinctively moral means to gaslighting someone is not a possibility she theorizes explicitly; nor, to the best of my knowledge, do other authors in the literature.

16. *Succession*, Season 1, Episode 7, "Austerlitz" (HBO, 2018). Later in the series (Season 2, Episode 6, "Argestes"), Logan slaps his son Roman viciously, sending him flying and knocking his tooth out. But Logan gaslights Roman into giving up his knowledge that the assault was quite deliberate, making it out to have been an accident—which indeed never even happened, as the dialogue continues. "That thing up in Argestes: I didn't even know you were there. I mean, if I did, I wouldn't, you know . . . That's not something I do, you know," he intones: a superficially descriptive statement intended to prescribe to Roman that he must buy, and echo, this false narrative. Roman accedes quickly—mumbling, avoiding eye contact—"I know, sure . . . I know that; I know, I know." "Did I even make contact?" Logan asks him, ensuring an answer in the negative. "Umm . . . I don't think . . . I'm not quite sure what we're talking about, to be honest," Roman

adds, obediently, as if the incident were nothing. And so it becomes nothing in family history.

17. Notice that, when beliefs are in question, this definition implies that you can't gaslight someone out of a belief to which they are not entitled (with the full implications of the definition being quite properly tied to the correct theory of our cognitive and affective entitlements, which is of course controversial). One cannot gaslight someone out of believing in a conspiracy theory, for example. I believe this consequence of my definition is as it should be, though we might still allow that someone employs techniques adjacent to gaslighting to improperly coerce someone out of beliefs she should not have held in the first place (or insincere avowals of belief, for that matter). It's also worth highlighting the intended consequence that, in cases of interpersonal gaslighting with respect to belief, my definition does not imply anything about whether or not the gaslighter himself believes the proposition he is pushing on the target. It thus allows for cases like that of Mr. Manningham, who gaslights his wife into believing that he's not creeping about in the attic upstairs at night, even though he knows full well that this is false; and it allows for cases like that of Dirty John, who gaslights Debra into believing that he is a good person, deep down, which he seems to believe himself (or at least we can imagine this).

18. Are all such defects either rational or moral? Or might some be prudential, for another salient possibility? I leave this question for another day, since I do believe that we can be gaslit out of certain broadly mental states, namely, appetite and hunger, by the prospect of not only seeming but also being "unhealthy." But given the difficulties of saying what this criticism amounts to, exactly—it seems partly prudential, partly moral, and also shares some linguistic features with pejoratives (perhaps surprisingly)—this topic would take me well beyond the scope of the present chapter.

19. I take this case from episode 16 ("Rob") of the podcast *Heavyweight*, produced by Jonathan Goldstein, October 4, 2018, https://gimletmedia.com/shows/heavy-weight/n8hoed.

20. Another question is whether an agent can gaslight herself, a possibility that my definition of gaslighting similarly leaves open. I believe the answer is "yes," but space considerations prevent my arguing as much here. For an interesting recent discussion of this phenomenon, see Dandelet (2021).

21. This is especially so given shared hermeneutical resources that marginalized people may develop, as a collective, which allow them to hang onto a sense of their own reasonableness in interpreting and navigating the social world.

22. For a classic discussion of the distinction between belief and acceptance, see Cohen (1989). I here rely on the fact that "acceptance" is an at least partly mental state, enabling it to count as the target of gaslighting on my account of it.

23. See the introduction of Manne (2017) for discussion.

24. Similarly, gaslighting is obviously more than mere lying, according to my account of it. However, repeated lies told to a particular end could be used

to gaslight someone, given specific background power dynamics. If a powerful and authoritative agent repeats a lie with enough confidence and brazenness, then their interlocutor or audience may reasonably feel loathe to question it, and even rationally or morally defective (confused, incompetent, or insolent) for doing so. This could then count as gaslighting; but many lies will not. Similarly, gaslighting is something more specific than manipulation, though it often involves it: for while manipulation may aim merely to change someone's behavior, gaslighting is aimed at achieving mental conformity: it aims to control what someone thinks or feels, and not merely what she does or refrains from doing.

Works Cited

Abramson, Kate. 2014. "Turning Up the Lights on Gaslighting." *Philosophical Perspectives* 28: 1–30.
Cohen, L. Jonathan. 1989. "Belief and Acceptance." *Mind* 98 (391): 367–89.
Dandelet, Sophia. 2021. "Epistemic Coercion." *Ethics* 131 (3): 489–510.
Davis, Angelique M., and Rose Ernst. 2019. "Racial Gaslighting." *Politics, Groups, and Identities* 7 (4): 761–74.
Dotson, Kristie. 2011. "Tracking Epistemic Violence, Tracking Practices of Silencing." *Hypatia* 26 (2): 236–57.
Duca, Lauren. 2016. "Donald Trump Is Gaslighting America." *Teen Vogue*, December 10, 2016. https://www.teenvogue.com/story/donald-trump-is-gaslighting-america.
Fricker, Miranda. 2007. *Epistemic Injustice: Power and the Ethics of Knowing*. Oxford: Oxford University Press.
Hamilton, Patrick. 1942. *Angel Street: A Victorian Thriller in Three Acts*. New York: Samuel French.
Heil, John. 1983. "Believing What One Ought." *Journal of Philosophy* 80 (11): 752–65.
Ivy, Veronica [Rachel McKinnon]. 2017. "Allies Behaving Badly: Gaslighting as Epistemic Injustice." In *The Routledge Handbook of Epistemic Injustice*, edited by Ian James Kidd, José Medina, and Gaile Polhaus Jr., 167–74. New York: Routledge.
Kline, Neal A. 2006. "Revisiting Once Upon a Time." *American Journal of Psychiatry* 163 (7): 1147–48.
Manne, Kate. 2017. *Down Girl: The Logic of Misogyny*. New York: Oxford University Press.
———. 2020. *Entitled: How Male Privilege Hurts Women*. New York: Crown.
Pilossoph, Jackie. 2019. "Beware of Dirty John." *Chicago Tribune*, January 30, 2019. https://www.chicagotribune.com/suburbs/ct-ahp-column-love-essentially-tl-0207-story.html.
Ruíz, Elena. 2020. "Cultural Gaslighting." *Hypatia* 35 (4): 687–713.

Serwer, Adam. 2018. "The Cruelty Is the Point." *Atlantic*, October 3, 2018. https://www.theatlantic.com/ideas/archive/2018/10/the-cruelty-is-the-point/572104/.
Sweet, Paige L. 2019. "The Sociology of Gaslighting." *American Sociological Review* 84 (5): 851–75.

5

Affective Gaslighting

KELLY OLIVER

Most philosophers writing about gaslighting maintain that it is a type of epistemic injustice because gaslighting undermines its target's status as a knower by making them question what they believe they know. In this chapter, I argue that limiting gaslighting to a form of epistemic injustice cannot adequately explain either unintentional gaslighting or the ways in which the targets of gaslighting accept their deficit status as knowers and become complicit with their own gaslighting. Some feminist philosophers argue that there is a moral dimension to gaslighting whereby the target is made to feel immoral for questioning the reality of the perpetrator. Here, I argue that in addition to epistemic or moral dimensions, there is an affective dimension of gaslighting. The affective dimension is essential to its functioning, including the ways in which gaslighting undermines knowledge claims or moral standing. In other words, for gaslighting to work on either the epistemic or moral levels, it must be working on an affective level too. In addition, if gaslighting is unintentional, then there are unconscious dimensions to gaslighting that influence the beliefs and actions of both the perpetrators and the targets. Yet, to date, the gaslighting literature does not account for either the affective or unconscious dimensions of gaslighting, which are essential to understanding how gaslighting works.

Following Miranda Fricker, theorists such as Kate Abramson, Rachel McKinnon, Cynthia Stark, and Kate Manne have argued that gaslighting is a form of epistemic injustice. In response to some interpretations of her notion of epistemic injustice as *intentional* manipulation and degradation, Fricker has argued that in a strict sense, both testimonial and hermeneutical injustice are necessarily *unintentional* (Fricker 2017, 54). Indeed, she distinguishes epistemic injustice from gaslighting by attributing malicious intentions to the latter, but not the former. Furthermore, she insists that epistemic injustice is structural or systematic, whereas gaslighting is an interpersonal form of domination. As we will see, feminist philosophers who articulate a concept of gaslighting most often acknowledge that it can be unintentional and that it necessarily involves some preexisting form of structural inequity or power imbalance.

In her seminal essay on gaslighting, Kate Abramson defines gaslighting as a form of moral and epistemic manipulation that aims to render its perpetrator beyond reproach and its victim beyond repair. She defines gaslighting as "a form of emotional manipulation in which the gaslighter tries (consciously or not) to induce in someone the sense that her reactions, perceptions, memories and/or beliefs are not just mistaken, but utterly without grounds paradigmatically, so unfounded as to qualify as crazy" (Abramson 2014 2). It is important to note that using the term "crazy" in this way is not only ableist but also could be seen as a form of gaslighting that denies grounded perception, memories and/or beliefs to people with mental illness. "Crazy," along with "insane" and "mad," are derogatory terms often used by gaslighters to manipulate. Calling someone "crazy" is a way to undermine them. It assumes that anyone with a mental illness is "crazy" and therefore not worth taking seriously. In this chapter, I continue to use the term in quotation marks to indicate that it is a derogatory term used by gaslighters to manipulate. Abramson insists that in most cases, the gaslighter is neither intentionally engaging in "crazy-making" activities nor consciously aware of his own motives. Rather, for Abramson, in an important sense, gaslighting operates at an unconscious level for both the perpetrator and the victim.

The target of gaslighting is susceptible to manipulation and mistrust of her own judgments because of social factors—institutional and systematic sexism and misogyny—that make her perpetrator valued as more credible than she is. Sexism is like the air that we breathe. It's all around us, but it is normalized and therefore usually we don't even notice it. Not only are we are surrounded by it, but also it permeates us and is internalized. So even the victims or targets of sexism believe themselves to be less deserving or less credible. Because of preexisting structural inequities and power imbalances, the victims—primarily women or other oppressed peoples—can be invested in maintaining their perpetrator's credibility and power.

For example, early in my teaching career, I taught an undergraduate course for the Women's Studies department on feminism. Most of the students were women. But there were a handful of men. On the first day of class, when I went around the room and asked each student why they were taking the class, one of the men in the back row said that he and his fraternity buddies had taken it on a dare. All of the men and some of the women snickered. As the professor, anticipating a semester of heckling from the bleachers, I was appalled.

We began the course with studies that demonstrated that in mixed-gender groups, men were more likely to talk and get uptake than women. The study even used an example of the classroom where men get called on more than women and men's voices are encouraged while women's are often discouraged. As an experiment, I decided to see what would happen if I reversed that dynamic to make the point. I was naive enough to be surprised that within only twenty minutes, not only the men in the class but all of the women got very upset when I called on women and not men. The women seemed more invested in the men's right to speak than in their own. For their part, the men stormed out of the class and went to my chair and the EEOO to complain, something women rarely ever do even when subjected to the same treatment.

As Abramson argues, gaslighting is most effective when deployed in the context of a power imbalance that favors the perpetrator and disadvantages the target. The perpetrator may tell his target that she is "crazy, paranoid, hysterical" or "overly sensitive or over-reacting," which are all traits already associated with women and other marginalized people within dominant culture. The victim comes to believe the perpetrator because she is already primed by the dominant sexist culture to believe that she is all or any of those. The victim has internalized the norms of her culture, which denigrate her in various ways, including as a rational agent, a moral agent, a knower, and an emotional being. Moral and epistemological injustice is already built into our society through institutional and systematic sexism. And so is affective injustice, wherein certain emotions (usually those with a negative valence) are associated with women and other feminized others.

What I've called *the colonization of psychic space* is the internalization of norms that undermine one's sense of oneself as a rational, moral agent, knower, and emotional being. Gaslighting works only because it happens in the context of the colonization of psychic space. Gaslighting depends on social and institutional factors that make the target susceptible to self-doubt and manipulation. Furthermore, the colonization of psychic space is *a form* of gaslighting that makes its targets complicit with their own victimization. As Abramson puts it, "part of the moral horror of gaslighting is that it makes one complicit in one's own destruction" (2014, 16–71).

For Abramson, the perpetrator's aims and desires are also, in at least some sense, unconscious. The perpetrator is not aware of the deep-seated reason he wants to dominate his target. He may not know why he wants to undermine her sense of herself as an epistemic or moral agent or undermine her trust in her own perceptions, judgments, and affects. On the contrary, Abramson describes gaslighting as akin to a form of pathology through which "the gaslighter [is] creating conditions such that his/her own deep anxieties are relieved by the successful gaslighting" (2014, 6). The gaslighter is not necessarily aware of these anxieties or their causes but uses gaslighting to satisfy his (perverse) desires. Abramson concludes that "the characteristic aim of gaslighting is interpersonal in the sense that it is a need gaslighters have of and directed towards particular persons" (2014 10). As we will see, other feminist theorists, Kate Manne and Cynthia Stark, for example, argue that gaslighting is not just interpersonal but also structural and systematic.

Cynthia Stark helpfully distinguishes manipulative gaslighting from epistemic gaslighting (2019, 223). In manipulative gaslighting, the perpetrator *intends* to undermine his target and uses the power imbalance between himself and his target to foster self-doubt in his victim. Epistemic gaslighting, on the other hand, is *unintentional* and involves social power imbalance based on prejudice that the perpetrator leverages to undermine the victim in her capacity as a knower. This second form is more in line with Fricker's concept of epistemic injustice, which requires social inequities and unintentional prejudice that result in credibility excesses and credibility deficits. Below, I return to a discussion of manipulative gaslighting as a form of *social* gaslighting.

Rachel McKinnon takes the importance of the perpetrator's unconscious bias one step further. In "Allies Behaving Badly," McKinnon gives examples of allies questioning the experience and testimony of marginalized people—in this case, trans women—not because they set out to manipulate but rather based on their unconscious prejudice (McKinnon 2017). Without intending harm, the gaslighter downplays or denies the marginalized person's experience and dismisses their testimony, even to their own experiences, as mistaken. In this way, the gaslighter calls into question the target's experience, testimony, and judgment, but does so without intending to harm that person. In fact, they may see themselves as intending to help.

So far, while Abramson and McKinnon agree that social inequities and power imbalance is a necessary background for gaslighting, most of their example are of individuals gaslighting other individuals. In other words, they do not discuss how the sexist, transphobic, or racist norms of dominant culture *are themselves* gaslighting marginalized people. They do not discuss how a society or culture can gaslight a group of people for the benefit of another group. Furthermore, while McKinnon analyzes unintentional gaslighting, and while Abramson discusses the psychology of gaslighting, neither of them spend much time discussing *how* this unintentional or unconscious bias/prejudice works.

Is it possible that unintentional or unconscious bias and prejudice work through gaslighting? In other words, is gaslighting an essential element of unconscious bias and unintentional prejudice? If gaslighting results in undermining the target's confidence in her own experience, testimony, judgments, and affects—her standing as a moral, epistemic, and affective agent, then does a sexist, racist, transphobic, ableist culture actually gaslight those people it pushes to the margins?

Discussing the 2016 election and why so many white women voted for Donald Trump (a known misogynist and sexual predator), Kate Manne asks whether women were "pre-gaslit" or "self-gaslighting" (Manne 2017, 15). In fact, she intends her work on misogyny "as a bulwark against gaslighting in this arena: the siphoning off of heat and light from the problem of misogyny, in both private life and public discourse, and the concomitant denialism" (Manne 2017, 12). In her second book, *Entitled*, Manne emphasizes the moral dimension of gaslighting over the epistemic. The target of gaslighting is made to feel that she is "committing a grievous sin" for challenging the worldview of the perpetrator (Manne 2020, 148). Believing and forgiving the perpetrator, and thus becoming complicit in one's own gaslighting, become a "moral imperative" (Manne 2020 153). As she explains it, gaslighting is a form of both epistemic and moral domination. The victim of gaslighting "has been epistemically dominated—*colonized*, even" (Manne 2020, 154, my emphasis).

What does it mean that the victim of gaslighting is epistemically dominated or colonized? Manne's account of logic and operation of misogyny suggest that it works through moral and epistemic domination and colonization. In fact, she argues that misogyny is a form of domination that aims to keep women under patriarchal control.

One of the most original aspects of Manne's theory is her distinction between misogyny and sexism. She maintains that misogyny is "like the shock collar worn by a dog to keep them behind one of those invisible fences that proliferate in suburbia. Misogyny can cause pain, to be sure, and it often does so. But even when it isn't actively hurting anyone, it tends to discourage girls and women from venturing out of bounds" (*Entitled*, 7). Sexism, on the other hand, is the "theoretical and ideological branch of patriarchy: the beliefs, ideas, and assumptions that serve to rationalize and naturalize patriarchal norms and expectations—including a gendered division of labor, and men's dominance over women in areas of traditionally male power and authority" (*Entitled*, 8). If sexism is the theory of male dominance, misogyny is the practice.

One of the most powerful tools in the misogynist toolbox is gaslighting. Indeed, sexism and misogyny work together to successfully gaslight women and girls. Going further, we could say that sexism and misogyny taken together become a form of gaslighting—gaslighting as the colonization of psychic space. In other words, gaslighting works as a form of domination through colonizing the psyche. For gaslighting to be successful, the target(s) must internalize the worldview, norms, and values of the perpetrator(s). This internalization is not benign. The internalization of norms that undermine one's sense of oneself as a reliable agent is essential to the operation of gaslighting—in this case, sexism norms enforced by misogynistic practices. Gaslighting turns its targets into unreliable narrators of their own experience. Its tactics are decidedly psychological.

Whether epistemic or manipulative, gaslighting is a form of psychological warfare that invades and colonizes the psyche of its targets. Given the unconscious dimensions of gaslighting in both perpetrators and victims, it cannot be reduced to an epistemic phenomenon alone. Gaslighting does not *just* work on the level of knowledge. It also and necessarily works on an unconscious level, which is to say a level antithetical to knowledge. What is unconscious is what we do *not know*. The unconscious is what falls outside of the epistemic. The unconscious is what has not, or cannot, come to consciousness. The operation of sexism and misogyny on the level of the unconscious makes it so much more dangerous. We cannot fight what we do not see.

The psychological dimension of gaslighting is perhaps the most complex and perplexing part of the phenomenon. Cynthia Stark discusses the connection between gaslighting and psychological oppression. She argues that there is a collective form of manipulative gaslighting that is not isolated to individual perpetrators and victims. What she calls misogynist gaslighting is a collective phenomenon, and "the psychological injuries produced by collective gaslighting are constitutive of the psychological oppression of women" (2019, 229). Following Manne's description of misogyny as the domination of women by men, Stark maintains that misogynist gaslighting is used to enforce the norms of patriarchy by undermining women's claims of abuse by men and thereby allowing men to get away with continued abuse and domination. This in turn helps consolidate men's power over women (2019, 230).

Misogynist gaslighting is a form of manipulation that operates on an unconscious level in both perpetrators and victims. Misogynist gaslighting "induces women to suppress or doubt their judgments in the domain of gender relations," and just as the perpetrators do "not see themselves as enforcing patriarchal norms, they also may not see themselves as participating in the mass manipulation of women" (2019, 230). Misogynist gaslighting, then, is the backdrop for patriarchy. It operates to normalize the domination of women by men through psychological manipulation that gives men a sense of entitlement and women a sense of self-doubt.

Stark identifies gaslighting as a form of psychological oppression, which she defines as "internalized subtle messages of inferiority sent to them [the oppressed] through entrenched social practices reserved specifically for the subordinated. Their sense of inferiority makes them, in a certain respect, their own oppressors, which, in turn, makes 'the work of domination easier'" (2019, 231). Still, like Abramson, McKinnon, and Manne, she limits gaslighting to the moral and epistemic realms without addressing the importance of the affective component. She concludes, "In distrusting their belief that an action done to them is in fact morally objectionable, they are doubting not only their ability to discern harm but their standing as one who is owed better treatment" (2019, 231). Thus, gaslighting not only undermines not only the target's confidence in their own judgments, but also their position as moral or epistemic agents who can make judgments.

The reason gaslighting is so successful in undermining both beliefs and one's sense of oneself as a moral or epistemic agent, however, is because it operates on an affective level. Without considering the affects of gaslighting or what we might call *affective gaslighting*, we miss a crucial part of the picture. In most of the examples used by the feminist epistemologists I've discussed so far, the victim is emotionally attached to the perpetrator. Even when gaslighting is social and not individual, it is the emotional impact that gives gaslighting its force. Through affects, gaslighting colonizes psychic space. If gaslighting is primarily epistemic and secondarily moral, then it influences the target's beliefs about what she knows and her status as both knower and moral agent. But without also influencing her very sense of herself in the depths of her psyche, the victim would remain detached from the experience of gaslighting, which would render it unsuccessful. For gaslighting to be successful, it must penetrate the very soul or psyche of the victim. Or, to put it less dramatically, to be successful, gaslighting must affect the target's sense of herself, not just as knower or even as moral agent, but as a *self*, full-stop. I return to this claim later.

While gaslighting creates epistemic uncertainty in its targets, this self-doubt is not *just* an epistemic phenomenon. The self-doubt in one's own experience, knowledge, beliefs, and judgment fostered by gaslighting is shrouded in affects and emotions of shame and worthlessness that make it effective. Take, for example, Patrick Hamilton's play *Angel Street*, which was performed on stage under the name *Gas Light* and became the basis for two subsequent films called *Gaslight*, from which the term gaslighting is derived. In the play and the films, the protagonist is being driven "mad" by her husband, who married her only to find her dead aunt's precious jewelry, which he assumes is hidden in the house his wife inherited from her aunt. Every night the husband secretly goes into the attic to search for the jewels. When he does so, he turns on the gaslights in the attic, and, as a result, the gaslights in the rest of the house dim.

The husband has been systematically convincing his wife that she is going "mad" (as her mother did before her). He hides things and then blames his wife, who does not remember moving those things. He tells her she is unwell so often that she begins to believe it. He humiliates her in public and forbids her from going out or receiving guests, thus isolating her from society.

What is interesting about *Gaslight*, and the way it has been used in some of the literature on gaslighting, is that it becomes obvious that *at some level* the wife knows that her husband is manipulating her. But because she *loves* him, she doesn't *want* to believe it. In the play and the films, arguably, it is not that she doesn't know what she has or has not done, but rather that she is made to *feel* as if she is "mad" because her husband tells her she is mad. Her husband is the arbiter of her reality. He invades her mind/psyche through psychological manipulation that plays on her insecurities (he is older than she, who was very young when they married). His gaslighting is successful on an emotional level—she accepts that she is sick because she loves him and wants to please him. But, as we will see, it fails on an epistemic level.

Ironically, given the contemporary meaning of gaslighting, it is the gaslights that reassure the wife that she is *not* going mad. The dimming of the gaslights proves that she is sane. The gaslights become the anchor for her resistance to her husband's scheme. The gaslights are the reality that cannot be controlled by her husband. The gaslights cast doubt on her husband's interpretation of the state of her mental health. If the gaslights flicker when her husband is gone, it proves that she is not "mad" after all. He really is up in the attic using gas when he turns on the lights.

The irony of the gaslights saving her rather than condemning her is further intensified by the fact that several scholars who cite the film to support their theories of gaslighting do so by *erroneously* claiming that the husband uses the gaslights to drive his wife "crazy," that he intentionally dims the lights and then denies it to drive her mad.[1] For example, Kate Abramson lists the husband's manipulation of the gaslights and subsequent denial as the final attempt to drive his wife "crazy." A conference poster on gaslighting organized by Amy Kind at Claremont McKenna College states:

> In this conference, we aim to focus specifically on distinctive forms of epistemic injustice produced through lying, misinformation, manipulation, and deceit. A paradigm example is the phenomenon known as "gaslighting." In the 1944 film *Gas Light*, Gregory Anton slowly and cruelly manipulates his wife Paula into thinking that she is going "insane." Having deliberately caused the lights in their home to dim, Gregory insists that Paula must be imagining it whenever the subject is raised. This depiction of Paula's plight—made especially poignant by a brilliant performance from Ingrid Bergman—has given rise to the term "gaslighting," used to refer to one individual or individuals causing another to question their own perceptions, beliefs, and memories through a series of manipulations, deceptions, and lies.

In an excellent presentation for NYC Law and Philosophy Colloquium, "Gaslighting Citizens," Eric Beerbohm and Ryan Davis define gaslighting based on this same error: "Our concept derives from the play and subsequent movie, *Gaslight*, in which Gregory intentionally attempts to cause Paula to doubt her sensory inputs. In the titular act of manipulation, Gregory changes the brightness of the gaslights in their home but insistently denies that there is any difference when Paula repeatedly notices that the lights have dimmed" (2019, 3). The fact is, Paula's husband doesn't know the lights are dimming when he is in the attic. He doesn't know that every time he's up there, the gaslights are giving him away.

When Paula gets a visit from a police officer informing her that her husband is a wanted criminal, it is the flickering of the gaslights that eventually convinces the wife that her husband has been manipulating her all along. The police officer uses the dimming of the gaslights as evidence that the husband really is in the attic looking for the aunt's jewelry. The gaslights become evidence not of the wife's lack of knowledge or discredited knowledge, but rather of the fact that at some level she knew all along. And it is this last shred of knowledge that saves her. In the end, the knowledge that the gaslights are really flickering allows the wife to turn her affects from love to hate and confront her conniving husband with a knife.

Why have so many scholars made the error of claiming that Gregory, the husband, intentionally adjusts the gaslights to drive his wife mad? There are no doubt many possible interpretations. One interesting possibility is that philosophers often talk about "shedding light" on a problem to better understand it. Understanding has been described in terms of illumination. To *shed light, illuminate, turn up the lights, shine a light on* are all phrases that indicate greater understanding through clearer vision. This underlines the connection within philosophical and popular discussions between seeing and knowing, vision and understanding. As some feminists, including me, have argued, this privileging of vision and knowledge over touch and feeling can be interpreted as perpetuating a tradition that values men over women and masculinity over femininity. While those distinctions may be old-fashioned today, still the telling error in gaslighting literature points to traces of this privilege still haunting recent philosophy, including feminist philosophy.

In addition, the mistake indicates how invested we are in the gaslighter's intentional manipulation of knowledge, his position of power over his victim. Gregory does not know the lights are flickering and giving him away. So what does the fantasy gain by believing that he controls the lights from the attic, from beyond Paula's field of vision? Again, a possible interpretation is the consolidation of the gaslighter's power over his victim. To the contrary, we could argue that the film precisely reveals that the gaslighter always will give himself away unwittingly. Within the very origins of the term *gaslighting* to describe the phenomenon of one person undermining another person's sense of knowledge/self/sanity is the resistance to gaslighting. In other words, some light still flickers somewhere, sometime, that reveals to the victim that she is right, that her perceptions and believes are true, that she is not going mad. Those flickering lights betray the gaslighter to his victim and threatened to render his manipulations ineffective.

So, if at some level, Paula knows her husband is manipulating her and the flickering gaslights are proof of his deception, why is she so affected by him? Why does he succeed in undermining her sense of herself? There must be more going on than meets the eye. Beyond the realms of perception, understanding, and knowledge, Paula is affected by her husband because she loves him. It Paula's affective connection to her husband, combined with his position of authority, that sets the stage for gaslighting. The epistemic considerations are secondary. Arguably, in all gaslighting affects play a central role. If gaslighting does not reach the affective dimension, it will not be successful. Then again, gaslighting's resulting self-doubt and doubt about reality do not come without affects. As I argued decades ago before the term gaslighting made it into public discourse, one of the primary affects through which patriarchy allows men to dominate women is shame. Gaslighting takes advantage of this shame and produces more shame.

In a culture where girls and women (and men of color and other marginalized people) have been pathologized, abjected, ridiculed, and hated, and where violence and abuse are normalized, it is difficult for marginalized people to resist incorporating at least some self-hatred or sense of inferiority or lack of legitimacy, along with some sense that they deserve abuse. The lack of positive images and reinforcement leads to feelings of emptiness, incompleteness, and worthlessness. These feelings are linked to shame. Gaslighting produces feelings of shame and worthlessness. Being ashamed is associated with one's identity rather than one's actions. In other words, one feels ashamed of themselves and not something they've done or not done.

Neither epistemic nor moral gaslighting can account for the *shame* at the heart of gaslighting. Epistemic gaslighting is about knowledge claims and the status as knower. And moral gaslighting is about obligations and moral claims and the status as moral agent. Most moral theories talk about the morality of actions or intentions, but not the morality of emotions. Shame is related to *one's sense of self* rather than to one's actions. Shame attacks the very core of identity. To feel shame is to feel like a bad person, not a person who has done something bad, which would be guilt rather than shame. Morally suspect actions or intentions might lead to guilt, and guilt in turn could produce shame. But guilt and shame are different emotions. Psychologists and early queer theorists have delineated the difference between guilt and shame as the difference between action and being or doing and self (cf. Lewis 1986, 1987; Tompkins 1995; Sedgwick 2003).

Those excluded or abjected by dominant values are made to feel ashamed, not about something that they have done, but about who they are. Shame is directed at the very being of the marginalized subject. In fact, shame is at odds with guilt insofar as it undermines the ability to act and to desire as a responsible agent. Stuck at the level of being, the shamed subject is cut off from the realm of meaning that engenders human agency and social legitimization. Shame undermines one's sense of agency and renders the shamed person passive. As I have argued elsewhere, oppression operates through an attack on subjectivity, particularly on the sense of agency inherent in subjectivity (see Oliver 2001, 2004). While one is held morally responsible for what one does and can therefore be praised or blamed, found innocent or guilty, shame is related less to morality than to inferiority. If guilt is associated with evil in a moral sense, then shame is associated with bad in the sense of inferiority. Shame brings with it the sense of being defective or flawed.

In an insightful study of shame and trauma in the writing of Toni Morrison, J. Brooks Bouson concludes that shame is related to feelings of inferiority that are internalized from early shaming interactions (Bouson 2000, 10; cf. 2009). Those excluded and abjected within mainstream culture are not only shamed, but also become the bearers of shame for the entire culture. Bouson makes this point in relation to Black Americans: "In a white male American culture that is 'shame phobic'—for it places value on 'achievement, competition, power, and dominance'—African Americans not only have been viewed as objects of contempt; they also have served as containers for white shame. Because white Americans have historically projected their own shame onto blacks, African Americans have been forced to carry a crippling heavy burden of shame; their own shame and the projected shame of white America" (2000, 15).

I would extend Bouson's claims to women, and other marginalized and abjected groups, who are made ashamed of their very being and forced to carry the shame of white men. For example, feminists have done important research on the emotional division of labor that assigns women, especially mothers, the lioness's share of affective burden so that men are free of it (cf. Brennan 1992; Bartky 1990; Oliver 2004; Whitney 2017). Shame is one of the heaviest parts of that affective burden.

Insofar as gaslighting is dependent on shaming its victims, it performs not only epistemic injustice, but also affective injustice. Victims of gaslighting are made to feel ashamed. Gaslighting, then, is not only about mistrust of one's own perceptions, understanding, and beliefs (epistemic dimension), or one's legitimacy or moral standing (moral dimension), but also about a deep sense of shame about being oneself (affective dimension). Gaslighting not only makes its victims feels like they'd made mistakes in judgment or understanding or that they aren't worthy in moral terms, but also that their very being is offensive. It creates a sense of being ashamed of existing.

In the systematic gaslighting that operates as part of oppressive dynamics, unwanted affects are projected onto the oppressed, who are then denigrated for being "too emotional." Anger directed toward the abuser turns inward and becomes anger and shame directed toward the self, which in turn flips over into the desire for recognition and love from those very same people who have rejected the target as hysterical, oversensitive, or "crazy" in the first place (cf. Oliver 2004). As we will see, this phenomenon is especially prominent in cases of sexual assault where victims blame themselves because they have internalized the norms of rape culture. The victims are expected to carry this affect without expressing it. Indeed, they are expected to carry the affective burdens of the culture. They are not only made ashamed of their very being but also forced to carry the shame of that culture.

Just as the gaslighter dominates his targets through manipulation of reality and denies the validity of the targets' experience, and makes his target feel ashamed of questioning his authority or standing up to him, so too the norms of dominant culture manipulate reality and deny the validity of marginalized people's experience, and then make them feel ashamed for standing up for themselves. When they do, they are often met with more gaslighting in the form of tone policing or dismissal as "snowflakes," "hysterical," "oversensitive," and so forth.

Following Frantz Fanon, we could say that negative affects of the oppressors are "deposited into the bones" of the oppressed (1968). Affects move between bodies. And colonization and oppression operate through depositing the unwanted affects of the dominant group onto those othered by that group to sustain its privileged position. Fanon describes the debilitating effects on the mind and body of taking on the colonizers' unwanted affects (1965, 1967, 1968).

Shiloh Whitney's recent work on affective injustice is instructive when considering the affective dimension of gaslighting (Whitney 2017, 2018). Although Whitney does not discuss affective injustice in terms of gaslighting or vice versa, she does describe what I'm calling affective gaslighting. Whitney's description of "byproductive affective labor" resonates with our discussion of gaslighting (see Whitney 2017). She maintains that those oppressed by sexism and racism are forced to carry the unwanted affects of their oppressors. Furthermore, women and people of color in sexist and racist societies become "affect disposals" who are then dismissed as "hysterical females" or "angry black women" or "overly sensitive" or "too emotional," and so forth.

Whitney maintains that affective labor is "byproductive" insofar as it produces affects for others to consume and creates affective byproducts in the worker, which then must be metabolized and often create harmful psychological and physical effects on the worker (2017). Affects are fabricated within exploitative economies, particularly within economies of coloniality and misogyny. I would argue that these forms of affective injustice are also forms of affective gaslighting.

Using Arlie Russell Hochchild's study of stewardesses as her example, Whitney argues that the commercialization of affect has feminized certain professions such that women or feminized men are expected to create a pleasant emotional response in the consumer. Stewardess are expected to produce "genuine" and "warm" rather than "forced" or "fake" smiles to make the flying experience more pleasant for the passengers (Whitney 2017, 644). Stewardesses are expected to conjure a cheerful affect to give to their customers. Compare this to Manne's argument that patriarchy demands that women legitimate men and do the emotional labor to make sure men continue to feel entitled.

But the stewardess's production of affect for the consumer—or the woman's production of affect for the man—has affective consequences for herself. She must "metabolize" the excess affect produced during the commercial flight, which means that after work they are still processing these negative emotions in ways that adversely affect their personal lives down to their very psyche or sense of self. As a result, they don't know which emotions are authentic and which have been produced for their jobs. Furthermore, they are forced to carry the hostility of their passengers home with them (Whitney 2017, 646). Since flights are often full of grumpy, anxious, and unhappy passengers, stewardesses must absorb those negative affects and return positive affects in their stead. The exchange is hostility for warmth. She takes on the passenger's hostility but makes them feel better by giving them cheerfulness in return. Again, compare this with Manne's argument that women are expected to prop up men's sense of themselves as authorities and entitled. And when women don't perform this affective service for men, they are subject to misogyny and abuse.[2]

Another example Whitney gives is domestic workers, who are expected to clean up both the physical and emotional messes of their employers and the children of their employers. Feminized service professionals such as nurses, childcare workers, and grade-school teachers are expected to manage not only their charges' bodies but also their emotions. Whitney concludes that even as these affective laborers produce the feeling of being cared for in their passengers or employers, they must mute their own affects. Furthermore, "affective hierarchies of gender and race," what we might call stereotypes of overly emotional women or people of color, play into feminized and racialized professions such as stewardess or domestic worker such that sexist and racist norms double down on affective gaslighting (cf. Whitney 2017, 665).

A prime example of the way affective gaslighting works in tandem with epistemic and moral gaslighting is rape culture. In rape culture, rape survivors are made to feel ashamed and even responsible for their own victimization. It is well-known that rape victims are often blamed for walking at night, or walking alone, or wearing provocative clothes, or leaving with the rapist, or drinking. Reporting rates for rape are astoundingly low because rape victims feel ashamed to report the assault. This is especially true on college campuses, where drugs and alcohol are often involved. When they do report sexual assault, survivors often report feeling interrogated by officials as if they were the criminals. Even when they do report sexual assault, it is rarely prosecuted. Until recently (thanks in part to the #MeToo movement), in a he-said-she-said situation, his word was always more credible than hers—a classic example of testimonial injustice (see Amber Carlson). Because of this testimonial injustice, when sexual assault is prosecuted, the perpetrators rarely get convicted. Even when they do get convicted, like the Stanford swimmer Brock Turner, they serve very little jail time.

Moreover, fraternity culture on college campuses promotes and valorizes so-called "nonconsensual sex" (see Oliver 2016). Even calling sexual assault *nonconsensual sex* instead of rape already suggests that rape is just another form of sex, which implicitly works to normalize sexual assault. There are too many cases to list where college women are welcomed to campus with signs and chants promoting rape (see Oliver 2016). The film *The Hunting Ground* shows case after case of college women who have been raped and then subjected to interrogations or blamed for being attacked. And, if they come forward and report their attacker, they are often blamed for ruining the life of a promising young man.

For example, in highly visible cases of sexual assault in Steubenville, Ohio, where high school football players sexually assaulted an unconscious girl, and in Nashville, Tennessee, where Vanderbilt University football players sexually assaulted a college junior, much of the initial public response was talk of "promising football careers ruined" (see Oliver 2016). Public reaction showed more sympathy for the perpetrators than the victims, what Manne calls "himpathy" (Manne 2020). The same is true of the Stanford swimmer whose father argued that the assault was just "twenty minutes of action" that shouldn't ruin the rest of his son's life. And what of the victim's life? What of the victim's promising career?

Perpetrators' appropriation of the discourse of victimhood is another form of gaslighting. They try to convince juries and their peers that they are the ones who are being harmed by the accusations of sexual assault, that they are the true victims (see Banet-Weiser 2021). Not only do they deny their violent actions and their victim's experience or trauma, but they also turn the tables such that they are the harmed party. Through manipulation of reality, they engage in gaslighting, which unfortunately is sanctioned by patriarchy and rape culture.

In addition to the physical pain of the attack, women must endure psychological abuse and emotional turmoil as a result of rape culture. The shame of being raped has led some girls and women to commit suicide, especially in cases where the assault was photographed or recorded and disseminated through social media (Oliver 2016). Some young women have gone so far as saying that the sexual assault itself was not the worst of their experience; rather the aftershocks of shame and humiliation were far worse, not to mention longer lasting. Some say they can heal from the physical pain of rape but not from the shame and humiliation heaped on them by rape culture (Oliver 2016).

When survivors of sexual assault are made to feel ashamed, or that they have ruined the life of their attacker, or that they are "damaged goods," they are the victims not only of rape but also of affective gaslighting.

Epistemic or moral gaslighting cannot explain the effect of rape culture on the victims of sexual assault. To understand the deep-seated shame and humiliation produced by rape culture in victims of sexual assault, we have to consider the affective dimension of gaslighting.

In sum, my claim is that gaslighting is *not merely* epistemic or moral. Rather, to be effective, gaslight is also necessarily affective. *Affect is the acid, so to speak, that burns the epistemic and moral uncertainty into the very identity of the target.* Shame is the byproduct of this process. Targets of gaslighting are made to feel ashamed. They are made to feel themselves as inferior or stupid or "crazy." And they are made to feel ashamed if they challenge the perpetrator. Gaslighting puts the victim in an affective double bind, damned if they do stand up to their abuser and damned if they don't. And it is this affective double bind, namely the affective injustice inherent in gaslighting, that makes its unconscious and unintentional perpetuation so pernicious and harmful to its targets, whose very souls are penetrated by debilitating affects through which they become complicit with their own gaslighting.

Notes

1. While teaching a graduate course on gaslighting in 2019, I saw this error repeated several times in the literature.

2. Of course, Mann and Whitney are not the first feminists to discuss women's emotional labor or the transmission of affect. Sandra Bartky, Teresa Brennan, Cynthia Willett, and my own early work, among others, take up these themes. And now there is a whole body of important research on affect theory, including work by Anne Cvetkovich, Sara Ahmed, and Lauren Berlant.

Works Cited

Abramson, Kate. 2014. "Turning Up the Lights on Gaslighting." *Philosophical Perspectives* 28: 1–30.
Ash, Allison, Redgina Hill, Stephen Ridson, and Alexander Jun. 2020. "Anti-Racism in Higher Education: A Model for Change." *Race and Pedagogy Journal* 4 (3).
Banet-Weiser, Sarah. 2021. "'Ruined' Lives: Mediated White Male Victimhood." *European Journal of Cultural Studies* 24 (1): 60–80.
Bartky, Sandra Lee. 1990. *Femininity and Domination.* New York: Routledge.
Bouson, J. Brooks. 2000. *Quiet as It's Kept: Shame, Trauma, and Race in the Novels of Toni Morrison.* Albany: State University of New York Press.

———. 2009. *Embodied Shame: Uncovering Female Shame in Contemporary Women's Writings*. Albany: State University of New York Press.

Brennan, Teresa. 1992. *The Interpretation of the Flesh: Freud and Femininity*. New York: Routledge.

Fanon, Frantz. 1965. *A Dying Colonialism*. Translated by Haakon Chevalier. New York: Grove Press.

———. 1967. *Black Skin White Masks*. Translated by C. L. Markmann. New York: Grove Press.

———. 1968. *The Wretched of the Earth*. Translated by Constance Farrington. New York: Grove Press.

Fricker, Miranda. 2007. *Epistemic Injustice: Power and the Ethics of Knowing*. Oxford: Oxford University Press.

———. 2017. "Evolving Concepts of Epistemic Injustice." In *The Routledge Handbook of Epistemic Injustice*, edited by Ian James Kidd, José Medina, and Gaile Pohlhaus Jr., 53–60. New York: Routledge.

Lewis, Helen Block. 1986. "The Role of Shame in Depression." In *Depression in Young People: Developmental and Clinical Perspectives,* edited by Michael Rutter. New York: Guilford Press.

———. 1987. "Shame and the Narcissistic Personality." In *The Many Faces of Shame,* edited by Donald L. Nathanson, 93–132. New York: Guilford Press.

Manne, Kate. 2017. *Down Girl: The Logic of Misogyny*. Oxford: Oxford University Press.

———. 2020. *Entitled: How Male Privilege Hurts Women*. New York: Crown Press.

McKinnon, Rachel. 2017. "Allies Behaving Badly: Gaslighting as Epistemic Injustice." In *The Routledge Handbook of Epistemic Injustice,* edited by Ian James Kidd, José Medina, and Gaile Pohlhaus Jr., 167–74. New York: Routledge.

Oliver, Kelly. 2004. *The Colonization of Psychic Space*. Minneapolis: University of Minnesota Press.

———. 2005. "Social Melancholy, Shame and Sublimation." In *Women and Children First,* edited by Patrice DiQuincio and Sharon Meagher. Albany: State University of New York Press.

———. 2016. *Hunting Girls: Sexual Violence from* The Hunger Games *to Campus Rape*. New York: Columbia University Press.

Sedgwick, Eve Kosofsky. 2003. *Touching Feeling: Affect, Pedagogy, Performativity*. Durham, NC: Duke University Press.

Stark, Cynthia. 2019. "Gaslighting, Misogyny, and Psychological Oppression." *The Monist* 102: 221–35.

Tomkins, Silvan Solomon. 1995. *Exploring Affect: The Selected Writings of Silvan S. Tomkins*. Edited by E. Virginia Demos. Cambridge: Cambridge University Press.

Whitney, Shiloh. 2017. "Byproductive Labor: A Feminist Theory of Affective Labor beyond the Productive–Reproductive Distinction." *Philosophy and Social Criticism* 44 (6): 637–60.

———. 2018. "Affective Intentionality and Affective Injustice: Merleau-Ponty and Fanon on the Body Schema as a Theory of Affect." *Southern Journal of Philosophy* 56 (4).

6

Anger Gaslighting as Affective Injustice

Shiloh Whitney

It is a tiresome truth of women's experience that our anger is not generally well-received. Men (and sometimes women) ignore it, see it as our being "upset" or "hysterical," or see it as craziness. Attention is turned not to what we are angry about but to the project of calming us down and to the topic of our "mental stability."

—Marilyn Frye, 1983

[B]ecause of the relation of feeling to significance, when our feelings are trivialized, ignored, systematically criticized, or extremely constrained by the poverty of our expressive resources, this situation can lead to a very serious kind of dismissal—the dismissal of the significance to a person of his or her own life, in a way that reaches down deeply into what the significance of a life can be to the person whose life it is.

—Sue Campbell, 1997

Gaslighting is currently discussed in feminist philosophy primarily as an epistemic injustice (an injustice related to knowledge and credibility).[1] However, I think gaslighting can also be an *affective injustice* (an injustice related to emotions and affective influence).[2] In this chapter I make an argument for that, sensitizing us to the affective dimension of gaslighting using *anger gaslighting* as a paradigm case.[3] Consider the following three quotes, each from a woman's testimony about her experience of anger:

> I could finally tell people on a Thursday that I'd been angry on a Monday. I couldn't tell them in real time. (Gloria Steinem quoted in Traister 2018, 57)

> [Anger] was so effectively severed from my use that, instead of being a catalyst for change, feeling angry invalidated both my confidence and my own experiences. (Soraya Chemaly 2018, 262)

> For years, I described myself as someone who wasn't prone to anger. "I don't get angry," I said, "I get sad" . . . at a certain point, I started to suspect that I was angrier than I thought. (Leslie Jamison 2018)

The women describing this experience—all in 2018—in each case connect it with an awareness of the same "tiresome truth" Frye observed in 1983: that her anger would not be "well-received" (see the first epigraph above). Variations of this experience are painfully familiar to me personally, and I have often commiserated about it with feminist friends. It is an experience not of anger merely dismissed, but anger impaired. In my 2018 article on affective injustice, I described it as a disjointed intentionality. Since then I have begun to think of it as "anger gaslighting." The advantage of this term is its ability not only to describe the injurious effect, but also to link that effect to the behavior that causes it: "gaslighting" names both. If garden-variety gaslighting makes me second-guess my perceptions, evaluations, or beliefs, anger gaslighting makes me second-guess my affective responses—specifically, my anger. If I have been successfully anger gaslit, then my anger has been impaired in its spontaneity (consider the first of my three quotes), its conviction (consider the second quote), or its legibility—not only to others, but also to myself (consider the third quote).

Affective injustice as an area of study is still quite new. Anger gaslighting has proven to be an instructive case for me as I work toward helping to build the theoretical scaffolding the field needs. The key concept I developed in studying anger gaslighting builds on Marilyn Frye's concept of *uptake*.[4] Uptake is a second-person affective behavior: it concerns how I am moved by someone else's affects. I define anger gaslighting behavior in terms of uptake. How do you gaslight someone's anger? Deprive it of uptake.

But the concept of uptake has special significance for the study of affective injustice because *it does for the theory of affective injustice what the concept of credibility does for the theory of epistemic injustice.* Just as the concept of credibility names the uniquely epistemic cooperative behavior whereby we take someone seriously as a knower, the concept of uptake names *the uniquely affective cooperative behavior whereby we take someone seriously as an affective being.* Establishing the importance of uptake and the uniquely affective social actions at stake in our second-personal affective behavior allows me to make a case for the unique importance of affective varieties of gaslighting.

To frame this phenomenon as anger gaslighting is to suggest that what is at stake here is not only whether others take me seriously as an affective being, but also whether I myself do so. As Campbell observes (see the second epigraph), our affects have a unique relationship to our ability not only to make sense of our own lives, but also to evaluate what is *significant* in them—not only to others, but also to ourselves in the first place. Like Frye, Campbell thinks that our episodic emotions are social actions, not only in the sense that they influence our social situation, but also in the sense that they are not unilaterally accomplished: emotions are actions that require cooperation from others to bring off. If that's so, it follows that our affective lives are a uniquely important site not only of collaborative sense-making, but also collaborative significance-making. But it also follows that affective sense-making and significance-making are uniquely vulnerable to distortion and sabotage by uncooperative others. This vulnerability is precisely what is in evidence in the phenomenon of anger gaslighting.

If that reliance of affective life on cooperation from others can be exploited not only in interpersonal abuse but also in domination and oppression, then this would make gaslighting's affective variety uniquely important. It would be akin to what Kate Manne has called "moral gaslighting," especially when the emotions being gaslit are performing moral functions (Manne 2023). But affective gaslighting would also exceed moral gaslighting, since its scope would include those evaluations of personal and interpersonal *salience* that are the purview of both the moral emotions and the pre-moral or non-moral ones. On this view, gaslighting's affective variation is an instrument that can be weaponized to distort our ability to not only make sense of the world, but also to evaluate what matters in it.

The Gaslighting of Anger Gaslighting

In each of the three testimonies of the anger gaslighting effect that I quoted in the introduction, the woman speaking does not merely report on the injustice and frustration of her anger being denied influence. She reports on a much deeper injury: one in which her own capacity to respond angrily to genuine insult or injury with spontaneity and conviction and legibility (even to herself) has been impaired. Critical phenomenologists would call this an inhibited or disjointed affective intentionality: an impairment of one's anger response in the first person.[5] This is how I initially described the phenomenon, and I still think it is a good phenomenological description of the injurious effect. What is at stake in the shift to the term "gaslighting"? In each testimony I quoted, the woman's goal in describing the injurious effect is not merely to report this injury. It is to link the injurious effect to its cause: the dismissal or uncooperative behavior she had come to expect from others in response to her anger. Her anger was being disabled by the way others responded to it. This link is what we bring into focus by identifying these experiences as cases of anger gaslighting.

"Gaslighting" names a unique injurious effect and also the behavior that tends to produce it.[6] When a person is successfully gaslit, they are not only doubted by others, but may begin to doubt themselves.[7] The concept of gaslighting includes the idea that the latter is accomplished by way of the former: casting doubt on someone is the means through which she was made to doubt herself. In gaslighting, the way others respond to me begins to impair an aspect of my relationship to myself. In particular, the non-cooperative response I receive from some second person(s) when I express my experiences to them begins to impair some aspect of my ability to make sense of my own experience to myself in the first person. In this way, gaslighting can function as a form of *violence*—not merely the status subordination of being dismissed.[8] What makes the concept of gaslighting so compelling and useful is its capacity to name this bidirectional expressive failure—both other-facing and self-facing—and to call out that failure as sabotage by linking its injurious effects for the self to its causes in someone else's uncooperative reception of them. Gaslighting expands our understanding of epistemic injustice by identifying a set of injurious effects that are not confined to its target's influence on others (testimonial credibility), but infect her relation to herself. Consider: while testimonial injustice produces a deficit of its targets' *perceived* or received competencies, gaslighting produces a deficit in its targets' *actual* capacities (to trust her own experience, to make sense of it to herself as well as to others, and similar). And to call it gaslighting is to observe that the one occurs by way of the other: the uncooperative reception of the target is what eventually incapacitated them in this way.

In the case of anger gaslighting, the sense-making abilities that are injured are affective. Consider again the testimony I quoted above: Steinem describes being able to identify her emotional state as anger, but only on a days-long delay, and that after decades of work. Jamison found that for years her own anger had only been intelligible to herself as sadness. Chemaly describes a different sort of alienation from her own anger: though she was not delayed or hermeneutically blocked from feeling anger, when she did, it undermined her confidence and her own experience. The person's whose anger has been successfully gaslit may have difficulty even identifying her own agitation as anger. Or she may be able to identify her emotion as anger, but experience that as undermining rather than motivating or empowering. Successful anger gaslighting thus constitutes a uniquely affective injury: an injury to the *spontaneity, conviction, and legibility of one's anger response*—not only within a given emotional episode, but on the scale of ones' emotional habits or characteristic affective traits.

What is impaired when our anger response is injured in this way? We will have to consider the functions of anger: what does it do, and why does it matter?

What Anger Does, and Why It Matters

Philosophers have long maintained that anger has unique moral and political functions. It has been called the political emotion par excellence: as our sense of injustice, anger enables us not only to register injustice but also to take a forceful stand against it, both singly and together.[9] Anger gaslighting can lead us to doubt ourselves in ways that sabotage those functions.

Some functions of anger are self-directed, but some are other-directed. The former fall into two categories. First, my *anger orients me*. Just as fear is my sense of alarm and grief is my sense of loss, anger is my sense of injustice.[10] Thus anger has a role in moral perception: it is an important part of our moral compass.[11] In making us second-guess our anger, anger gaslighting is morally disorienting, spinning our moral compass. That makes it is a uniquely powerful tool of subordination.

Second, anger *takes a stand*. I mean not only that an angry response expresses an evaluation (denouncing its object as a wrongdoing or its target as a wrongdoer), but also that in doing so anger enacts an *entitlement* to make such evaluations. Anger takes a stand not only about the *sense* but also the significance of a shared situation, about what is *salient* in it; and makes demands on oneself and others accordingly. And in doing so, it claims for the angry person the entitlement to make such demands: to participate in the affective adjudication of what is in and out of bounds, and what most deserves our attention; and to hold others accountable to these demands.[12] Marilyn Frye's illustration is helpful:

> You walk off with my hammer and I angrily demand that you bring it back. Implicitly, I claim that my project is worthy, that I am within my rights to be doing it, that the web of connections it weaves rightly encompasses that hammer . . . Anger implies a claim to a domain—a claim that one is a being whose purposes and activities require and create a web of objects, spaces, attitudes and interests that is worthy of respect, and that the topic of this anger is a matter rightly within that web. (Frye 1983, 87)

In Frye's example, my anger takes a stand about you and me with respect to the hammer: that you wrong me in walking off with it. But, as she suggests, my anger also takes a stand about something much more fundamental: my entitlement to a degree of affective meaning-making jurisdiction in our shared situation. It takes a stand regarding not only this particular project with the hammer, but also the entitlements of my affective agency to determine salience generally: my entitlement to care about and become affectively invested in things like hammers and construction projects, and for those investments to have weight or be salient not only to me, but also for others concerned. Anger takes a stand, not only on the *significance of its objects*, but on the *significance-making jurisdiction of its subject*. Even if I turn out to be wrong about the hammer-related specifics of my anger's demand (perhaps in fact you had prior claim, or a more urgent concern), my anger can still be right to take a stand about this more fundamental demand that my affective investments should be taken seriously by others, that my emotions have a place in the collaborative process of establishing what matters. In being angry that you took my hammer, I assert myself as someone whose projects and interests are worthy and weighty, someone who is a player in negotiating salience: what matters in our shared situation. Anger gaslighting threatens our capacity to stand up for ourselves and others in this uniquely affective way.[13]

Anger also has an other-directed function: *anger is influential*. Frye says that anger is a *"social act"*: anger is a way of directing and focusing the perception and attention of others, orienting them toward my affective investments (Frye 1983, 89, emphasis mine). I already said that my anger functions to orient me. What I am adding now is that (with a little cooperation from you) my anger can also function to orient *you*. I said that my anger functions to take a stand and enact the affective entitlement to do so; now I am adding that this meaning-making action is not only personal, but also interpersonal and social. Anger is a social action in the sense that its significance is social: it aims to act not only on oneself, but also on others. When anger makes sense of you grabbing my hammer as a wrongdoing, it aims to make this sense of the situation not only privately, but also publicly. It aims to publish this sense of the situation, to broadcast it to others. But it is also social action in the sense that it is an action that cannot be accomplished unilaterally: my anger offers you an orientation, but it cannot complete this act without a little cooperation from you. Borrowing from J. L. Austin's account of the cooperative behavior speech acts require to come off, Frye calls this cooperative behavior "uptake."

Frye says that anger, like a speech act, not only communicates something, but *does* something. The difference between saying "you wronged me" dispassionately versus saying it angrily is that "you do not just assert or report something . . . you also reorient yourself *and another person*" (Frye 1983, 88, emphasis mine). My anger offers me an orientation in our shared situation. But it also offers *you* an orientation in our shared situation. My anger is a way for me to get my bearings, but it is also a way for *you* to get my bearings. What is at issue is not merely knowledge, but also an affective orientation: being moved. By directing attention toward wrongdoing and wrongdoers, anger not only communicates a message, but also conveys influential attention-directing force. For my anger about the hammer to be successful in moving you, it need not overwrite your own evaluation of the situation; but it amplifies the salience of the hammer and your act of taking it, insisting that what matters to me command your attention as well as mine. Frye says that anger is like a speech act, not only reporting on the world, but also acting on it. And that what anger does—as long as it receives uptake—is reorient us: not only the angry agent, but also those who gave uptake. In this way, anger is a potent source of moral and political influence, commanding attention and fueling solidarity.[14] It directs our conversation and our projects—most basically, our project of making sense of our world together and establishing what is salient in it, what most deserves our attention individually and collectively. Anger gaslighting is a tool for making this other-oriented function backfire, redirecting attention away from what I'm angry about and onto scrutiny of me and my emotional state instead.

This is especially significant since the orientation my anger offers you is not only an orientation toward the anger's object (in the hammer example: my anger offers you an orientation toward the hammer as something I have a prior claim on; a claim that you violated in grabbing it), but also toward me as its subject. My anger offers you an orientation toward my affective agency: an orientation toward me as someone whose projects and interests are worthy and weighty, someone who is a player in negotiating the salience of the situation. And this is not only an orientation toward me, but toward my affective investments, and my entitlement to have them: the web of projects, interests, and attitudes that radiates out from me. Indeed, it is an orientation toward our whole shared situation as remapped by the contours of my concerns. Thus my anger offers you an orientation toward me as someone whose affective investments are to be taken seriously; someone whose affective life matters in your own negotiation of our shared situation. Thus to have my anger dismissed would be a very serious dismissal indeed: it would disable this other-directed function and marginalize me from participation in the negotiation about what is salient in our shared situation. But if anger can be gaslit, then *non-cooperation with the other-directed functions of anger can eventually disable the self-directed ones as well*. What is at stake is not only being dismissed from my participation in that negotiation, but my being denied the hermeneutic resources to formulate my affective orientation in the first place.

It may be tempting to reduce anger's other-directed function to a special case of testimony. To understand why there is something uniquely affective at stake here, it helps to focus on the "act" part of Frye's speech act analogy for anger. My anger is doing more than carrying a message to you. It can (re)orient you. It can sensitize you to what matters to me: the affective geography of our situation according to me, the landscape of salience that is being worked out in the complex pushes and pulls of my affective life (all the more difficult to communicate in any other way because of their complexity and ambivalence, the famous capacity of emotional life to accommodate otherwise incompossible vectors). This is communication, but not in a manner that can be liquidated into a more strictly epistemic framework. Anger communicates, not only *diegetically* (telling), but also *mimetically* (showing). Anger doesn't just *tell* you what matters to me, it also *shows* you; it gives you a *feel* for the world according to me.[15] Instead of merely indicating or reporting about its object, anger summons or evokes its object: makes its presence felt. Anger is moving.

Notice how this other-directed function of anger exceeds that of testimony in ways that are especially socially and politically important in cases where there is significant hermeneutical injustice—for example, where my social group's experiences have been marginalized in the dominant discourse.[16] Like Lugones's "hard-to-handle anger," I may struggle with a sentiment of injustice that frustrates my attempts to make it legible and respectable.[17] In these circumstances, my anger response is a vital form of agency. It connects me with others who share my predicament and serves as the raw material out of which we build new sense-making conditions to make our anger intelligible and respectable (consider the role of anger in feminist consciousness-raising practices that eventually produced a conceptual vocabulary for sexual harassment). With a little cooperation from you, my anger makes it possible for me to show you my concerns even when the dearth of hermeneutic resources makes it impossible for me to *tell* you my concerns in a dispassionate report. In such cases, a demand from you that I swallow my anger in the service of dispassionate communication may appear an innocent call for reason and calm, but it functions to preserve hermeneutical injustices, disabling one of our key tools for repairing them.

The political power of anger's functions makes it uniquely attractive target for intersecting oppressive structures. Soraya Chemaly writes that "the dynamic of who gets to express anger matters in all unequal social relationships" (Chemaly 2018, 261). Race, class, and age are also sites of anger gaslighting, and they ramify the ways that gender is a site of it. For example, whether a woman's anger is given or refused uptake may depend on social factors including not only her gender, the gender of her anger's target, and gendered associations with the domain of her anger's object, but also her race, the race of her anger's target, and any racialized associations with the domain of her anger's object (for example, white women angry about school desegregation and its perceived harm to white children might reasonably expect uptake even in social environments that generally refuse uptake to women's anger). Anger gaslighting is a multipurpose tool of subordination.

Anger's unique sociopolitical salience makes anger gaslighting a singularly important case of affective injustice, but also a uniquely instructive paradigm case for understanding how emotions can be weaponized in social power struggles and why it is crucial to study the varieties of injustice that target the affective capacities of a person or group.

Uptake: Anger Gaslighting Behavior

What is the cooperative behavior that anger gaslighters withhold? Marilyn Frye calls it "uptake": "It is a tiresome truth of women's experience that our anger is generally not well-received. . . . Attention is turned not to what we are angry about but to the project of calming us down and to the topic of our 'mental stability.' It is as common as dirty socks. . . . [Our anger is d]eprived of uptake" (Frye 1983, 84). Anger uptake refusers engage with my anger as an obstacle rather than an orientation. They do not permit my anger to orient them, to direct their attention toward its concerns, and toward me as entitled to be a player in negotiating the affective significance of our situation, what is salient in it. Instead, they treat my anger as an obstacle. They focus on scrutiny of my emotional state and the question of whether I am regulating my emotions properly. Anger gaslighting behavior is constituted by persistent, pervasive refusal of uptake for apt anger.

Uptake is a second-person affective behavior. It's not a matter of how one feels oneself, but of how one responds to someone else's feelings. More precisely: uptake is not a matter of producing an emotion myself, but of *cooperating with another person's emotion in a manner that provides their emotion the conditions needed to complete its social action*, its other-directed function of affective influence. Frye writes that when my anger is deprived of uptake, it "is left as just a burst of expression of individual feeling. As a social act, an act of communication, it just doesn't happen": its other-orienting action is "non-played" (Frye 1983, 89). The conditions needed to complete its social action, its other-directed function, have been withheld. When you refuse my anger uptake, you scuttle its potential to *show* you how I feel, to sensitize your perception and attention toward what matters to me in our situation. You neutralize (or backfire) my anger's influence.

Refusing anger uptake need not take the form of an erroneous evaluation of its aptness. Indeed, it is much more effective to remain unmoved, affectively aloof, and insist on dispassionate communication. Frye describes uptake refusers as focusing on the project of calming down the angry person. Alicia Garza observes: "[Black women's] anger gets dismissed and devalued and gaslighted. . . . We get told all the time that our anger is disruptive, that it is a distraction, that it is . . . divisive and moving us backwards. . . . Yet nobody ever seems to question: why are you so fucking mad?" (Alicia Garza quoted in Traister 2018, 54). On Garza's description, these anger gaslighters need not claim that Black women's anger is inapt. They only need to insist that it is disruptive, distracting, divisive, or otherwise counterproductive. They remain affectively aloof from the anger themselves, refusing to be moved by it: refusing to allow it to sensitize them to the world according to Black women. Audre Lorde's white feminist anger gaslighters treat her anger similarly: "I speak out of a direct and particular anger at an academic conference, and a white woman says, 'Tell me how you feel but don't say it too harshly or I cannot hear you'" (Lorde 2017 [1984], 125). Lorde's anger gaslighter responds to her anger by demanding calm, holding communication hostage until Lorde swallows her anger, liquidating its concerns into a dispassionate report. Like Garza's anger gaslighters, Lorde's anger gaslighters seize on her anger itself as the real problem. They react to her anger as if the proper locus of concern in the situation is not what she is angry about, but rather the fact of her anger. They decline to let her anger inform their feel for what is salient in the situation.

Anger gaslighting may also be more active and pathologizing. In Frye's description of women's anger uptake refusers, they might also take her anger as an occasion to redirect focus to questions of her mental stability, or they might focus on the project of calming her down in a way that accomplishes this more implicitly. Anger gaslighters might seem to be complimentary ("You're cute when you're mad") or benevolent ("I'm so sorry you feel that way"). Whichever approach they use, the definitive aspect of the anger gaslighting behavior is that anger gaslighters *refuse to cooperate with anger's other-directed function*. Anger gaslighters treat my anger as if what it offers to them is an *obstacle* rather than an *orientation*. In doing so, *they fail to take me seriously as an affective being*.

Even in an isolated episode, the anger gaslighting behavior disables my affective influence on others. But when it is persistent and pervasive, targeting a particular individual or social group, anger gaslighting also threatens to injure one's sense of injustice in the first person as well. This is what is at stake in conceptualizing this behavior as anger gaslighting rather than merely dismissal. To call this anger gaslighting rather than mere dismissal is (a) to position it as part of an actual or potential pattern of persistent anger-uptake-refusing behavior, and (b) to suggest that if this treatment is persistent and pervasive, then *it will tend to undermine my capacity to take myself seriously as an affective being*. Thus the injurious effect of anger uptake refusal should not only be assessed in its impact on anger's other-directed functions. Eventually the *self-directed functions* of my anger may also be impaired.

When you give uptake to my anger, you permit it to direct your attention toward its concerns, its object and target. My anger orients you: you get your bearings by it. When you refuse uptake, you take my anger as an occasion to scrutinize my emotional state, directing your attention away from my anger's concerns and toward the question of my emotional competency instead. Instead of receiving my anger as a way to get your bearings, you treat it as an indication that I have lost mine. Hence what is at stake in anger uptake is not just whether a particular episode of anger gets the reception it deserves, or whether an angry person received the recognition or respect she deserves. What is at stake is whose emotions get to be influential, the ones by which we get our bearings in a shared situation. And it is not only this episodic situation that is at stake, but the broader sense-making conditions of our shared world.

What is it like to give anger uptake?[18] Discussing with a Black colleague what uptake for the protest anger of the Black Lives Matter movement has meant in her life, she told me that what her neighbors paid attention to had changed. Her sons had a habit of stopping at the corner store on their way home from school. The proprietor called her one day when he did not see them, checking to make sure they got home safe. Another neighbor offered rides. What mattered to my colleague was not that her neighbors recognized and validated or joined her in her feelings about racial injustice: her anger, her fear as a parent of Black children. What was important, she told me, was that *her neighbors had become sensitized to the world according to those feelings*. Instead of rejecting Black Lives Matter anger as inappropriate or out of bounds, it began to have weight in how they got their bearings, part of what must be taken into account in distinguishing what is in and out of bounds in the first place.

My own experience as a white woman of giving uptake to the anger of Black people at racial injustice involves not stepping into their shoes, but experiencing the weight of my own white skin in the world differently. Resentment flashes once again across the face of a student in one of my classes, and while I had found it incomprehensible before, knowing I had not personally done anything to deserve it from him, something shifts when I suspend my defensiveness and tune in to his anger, getting a feel for myself and our situation by its lights. No, it wasn't something in particular I did, but that's exactly it: here I am, one more white authority figure in an institution full of them. This experience of anger-plus-uptake has the potential to accomplish something much more profound than mere understanding of an injustice or recognition that repairs a status injury. It reorients us, giving the angry person a uniquely affective kind of power: affective influence in our shared situation, jurisdiction in establishing what is salient in it.

Notice that giving uptake is not itself necessarily a mimetic behavior even though it is still an affective behavior: you don't have to join me in my anger to give uptake to it. In giving uptake, you become a receiver or amplifier tuned in to my anger, not necessarily a transmitter of your own. Uptake is an affective behavior insofar as it is a way of being moved. But it is a way you are moved by *my* anger, rather than simply being moved to your own.[19] To give uptake, you need not get mad on my behalf or put yourself in my shoes. When you give uptake to my anger, this is not a vicarious experience: you are not put in my place in our situation. Instead you stay in your own place in our shared situation but become sensitized to it differently, as remapped by the contours of my concerns.[20]

Undoubtedly there are many more questions to be pursued about uptake. Some of them I discuss elsewhere.[21] But there is one additional reflection that I will share here. Increasingly I am inclined to think about uptake, not as a singular affective gesture with two binary modes (given vs. refused), but as a name for a whole genre of affective behavior with a wide spectrum of modes and gestures: a uniquely affective hermeneutic process that cannot be successfully completed privately, but that is fundamentally interpersonal or social. If anger gaslighting is possible, this suggests that philosophers of emotion like Sue Campbell are correct to say that there is a "power of our interpreters to affect how we feel" through the way that they "view the occasions of our lives and respond to our expressive acts," and that this is a necessary rather than incidental part of affective life (Campbell 1997, 10, 135). Campbell has called this *triangulation*: I am being moved by some occasion, and you are responding to my response; and this triangle is the basic condition of affective meaning, of establishing the personal significance of the occasions of our lives, not only to others, but also to ourselves.[22] Giving uptake, then, becomes a name for serving as the third apex of this triangle: the responder to another's response, a kind of affective midwifery required for the "facilitation of affective significance" (Campbell 1997, 155). In anger gaslighting, this cooperative affective response is systematically withheld, and we are denied a basic hermeneutic resource needed for successfully making affective meaning.

If uptake is an interpersonal hermeneutic process that is endemic to affective life, then there is a great deal of uptake work to do. How is this labor divided? Another thought: the dearth of uptake for women's anger may be the corollary of a demand that we do this service of facilitating affective significance for others. Drawing on Sandra Bartky's analysis of the feminized emotional labor, Ellie Anderson gives an account of feminized "hermeneutic labor": "hermeneutic labor is the burdensome activity of a) understanding one's own feelings, desires, intentions, and motivations, and presenting them in an intelligible fashion to others when deemed appropriate; b) discerning others' feelings, desires, intentions, and motivations by interpreting their verbal and nonverbal cues, including cases when these are minimally communicative or outright avoidant; and c) comparing and contrasting these multiple sets of feelings, desires, intentions, and motivations for the purposes of conflict resolution" (Anderson, 2023, 178). Even as anger gaslighting and related phenomena deny us the resources to make our own emotions legible and orienting for ourselves as well as others, we are tasked with the uptake work of facilitating this affective process for more privileged others. As Bartky points out, the injustice of this is not only exploitation—the systematic appropriation of our emotional resources in the service of others—but also an alarmingly profound disempowerment and subordination. As Bartky describes it, in this feminized emotional labor, part of being identified as a woman is being systematically enlisted in "an active and affective assimilation of the world according to men" (Bartky 1990, 117). If what is fundamentally at stake in making affective meaning is establishing salience or personal significance, then an affective assimilation of this sort is a devastating divestment of the conditions, not only of self-determination, but of self-development in the first place.[23]

Anger Gaslighting as Moral Gaslighting?

Given my emphasis on anger's moral functions, we might think that anger gaslighting is an instance of what Kate Manne has called "moral gaslighting" (Manne 2023). If affective responses like anger are part of our moral perception (setting our moral compass by sensitizing us to wrongs and enabling a sense of injustice and self-respect in the face of being wronged), our moral motivation and action (how we take a stand against wrongdoing), and our ability to function well in a moral community (how we direct attention and conversation toward wrongdoing and build solidarity with others who stand against it), then anger gaslighting can lead us to doubt ourselves in ways that injure those unique and important functions.[24] Thus anger gaslighting constitutes a significant moral injury. More than sabotaging particular moral and political projects, it can also wound our abilities to register injustice in the first place as well as to take a forceful stand against it, both singly and together.[25]

Is there anything left that is distinctively affective about the gaslighting of anger gaslighting, or can it be reduced to moral gaslighting? Let us consider the gaslighting of a non-moral emotion. Fear constitutes its object as a danger rather than a wrong, and so is not necessarily a moral emotion; yet in sensing danger and orienting me toward it, fear orients me toward what *matters* in my situation, what is worthy of attention and action, what is salient. I think we can be gaslit about these non-moral affective orientations. Brittany Cooper writes: "White fears are routinely treated as fact rather than fantasy. . . . [E]veryone who is nonwhite is treated as though their fears are the stuff of fantasy" (Cooper 2018). In a white supremacist society, racial bias skews our sense of alarm, so that a Black person's apt fear may be refused uptake ("That cop's not following you; you're just paranoid") even as a white person's inapt fear may be given uptake ("Well, the officer said he feared for his life"). This is fear gaslighting: persistent and pervasive uptake refusal for apt fear. It functions to sustain white supremacy by reproducing a racially biased sense of alarm (Cooper 2018, 204).

Thus I think that any episodic emotion can be gaslit, but this is only moral gaslighting when the emotion is a moral one. Still, I suspect non-moral affective gaslighting has more in common with moral gaslighting than with garden-variety gaslighting. Manne's key insight about moral gaslighting is that gaslighting is especially—or at least, uniquely—alarming and injurious where it affects not only our beliefs but also our *evaluations*. I think we undersell the importance of this observation if we limit it to moral evaluations rather than extending it to all our ways of orienting ourselves in some gradient of valence. To countenance what is uniquely alarming about affective gaslighting, we must include uniquely affective orientations such as attractions and aversions, which may have moral valence in some cases, but may also be appetitive, sensorimotor, and aesthetic orientations. While not all emotions constitute their objects in explicitly moral terms like anger does, even so, all emotions do enact an orientation toward the world that takes a position on what is *salient* in it: what is worthy of attention and action, what attracts or repels. Conversely, emotions with uniquely moral functions *also* have this uniquely affective salience-making function. Consider: anger's functions too are not exclusively moral. As I argued earlier in this chapter, even where anger orients us toward moral salience, it also orients us toward personal and interpersonal salience: which projects, interests, and attitudes matter and are worthy of our collective attention. And to be gaslit about this is a profound and devastating means of subordination—at least as serious as being gaslit about one's perceptions or factual beliefs—and one's moral intuitions.

Yet, as Manne observes, it is probably both easier and more common to gaslight people about values than about perceptions or factual beliefs. So this too would be a feature shared between affective gaslighting and moral gaslighting. Indeed, I suspect it is even easier and more common to get people to doubt their affective orientations than their moral ones.

Affective Injustice

No doubt it is frustrating and even injurious when our apt anger is refused uptake. But how might it constitute an injustice?

Frye emphasizes the power the refusal of uptake has to hijack anger's function as a social act. When "[d]eprived of uptake, the woman's anger is left as just a burst of expression of individual feeling. As a social act, an act of communication, it just doesn't happen."[26] To be deprived of the capacity to act in this uniquely affective way is a substantial disempowerment. Studies show that women's anger tends to be less influential or even directly counterproductive for women even where it can be productive for men: while anger decreases the persuasiveness of women's arguments on others, it increases the persuasiveness of men's (Brescoll and Uhlman 2008). As Rebecca Traister observes: "[A]nger works for men in ways that it does not for women. . . . [M]en like both Donald Trump and Bernie Sanders can wage yelling campaigns and be credited with . . . compellingly channeling the rage felt by their supporters while their female opponents can be jeered and mocked as shrill for speaking too loudly or forcefully into a microphone" (Salerno and Peter-Hagene 2015). Thus anger gaslighting behavior constitutes an injustice insofar enables and disables the influence of our anger in ways that reproduce social hierarchies. When a woman's anger is refused uptake, the interpersonal or social impact of her anger backfires. Instead of directing others' attention toward the object and target of her anger—the situation in our shared world that she is angry *at* with its wrongdoing and wrongdoer—her anger functions to direct attention toward her self and her emotional state and the question of her emotional competency. Anger gaslighters have changed the subject: now what is at issue is not the wrongdoing, but the woman's tone, demeanor, and attitude; instead of gathering around the project of determining what, if anything, should be done about the alleged wrongdoing, her anger gathers people around the project of calming her down and policing her attitude.

Notice that in a world where emotionality is widely figured as a deficiency of rationality, simply pivoting to attending to the emotional state of the agent may be enough to undermine her emotion's influence on others. This is especially so if the agent belongs to a social group that is traditionally associated with emotionality or unruly affects. In that case, the undermining effects of refused uptake will be more likely to stick to the agent rather than the episode. For example, a powerful white man's outburst might be chalked up to a cranky mood or a stressful week, while a Black woman who fails to meet smile expectations may be branded as an "angry black woman" and undermined indefinitely. The question of affective competency sticks to her as an agent, while for him it only sticks to the isolated episode.

But we do not have to accept this injury as an intrinsic violation to see the injustice here. For that, we need to observe the economy of affective influence parallel to Fricker's economy of credibility. Just as there are deficits and surpluses of credibility that are constitutive of epistemic injustice, there are *deficits and surpluses of uptake that are constitutive of affective injustice*. We need not appeal to a set of intrinsic or universal set of affective goods that a just social world must protect in order to be just (Traister 2018). The injustice can be found in the large-scale pattern of enabling affective capacities for some individuals and social groups at the expense of disabling them for others. When an individual or social group is pervasively, persistently targeted for uptake refusal, this is unjust regardless of whether each and every episode of anger denied uptake was apt, since the persistent uptake refusal amounts to disabling a uniquely affective agency for that individual or social group.

Anger gaslighting is thus a uniquely affective injustice, not merely in the sense that it is an affective dimension of the experience of injustice. Rather, it is an injustice that is constitutively affective. *There is a uniquely affective power of action at stake, and anger gaslighting does not merely reflect but rather helps to directly constitute the social hierarchies that enable that power for some at the expense of others.* Insofar as the injustice is one of blocking or constraining a given social group from engaging in certain affective actions, it is a kind of disempowerment. But it can also be the injustice of blocking or constraining that social group from being taken seriously as the kind of agent who can engage in such actions at all: undermining their affective capacities and jurisdiction wholesale.

All of this can be maintained just insofar as anger gaslighting affects anger's other-directed functions, since they concern the success of our anger as a social action and the way anger gaslighting sabotages it, muting and even backfiring our anger's interpersonal or social impact. Persistent, pervasive refusal of uptake can make anger non-productive at its other-directed functions (I call this anger muting) or counterproductive at them (I call this anger backfiring). In anger muting, anger gaslighting behavior has succeeded in diminishing the influence of the anger on others' attention and energy. The anger is rendered incapable or less capable of directing others' attention toward the anger's target or object of concern. Instead of being engaged as an orientation, the anger is treated as noise and tuned out or turned down. Anger muting is often combined with anger backfiring, in which anger gaslighting behavior not only has succeeded in diminishing the anger's productive influence, but has succeeded in making it a counterproductive influence. Even when the agent's anger is apt, anger backfiring makes it a danger to the agent and a threat to her chances to redress the wrong that angers her. Anger *muting* decreases the *incentive* to respond angrily even in the face of genuine insult or injury, whereas anger *backfiring* increases the *risk*.

These are direct results of anger gaslighting behaviors, but what's injurious and unjust about them exceeds the gaslighting effect. Even if the target never doubts herself, persistently refusing uptake sabotages her anger's capacity to demand respect and influence others. Uptake refusal *makes* the target's anger counterproductive. Even when it fails to impair the target's anger at its source in her own affective capacities, jamming its *intrapersonal* spontaneity or conviction, uptake refusal can impair the transindividual or *interpersonal influence* of the target's anger. This is unjust wherever it is constitutive of a larger pattern of domination or oppression, enabling affective influence for some social groups at the expense of others.

However, where anger gaslighting is successful at obstructing anger's self-directed functions, more can be said. For one, when anger gaslighting is successful, this constitutes violence: a disabling of our capacities, not merely once they radiate forth from us and aim at the world, but rather a disabling that withers them at the root. Anger gaslighting can mute our anger's influence on others, but it can also jam the signal at its source. This brings out the hermeneutic dimension to the affective injustice of anger gaslighting. When a social group is targeted for anger gaslighting, we are denied the interpretive resources to make sense of our experience.

Anger can also be self-muted: to swallow one's anger is to metabolize it inwardly rather than express it outwardly. Persistent, pervasive refusal of uptake incentivizes the angry agent to swallow her anger in anticipation of its muted or backfired reception. Traister describes this deliberation:

> I value my own rage and the rage of others, especially of women. But I also live in the world. I have, for years, made the rage that guided my work appear palatable . . . I was funny! And playful, cheeky, ironic, knowing! I worked to make it clear that I am a fun person who enjoys friends and beer and laughter. I took great care to be nice . . . To full-throatedly express my ire would have been alienating, tactically unsound. I have watched as my peers have made similar choices. (Traister 2018, xxix)

If we anticipate uptake refusals that will mute our anger, this is an incentive to swallow it, and anger backfiring makes it a risk not to swallow it. While I reserve the name "anger swallowing" for the act of an angry agent adapting strategically to a non-choiceworthy situation, I like Alison Bailey's term "affective smothering" as a name for the demand to swallow one's anger or other outlaw emotion.[27] The injustice of this demand is that it forces a choice between two bad options, both tending to reproduce social hierarchies. Amia Srinivasan offers an interesting account of the unique affective injustice of the demand to swallow one's anger in the face of expectations of its poor reception in others. On my own view, the injustice is found in the deficits and surpluses of uptake in the background affective economy such that one social group's emotional *incompetency* can function to further privilege them, while another group's emotional competency functions as a burden of labor or a liability they must hide.

Frye claims that tracking anger uptake is an "instrument of cartography": anger uptake maps power (Frye 1983, 93–94). If we track whose anger gets uptake (from whom, with respect to what domain, etc.), that will yield a map of social hierarchies. This is a fascinating claim, positioning anger uptake as a potent tool for mapping complex intersections of power. In the context of a discussion of anger gaslighting, I think we can draw a bolder conclusion. Uptake distribution doesn't just map power; it shapes the territory. Uptake has a constitutive role, not merely a representational one. Giving and refusing uptake is an instrument, not only of the cartography of power, but of power itself. It is one of the ways that social hierarchies are made.

Epistemic Injustice or Affective Injustice?

No doubt all or most epistemic injustice may have an affective dimension. Consider Fricker's paradigm case of testimonial injustice: the fictional case in which the character Marge Sherwood's suspicion of Tom Ripley is dismissed as "female intuition" rather than "facts."[28] Fricker treats this as a diminishment of Marge's status in the credibility economy due to her gender. And it no doubt is that. But consider how this same incident is also a case in which Marge's emotion—her suspicion or alarm, a species of fear—is refused uptake.

Indeed, it may fit the particulars of this example better to understand it as an affective injustice. It is debatable whether Marge has knowledge of Tom Ripley's guilt in the strictest sense: the character herself is not in a position to have evidence beyond the circumstantial, so while the audience of the film knows her suspicion to be true, it would stretch a point to say it is justified. What Marge has is indeed an intuition: an epiphany that is perhaps more fittingly read as moral or interpersonal discernment about Tom Ripley's character than as insight into the facts of the case. Her sense of alarm is apparently more well calibrated than her father's, and it goes off, a flash of fear that reorients what is salient in the shared situation. Suddenly, finally, with growing horror, she perceives Tom Ripley not as a loyal family friend and harmless social climber, but rather as the threat he is: a desperate person capable not only of grifting but of murder and extended cover-up to satisfy his appetites for luxury and status. Is it Marge Sherwood's knowledge of the facts that is dismissed by the Herbert Greenleaf character? Or is it her fear? It can be both. But it seems to me that her affective evaluation of what is salient in the situation is doing more work in the (fictional) scenario than her knowledge of the facts. After all, she has not witnessed anything more than what they all have. So Herbert Greenleaf errs, not in failing to grant credibility to her testimony about the facts, but rather in failing to give uptake to her affective response.

And if fear—or in this case suspicion, its subtler variation—is our sense of alarm, then Marge's suspicion is refused uptake: she is being "suspicion gaslit." I hope I have shown how this can constitute an injury and an injustice that is affective, not only epistemic; an injury that is appropriately called gaslighting because of its potential to make one doubt oneself.

Notice too that the sort of moral discernment via emotional sensitivity that Marge evinces in this scene (as I am interpreting it) is especially important for marginalized people who find themselves in circumstances of hermeneutical injustice. Endemic to many forms of oppression is a hermeneutical injustice in which the threats the oppressed face are not intelligible to more analytical forms of knowing, at least in the terms for sense-making that predominate. That is already a powerful form of subordination. But to gaslight oppressed people about our anger or fear threatens to extend its injurious effects into our ability to make sense of our situation emotionally as well (to ourselves and others), and to exercise uniquely affective resources and influence toward the ends of remedying the hermeneutical justice.

Conclusion

My overall claim about gaslighting, then, is that it can be an affective injustice. Gaslighting is not only an epistemic and perceptual destabilization. It can also be an affective one. We see this in my paradigm case of anger gaslighting: we cannot account for the mechanisms of anger gaslighting or its injurious effects without attending to its uniquely affective dimension.

But I am also making a larger claim about the nature of injustice: just as there are uniquely epistemic forms of injustice, there are also uniquely affective ones. In analyzing gaslighting as affective injustice, I hope to provoke awareness of the affective forces that are bent in the service of domination and oppression and to provoke interest in cultivating those forces into instruments of justice.

Notes

1. In 2017 an entire philosophy conference dedicated to "Gaslighting and Epistemic Injustice" was held at Carnegie Mellon University, and in 2020 *Hypatia* published a special issue "On Gaslighting and Epistemic Injustice."

2. I first wrote about affective injustice in 2018 ("Affective Intentionality and Affective Injustice"), giving an account of variations of affective injustice that corresponded to some of Iris Young's five faces of oppression in her account of social injustice: uniquely affective varieties of marginalization, exploitation, powerlessness, and violence (*affective marginalization* disables or withholds social or interpersonal sense-making conditions for the affects of a targeted social group, *affective powerlessness* deprives a social group's affects of their influence, *affective exploitation* deploys the affective resources of one social group in a manner that systematically transfers power to another (see also my work on affective and emotional labor in my article "Byproductive Labor"), and *affective violence* injures or impairs the affective capacities of a targeted social group). Alfred Archer and Benjamin Matheson have since published an important extension of my account to Young's fifth category of oppression: cultural imperialism ("Commemoration and Emotional Imperialism"). Amia Srinivasan also published a piece in 2018 coining the same term to more narrow ends ("The Aptness of Anger.") More work is accumulating, including a special issue of *Philosophical Topics* (my article in that issue contains a more in-depth account of the themes I explore in this chapter). See also Francisco Gallegos, "Affective Injustice and Fundamental Affective Goods"; Alfred Archer and Georgina Mills, "Anger, Affective Injustice, and Emotion Regulation." José Medina has called for a discussion of the affective dimension of epistemic injustice (*The Epistemology of Resistance*). Two thinkers who are particularly influential for my understanding of affect are Teresa Brennan (*The Transmission of Affect*) and Sara Ahmed (*The Cultural Politics of Emotion*). Iris Marion Young is particularly influential for my understanding of injustice.

3. Both Alison Bailey ("On Anger, Silence, and Epistemic Injustice") and Myisha Cherry (*The Case for Rage* and "The Errors and Limitations of Our 'Anger-Evaluating' Ways") have written about anger gaslighting in ways that inform my discussion of it as affective injustice. However, neither seems to have in view the full-blown anger gaslighting effect as I describe and illustrate it in the next section: when anger gaslighting is completely successful, the target's affective responses are injured by it. Interestingly, the fact that affects could be targeted in

some cases of gaslighting was already noticed in the clinical psychological literature on gaslighting. For example, Dorpat grounds his 1996 analysis of gaslighting in psychological literature as early as 1959 about techniques that undermine not only the other person's "perception of reality," but also their "confidence in his [sic] affective reactions" (Dorpat, *Gaslighting*, 32).

4. Frye's adaptation of the notion in "A Note on Anger" borrows it from Austin's speech act theory. María Lugones's continues Frye's investigation ("Hard-to-Handle Anger").

5. See my work on anger as a "disjointed intentionality" ("Affective Intentionality and Affective Injustice") and Young on "inhibited intentionality" ("Throwing Like a Girl").

6. This is consistent with its roots as a diagnostic term in clinical psychology: diagnostic terms often identify a disease by its symptoms and call them by the same name to relate them.

7. Abramson writes that gaslighting is unique from mere dismissal, since "dismissal simply fails to take another seriously as an interlocutor, whereas gaslighting is aimed at getting another not to take herself seriously" (Abramson 2014, 2). Of course, what is interesting about the phenomenon of gaslighting is that the latter is accomplished by way of the former. As Laura Thomas notes in her discussion of gaslighting, "[w]ithout people to back us up, it is hard to trust ourselves wholly" (2018, 118).

8. See Veronica Ivy (writing as Rachel McKinnon), "Gaslighting as Epistemic Violence"; see also my work on affective injustice as including uniquely affective forms of violence (Whitney, "Affective Intentionality and Affective Injustice").

9. To be sure, what anger's functions may be and whether they should be enabled or disabled is a topic of some philosophical controversy. In the Western tradition, we may look back to the ancient debate between Aristotle and Seneca about whether anger is always a vice or can be a virtue. Happily for my argument, feminist philosophers have been less divided on the uses of anger. There one finds a robust contemporary conversation defending anger at injustice in particular (see Cherry, Tessman, Bell, and Srinivasan, among others; for an exception to the pro-anger consensus, see Nussbaum's *Anger and Forgiveness*). This inherits a twentieth-century feminist discussion defending anger at injustice (see Lorde, Jaggar, Spelman, Frye, and Lugones, among others).

10. Here I give my own view, whose first two features are shared to some degree by many feminist philosophers contributing to the excellent body of scholarship on the moral and political psychology of anger. Here are several who have been particularly influential for my own view of its moral functions: not only Cherry (*Rage, Errors*), Frye (*Politics*), Lugones (*Pilgrimages*), and Srinivasan ("Aptness"), whom I have already cited, but also Audre Lorde (*Sister Outsider*), Callard ("On Anger"), Elizabeth Spelman ("Anger and Insubordination"), Lisa Tessman (*Burdened Virtues*), and Macalester Bell ("Anger, Virtue, and Oppression").

For an opposing view (that anger is always a vice), see Martha Nussbaum (*Anger and Forgiveness*).

11. This view follows sentimentalist views of emotion, like Adam Smith's. See Agnes Callard ("On Anger") for a contemporary gloss of the sentimentalist position.

12. See Callard ("On Anger") for one account of anger's perceptual role in our moral psychology. Srinivasan ("Aptness") offers another. Tessman (*Burdened*) and Bell ("Anger") are also relevant.

13. No doubt episodic emotions other than anger also have this more fundamental function of publishing and negotiating the meaning of a shared situation. Anger is again helpful as a paradigm case insofar as its specific scope tends to express jurisdictional disputes in this meaning-making activity. See my account of this in Whitney, "Anger and Uptake" (2023).

14. Here my view adds something that is not already a broadly shared view in the literature on the moral psychology of anger by emphasizing not only its intelligibility as sense, but also its influence as force. I have theorized this forceful aspect of affective life in a relevant way in published work (Whitney, "Affective Intentionality and Affective Injustice"). But the idea is not exclusively mine. For instance, Randall Collins identifies the sort of phenomenon I have in mind as "emotional energy" and traces his conceptualization to Durkheim's notion of "moral force" and Mauss on *mana* (see Randall Collins, "Social Movements and the Focus of Emotional Attention"). My own thinking about affective force is especially indebted to Lorde's account of anger's energetic dimension. But she tends to describe this as intrapersonal: one's own anger can be metabolized as fuel (*Sister Outsider*, 124–33 and 145–75). I think that anger is transindividually or interpersonally forceful as well. Brennan has also been influential on my thinking in this respect (*Transmission*), as has the sociological literature on emotional labor/work. For the purposes of this chapter, it may be helpful to flag that I think we cannot explain the injurious effects of anger gaslighting without invoking this energetic dimension of the affect's role in our moral psychology. While I do not make the argument for that here, in the "Affective Intentionality" piece I build the theoretical resources to make it by developing a theory of affective force or influence grounded in Merleau-Ponty's and Fanon's accounts of the body schema.

15. For an account of affect as mimetic rather than diegetic communication, see Anna Gibbs, "After Affect: Sympathy, Synchrony, and Mimetic Communication."

16. See Fricker on hermeneutical injustice; she points to the lack of a concept of sexual harassment as a paradigm case (2007).

17. See Lugones 2003; also Cooper 2018.

18. I offer a more in-depth account of giving uptake in "Anger and Uptake" and "Anger Gaslighting and Affective Injustice."

19. Giving uptake can thus be distinguished from emotional contagion, as well as from sympathy and empathy—at least in their vernacular sense; philosophical accounts of sympathy and empathy are legion, and some may include

what I call uptake here. In the relevant vernacular notion of sympathy, you have (or induce) a sympathetic anger in yourself: you get mad on my behalf. In the relevant vernacular notion of different empathy, you have (or induce) a vicarious experience of my anger: you put yourself in my shoes. Uptake is distinct from these because when you give uptake, your perception and attention are oriented by my anger. There is a single episode of anger (mine), and you cooperate with it enough for it to complete its own function as a social act. The anger thereby does not become yours, or put you in my place.

20. Though if you repeatedly lend your affective capacities to my anger in this way, your affective capacities may become educated/trained: for better or worse, in giving uptake, you may become sensitized to what moves me at the level of your own emotional habits.

21. See Whitney, "Anger and Uptake" and "Anger Gaslighting and Affective Injustice."

22. Campbell is drawing on Donald Davidson to give an account of affective meaning (see Campbell 1997, 111–20).

23. I am thinking here of Young's distinction between domination, which institutionalizes constraints on the self-determination of some social group, versus oppression, which institutionalizes constraints on the self-development of that social group in the first place (see *Justice and the Politics of Difference*, 37).

24. Lugones (*Pilgrimages*), Lorde (*Sister*), and Cherry (*Rage*) offer accounts of anger's role in this regard.

25. For recent philosophical work on the importance of anger in our moral apparatus, see Cherry, Cherry and Flanagan, Bell, Tessman, Srinivasan, and Callard. For older feminist philosophy on the topic, see Jaggar, Superman, Frye, Lugones, and Lorde. For an opposing view, see Nussbaum.

26. See Whitney, "Affective Intentionality and Affective Injustice."

27. Alison Bailey calls this phenomenon "anger smothering" to relate it to Dotson's notion of "testimonial smothering" (Bailey, "Silence"). While smothering is, *ceterus paribus*, a somatically dangerous action, swallowing is ambivalent: its valence depends on what you swallow, and how much (in a given duration). Calling the action "anger swallowing" allows me to distinguish the action from the demand to do it, which allows me to preserve the normative ambiguity of the action even while condemning the demand for it. Swallowing anger—even apt anger—can be an adaptive preference, a strategic response to a non-choiceworthy situation.

28. See Fricker 2007, 9.

Works Cited

Abramson, Kate. 2014. "Turning Up the Lights on Gaslighting." *Philosophical Perspectives* 28 (1): 1–30. https://doi.org/10.1111/phpe.12046.

Ahmed, Sara. 2004. *The Cultural Politics of Emotion*. Edinburgh: Edinburgh University Press.

———. 2010. *The Promise of Happiness*. Durham: Duke University Press.

Anderson, Ellie. 2023. "Hermeneutic Labor: The Gendered Burden of Interpretation in Intimate Relationships Between Men and Women." *Hypatia* 38 (1): 177–97.

Archer, Alfred, and Benjamin Matheson. 2020. "Commemoration and Emotional Imperialism." *Journal of Applied Philosophy* 39 (5): 1–17.

———, and Georgina Mills. 2019. "Anger, Affective Injustice, and Emotion Regulation." *Philosophical Topics* 47 (2): 75–94.

Bailey, Alison. 2018. "On Anger, Silence, and Epistemic Injustice." *Royal Institute of Philosophy Supplement* 84: 93–115. https://doi.org/10.1017/S1358246118000565.

———. 2020. "On Gaslighting and Epistemic Injustice: Editor's Introduction." *Hypatia* 35 (4): 667–73.

Bartky, Sandra. 1990. *Femininity and Domination*. New York: Routledge.

Bell, Macalester. 2009. "Anger, Virtue, and Oppression." In *Feminist Ethics and Social and Political Philosophy: Theorizing the Non-Ideal*, edited by Lisa Tessman, 165–83. New York: Springer.

Berenstain, Nora. 2016. "Epistemic Exploitation." *Ergo, an Open Access Journal of Philosophy* 3 (20201214). https://doi.org/10.3998/ergo.12405314.0003.022.

Brennan, Teresa. 2004. *The Transmission of Affect*. Ithaca: Cornell University Press.

Brescoll, Victoria L., and Eric Luis Uhlmann. 2008. "Can an Angry Woman Get Ahead? Status Conferral, Gender, and Expression of Emotion in the Workplace." *Psychological Science* 19 (3): 268–75.

Callard, Agnes. 2020. "On Anger." *Boston Review Forum* 13 (45.1): 9–27.

Campbell, Sue. 1997. *Interpreting the Personal: Expression and the Formation of Feelings*. Ithaca: Cornell University Press.

Chemaly, Soraya. 2018. *Rage Becomes Her: The Power of Women's Anger*. New York: Atria.

Cherry, Myisha. 2018. "The Errors and Limitations of Our 'Anger-Evaluating' Ways." In *The Moral Psychology of Anger*, edited by Myisha Cherry and Owen Flanagan, 49–65. New York: Rowman & Littlefield.

———. 2021. *The Case for Rage: Why Anger Is Essential to Anti-Racist Struggle*. Oxford: Oxford University Press. https://doi.org/10.1093/oso/9780197557341.001.0001.

Collins, Randall. 2001. "Social Movements and the Focus of Emotional Attention." In *Passionate Politics: Emotions and Social Movements*, edited by Jeff Goodwin, James M. Jasper, and Francesca Polletta, 27–44. Chicago: University of Chicago Press.

Cooper, Brittany. 2018. *Eloquent Rage: A Black Feminist Discovers Her Superpower*. New York: St. Martin's Press.

Dorpat, Theo. 1996. *Gaslighting, the Double Whammy, Interrogation, and Other Methods of Covert Control in Psychotherapy and Analysis.* London: Jason Aronson.
Fricker, Miranda. 2007. *Epistemic Injustice: Power and the Ethics of Knowing.* Oxford: Oxford University Press.
Frye, Marilyn. 1983. *The Politics of Reality: Essays in Feminist Theory.* Berkeley: Crossing Press.
Gallegos, Francisco. 2021. "Affective Injustice and Fundamental Affective Goods." *Journal of Social Philosophy* 1–17.
Ivy, Veronica [McKinnon, Rachel]. 2017. "Allies Behaving Badly: Gaslighting as Epistemic Injustice." In *The Routledge Handbook of Epistemic Injustice*, edited by James Kidd, José Medina, and Gaile Pohlhaus, 167–74. London: Routledge.
———. 2019. "Gaslighting as Epistemic Violence: 'Allies,' Mobbing, and Complex Posttraumatic Stress Disorder, Including a Case Study of Harassment of Transgender Women in Sport." In *Overcoming Epistemic Injustice: Social and Psychological Perspectives,* edited by Benjamin R. Sherman and Stacey Goguen, 285–301. New York: Rowman & Littlefield.
Jaggar, Alison. 1989. "Love and Knowledge: Emotion in Feminist Epistemology." *Inquiry* 32 (2): 151–76.
Jamison, Leslie. 2018. "I Used to Insist I Didn't Get Angry. Not Anymore: On Female Rage." *New York Times Magazine.* https://www.nytimes.com/2018/01/17/magazine/i-used-to-insist-i-didnt-get-angry-not-anymore.html.
Lorde, Audre. 2007 [1984]. *Sister Outsider.* Berkeley: Crossing Press.
Lugones, María. 2003. *Pilgrimages/Peregrinages: Theorizing Coalition against Multiple Oppressions.* New York: Rowman & Littlefield.
Manne, Kate. 2017. *Down Girl: The Logic of Misogyny.* New York: Oxford University Press.
———. 2023. "Moral Gaslighting." *Aristotelian Society Supplementary Volume* 97 (1): 122–44.
Medina, José. 2013. *The Epistemology of Resistance: Gender and Racial Oppression, Epistemic Injustice, and Resistant Imaginations.* New York: Oxford University Press.
Nussbaum, Martha. 2016. *Anger and Forgiveness: Resentment, Generosity, Justice.* New York: Oxford University Press.
Potter, Nancy. 2000. "Giving Uptake." *Social Theory and Practice* 26 (3): 479–508.
Salerno, Jessica M., and Liana C. Peter-Hagene. 2015. "One Angry Woman: Anger Expression Increases Influence for Men, but Decreases Influence for Women, during Group Deliberation." *Law and Human Behavior* 39 (6): 581–92. https://doi.org/10.1037/lhb0000147.
Sanders, Ash. 2021. "Under the Weather." *In All We Can Save: Truth, Courage, and Solutions for the Climate Crisis,* edited by Ayana Elizabeth Johnson and Katharine K. Wilkinson, 231–47. New York: One World.

Spelman, Elizabeth. 1989. "Anger and Insubordination." In *Women, Knowledge, and Reality: Explorations in Feminist Philosophy*, edited by Ann Garry and Marilyn Pearsall, 263–73. Boston: Unwin Hyman.

Srinivasan, Amia. 2018. "The Aptness of Anger." *Journal of Political Philosophy* 26 (2): 123–44.

Tessman, Lisa. 2005. *Burdened Virtues: Virtue Ethics for Liberatory Struggles*. New York: Oxford University Press.

Thomas, Laura. 2018. "Movies of the Mind: Gaslight and Gaslighting." *Lancet* 5: 117–18.

Traister, Rebecca. 2018. *Good and Mad: The Revolutionary Power of Women's Anger*. New York: Simon and Schuster.

Whitney, Shiloh. 2018. "Affective Intentionality and Affective Injustice: Merleau-Ponty and Fanon on the Body Schema as a Theory of Affect." *Southern Journal of Philosophy* 56 (4): 488–515. https://doi.org/10.1111/sjp.12307.

———. 2019. "From the Body Schema to the Historical-Racial Schema: Theorizing Affect between Merleau-Ponty, Fanon, and Ahmed." *Chiasmi International* 21: 305–20.

———. 2023. "Anger and Uptake." *Phenomenology and the Cognitive Sciences* 22 (5): 1255–79.

———. 2023. "Anger Gaslighting and Affective Injustice." *Philosophical Topics* 51 (1).

Part II
Experiences of Gaslighting

7

Allies Behaving Badly

Gaslighting as Epistemic Injustice

Veronica Ivy [Rachel McKinnon]

Preface to the Original Essay

I first began work on gaslighting in 2013. At the time, no philosophical work was yet published. Kate Abramson's paper was yet to be the first philosophical article published on the topic. Fortunately, it's now fair to say that philosophical work on gaslighting has exploded. Partly as a consequence of this, I've had time to revisit some of what I argued in my earlier work. More importantly, there are more philosophical interlocutors available to help push on weaknesses in my earlier account. In short, my earlier account did not go far enough.

In my earlier work on gaslighting, reprinted below, I focused on explicating the epistemic harms of gaslighting in terms of epistemic injustice, and specifically as a form of *testimonial injustice*. I want to take this opportunity briefly to correct what I now see to be two shortcomings in that account.

First, rather than viewing gaslighting as a kind of epistemic injustice, we should understand it as a kind of *epistemic violence*. Second, I didn't go far enough in replacing "ally culture" with merely the active bystander model. Instead, I should have replaced "ally culture" with the concept of the *accomplice*.

The first issue with my earlier account of gaslighting is that I inappropriately shoehorned my epistemic account of gaslighting into Fricker's (2007) account of testimonial injustice. The problem is in explicating the epistemic nature of gaslighting as a form of credibility deficit due to an identity prejudice against the victim. For Fricker, testimonial injustice is caused, at its root, by an identity-based prejudice. For example, someone discounts a woman's testimony because women are emotional, and emotionality is inconsistent with reliable perceptions. Fricker's case is Marge in *The Talented Mr. Ripley*. In the case of the mispronouning of the trans woman by an "ally," I suggested that it's a core stereotype that trans women are perceived as especially overemotional due to estrogen-based hormone replacement therapy.

However, I'm no longer convinced that the source of the credibility deficit being an identity-based prejudice is a necessary condition for testimonial injustice (and thus gaslighting, if gaslighting is properly understood in terms of testimonial injustice). Some people simply give their own perceptions too much credence such that the contrastive nature of epistemic credibility—particularly when confronting information contrary to background beliefs—produces an inappropriate credibility deficit in a speaker, thus producing testimonial injustice. I think what's more important is when we can speak to structural patterns in such credibility deficits without requiring reference to identity-based prejudices.

Instead, I want to expand our understanding of epistemic violence to include gaslighting. In my previous work, I focused on gaslighting as a betrayal of trust by someone who purports to support the victim—an "ally." I noted that one of the consequences of this is isolation and withdrawal: if someone we trusted betrays that trust, we're less likely to go to them for support again. And if the people who claim to support us betray our trust, then a natural response is withdrawal and isolation. But at the time I didn't appreciate just how serious these effects can be. In [McKinnon] (2019), I show how gaslighting can cause posttraumatic stress disorder (PTSD). In many cases, the effects of the gaslighting can be far more serious than the harm for which the victim was seeking the "ally's" help, or even merely to be heard and believed. Epistemic violence and trauma are *violence*.

On the second point, perhaps the most important work on this issue is "Accomplices Not Allies: Abolishing the Ally Industrial Complex" by Indigenous Action Media (2014). They define an accomplice as "a person who helps another person commit a crime." One persistent problem that has evolved in ally culture is that "allies" are unwilling to take real personal risks, including social risks like upsetting a "friend" or co-worker. They tend to choose their own comfort over concretely helping the marginalized people they claim to support. They can take off the ally "hat"—or the button, oh my goodness the *buttons*—when it no longer serves their purposes, but the marginalized folx don't have the same luxury to escape their identity-based oppression.

The way I like to put it is that an "ally" will put on a button, but an accomplice will grab and throw a brick. This can be literal: after all, the Stonewall Riot was a *riot* against police violence and harassment of queer and trans people, which involved literal brick throwing. The brick has become a symbol for trans* liberation. Far more commonly, though, "throwing a brick" is metaphorical. If someone says something racist, immediately calling that person out is "throwing a brick." It's standing up for and with the marginalized and taking on considerable personal risk in whatever form (economic, physical safety, social, political, etc.). An accomplice is willing to lose friends over their being racist/sexist/homophobic/transphobic and so on.

To put it succinctly: fuck "allies." "Accomplices are realized through mutual consent and build trust. They don't just have our backs, they are at our side, or in their own spaces confronting and unsettling colonialism. As accomplices we are compelled to become accountable and responsible to each other, that is the [nature] of trust." The active bystander model is insufficient to capture the risk that accomplices are, and need to be, willing to take when someone sees an injustice taking place. If you want to help, you have to be willing to throw a "brick."

Trans* Epistemology and "Allies" (Original Article)

There isn't a great deal of work that we might call "trans* epistemology," although there is certainly increasing attention being given to epistemological insights to be gained by considering trans* perspectives.[1] Taking trans* perspectives seriously allows us to shed light on some problems, particularly with how "allies" behave toward those they claim to support. Talk of "allies" is everywhere in queer politics and activism.[2] There are "safe spaces" and "ally" training programs at most universities and colleges. In many cases, one can acquire a sticker, sign, or plaque to display, maybe even a button, badge, or pin that denotes one as an "ally." However, the concept of an "ally" and how this concept has translated into what we might call "ally culture" has started receiving increasing attention and criticism, mostly by the very people it's meant to support. One prominent example is Mia McKenzie's 2013 blog post (reprinted in McKenzie 2014) "No More 'Allies,'" where she discusses some problems endemic to the behavior of allies. In many cases, allies have been behaving badly. In some cases, "allies" are further harming victims.

My focus in this chapter is the bad epistemic behaviors of "allies," approached from a trans* perspective. One common form of bad behavior is that when "allies" are confronted with their bad behavior, they use their identity as an "ally" as a defense; other times, people will do so on an "ally's" behalf ': "Dave couldn't have behaved that badly, he's an ally!" Another bad behavior I focus on is known as gaslighting. I argue that we can best understand gaslighting as an instance of epistemic injustice—more specifically, as an instance of testimonial injustice. I discuss this through the lens of trans women's experiences with "allies," since a common form of epistemic injustice that trans* people face is gaslighting at the hands of "allies."[3] I close with some considerations on what this means going forward for "allies" and "ally culture." In short, I argue that we should abandon "allyship" and replace it with a focus on cultivating active bystanders.

For the purposes of this chapter, I should briefly comment on what I mean by "allies." I take it as given that "[e]ach person has a complicated intersectional identity, composed of various socially and biologically constructed factors.[4] These factors include race, gender and gender identity, sexual orientation, socioeconomic status, education, religious affiliation, nationality, and so on" (McKinnon 2015a: 428). Following Brown and Ostrove (2013), "[a]cross these various settings and identities, allies are generally conceived as dominant group members who work to end prejudice in their personal and professional lives, and relinquish social privileges conferred by their group status through their support of nondominant groups" (2013: 2211). On this view of "allies," a cisgender person may act as an "ally" to a trans* person, a white person can act as an "ally" to a person of color, a man can act as an "ally" to a woman, and so on.[5]

Gaslighting as Epistemic Injustice

There's been a recent resurgence in interest in a kind of behavior called gaslighting.[6] It generally takes one of two forms: a psychological abuse form and a more subtle epistemic form. The term originates from a 1938 Patrick Hamilton play and subsequent 1944 film called *Gaslight*. In it, the protagonist engages in psychological warfare on his wife with the aim of having her hospitalized for mental instability. He does this by trying to convince his wife that she's crazy and suffering delusions.[7] He wants her to doubt her memory and sense perceptions. And it works. However, this isn't the form of gaslighting that I'm interested in for the purposes of this chapter. Instead, I'm interested in the more subtle form, often unintentional, where a listener doesn't believe, or expresses doubt about, a speaker's testimony. In this epistemic form of gaslighting, the listener of testimony raises doubts about the speaker's reliability at perceiving events accurately. Directly, or indirectly, then, gaslighting involves expressing doubts that the harm or injustice that the speaker is testifying to really happened as the speaker claims.

Here's the sort of case I want to focus on.[8] Let's say that a trans woman, Victoria, is at a department holiday party. Victoria uses the feminine pronouns she/her/hers. It's the end of a long semester, and a long week for everyone. So people are looking forward to cutting loose a little. After a couple drinks, she's in conversation with a few people when one of her colleagues, James, begins telling an amusing anecdote about her. The story is about how she didn't notice a particular feature about his house at a previous department party. James continues the story: when Victoria gets into an involved conversation about her field of work, she gets a sort of tunnel-vision focus. He then says, "So of course he wouldn't notice something like that. When he gets talking epistemology, he doesn't notice anything about his surroundings. He . . ." In rapid-fire fashion, James mispronouns Victoria five times. Mispronouning is a serious offence for trans people: it's one of the most common forms of harassment that they face. In many jurisdictions where gender identity is included as a protected class with respect to harassment, mispronouning counts as gender harassment.[9]

We don't yet have our case of gaslighting, though. Suppose that Victoria goes to a mutual colleague, Susan, to complain about James's mispronouning her at the party and to raise worries about the workplace climate given that this isn't the first time James has done this. And suppose that they have this conversational exchange:

SUSAN: "I'm sure you just misheard him: you're on edge and expect to hear mispronouning. I just don't believe that James would do that. He won a university diversity award for his supporting queer issues, after all. Besides, he's been a supporter of yours in the past too. He really is your ally."

VICTORIA: "Well, he's done it a bunch of times in the past few months. The last time was two weeks ago in his office."

SUSAN: "You say that he's done it before, and maybe he has, but I've never heard him do it before."

At first, many cases of gaslighting don't seem clearly to arise from a speaker identity prejudice or stereotype. And to properly count as testimonial injustice—following Fricker's (2007) framework—the credibility deficit that Victoria suffers would have to be due to an identity prejudice.[10]

Two things are happening in Victoria's case when Susan discounts Victoria's testimony. First, one common stereotype of trans women is that they're overly emotional, perhaps particularly if they're on estrogen-based hormone replacement therapy.[11] And since it's also a common view, particularly in many Western patriarchal societies, that emotionality is at odds with rationality, a common way of discounting a woman's testimony (whether cis or trans*) is to point to her being emotional.[12] This is at play when Susan responds by doubting Victoria's perceptual reliability: Victoria is probably hearing things she expects to hear because she expects mispronouning and discriminatory behavior, for example. Victoria suffers a credibility deficit due to an identity stereotype or prejudice: (trans) women are emotional, and emotionality undermines rationality and perceptual reliability. This is classic testimonial injustice, then.

As a short detour, though, one pattern that I notice is what I often refer to as the "epistemic injustice circle (of hell)." This happens when something such as an identity prejudice based on emotion is treated as a reason to discount a speaker's testimony, whereby a normal response to this testimonial injustice is to become more emotional (e.g., angry, frustrated, etc.). But this subsequent emotionality is treated as a further reason to discount the speaker's testimony. And so on: it's a positive feedback loop. Testimonial injustice tends to cause victims to become emotional, which is often used as a reason to further victimize them. Drawing on one of Fricker's examples, observe Marge Sherwood's behavior in *The Talented Mr. Ripley*, particularly the last scene where we see Marge. She has an emotional outburst, crying (while hitting Tom Ripley), "I know it was you! I know it was you!!" But

Herbert Greenleaf shuttles her away: she's just another distraught woman lashing out. "Allies" also engage in this with those they purport to support: their gaslighting of victims tends to cause the victims to become more upset, which the "allies" take as further reason to discount the victim's testimony. In more extreme cases, it leads to writing off the victim as worthy of any credibility at claims of harassment or harm. In Dotson's (2011) terms, this constitutes *testimonial quieting*: the speaker suffers such a severe credibility deficit that it's as if they never spoke at all.

Second, Susan doubts Victoria's testimony—that James mispronounced Victoria repeatedly at a recent party—by appealing to James's "identity" as an "ally."[13] Susan thus lends inappropriate weight to her background knowledge[14] of James, particularly in relation to her observation of James's past behavior with respect to Victoria, and thus produces a credibility deficit for Victoria's testimony. And yet it's entirely consistent that James's past behavior has been good with respect to Victoria in other contexts. When Susan says, "You say that he's done it before, and maybe he has, but I've never heard him do it before," she is at least expressing the implicature that she doubts Victoria's testimony of James's previous bad acts.[15] But why should the listener privilege her own perceptions, rather than trust Victoria's testimony? I suggest that this is another site of subtle, but deeply troubling, epistemic injustice.

In many cases, "allies," when listening to a person's testimony, privilege their own firsthand experience over the testimony of the person they're supposed to be supporting.[16] Probably the "ally" suspects that the affected person isn't properly epistemically situated—perhaps they're not suitably objective—to properly assess the situation. Maybe the "ally" thinks the person is expecting to see harassment, so they perceive harassment when it's not really there (but, of course, this is used to doubt accurate claims of harassment).

But why would this be a readily observable pattern, one that I know many trans* people have experienced with their "allies"? I suspect that the listener (the "ally") thinks that the speaker is misperceiving events, or maybe that they're reading into situations things that just aren't there. These are taken as good reasons to doubt the speaker's testimony. They may not be taken as reasons to think that the speaker is wrong in what they say, per se, but they'll be taken as reasons not to believe. But this gets things exactly backwards. The affected person is particularly *well* epistemically situated to perceive events properly. In the following section, I turn to some discussions about why.

Trans* Epistemology and First-person Authority

As I noted at the outset, there isn't a great deal of work that we might call "trans* epistemology," although there is certainly increasing attention being given to epistemological insights to be gained by considering trans* perspectives. Two contributions I want to focus on here involve arguments for taking the assertions of trans persons as prima facie reasons for believing what they say. Part of my view is that to fail to do this constitutes testimonial injustice. Building on what I argue in McKinnon (2015a), we have strong prima facie reason to believe what someone tells us with respect to harassment and discrimination. And combining that with what Bettcher (2009) argues, we have a moral responsibility to afford speakers with disadvantaged identities first-person authority. My argument is that gaslighting, particularly by "allies," constitutes a failure to afford the first-person (epistemic) authority of disadvantaged speakers their appropriate epistemic weight.

Gaile Pohlhaus Jr. (2012) nicely captures the behavior that I'm highlighting in "allies," which she describes as willful hermeneutical ignorance. In short, willful hermeneutical ignorance happens when "marginally situated knowers actively resist epistemic domination through interaction with other resistant knowers, while dominantly situated knowers nonetheless continue to misunderstand and misinterpret the world."[17] Key to this phenomenon is taking seriously the idea that who knowers are, and their social situatedness, matters to their epistemic positions with respect to themselves, the world, and others. As Pohlhaus Jr. notes: "[T]he situations resulting from one's social positioning create 'common challenges' that constitute part of the knower's lived experience and so contribute to the context from which she approaches the world (Alcoff 2000, 2006; Collins 2008). Repeated over time, these challenges can lead to habits of expectation, attention, and concern, thereby contributing to what one is more or less likely to notice and pursue as an object of knowledge in the experienced world (Alcoff 2006, 91)" (Pohlhaus 2012, 716–17). The key here is that one's social situatedness—which involves various social identity features such as gender, race, socioeconomic status, sexual orientation, disability status, and so on—impacts *how and what we perceive* in the world.

The point is that one's situatedness impacts whether one is sufficiently well epistemically positioned to even properly perceive the world—whether one, for example, is likely to perceive harassment as harassment. Applying this to Victoria's case, Victoria, on account of her being a trans woman and marginally situated, is far better epistemically positioned than her cis "ally" Susan both to perceive mispronouning (and to perceive it as mispronouning) and to understand the depth of the harm of being mispronouned. Those who don't personally experience a category of harms are likely to underappreciate its severity. There is thus an important epistemic asymmetry between those with marginalized situatednesses and their "allies." The marginalized people tend to be better epistemically situated to perceive harassment as harassment.

Willful hermeneutical ignorance, then, is how those with dominant situatednesses fail to develop their epistemic resources to better perceive the world and others. I suspect that one mechanism for this is that these people—such as "allies"—fail to give the testimony of marginalized persons' testimony adequate epistemic weight. The "allies" place too much weight on their own firsthand experiences and perceptions of events. And when their perception of things conflicts with the testimony of the marginalized person's, this is taken as a reason to doubt (or reject) the testimony.

There are both epistemic and moral upshots of this. The epistemic upshot is that dominantly situated knowers—that is, "allies"—ought to place more epistemic weight, credibility, and trust in the first-person reports of marginalized situated knowers. It was epistemically inappropriate for Susan to treat her perceptions and experiences of James as equally credible or with equal weight as Victoria's testimony that James has mispronouned her in the past, and on more than one occasion.[18] "Allies" ought to put their own perceptions largely aside and trust the testimony of the marginalized person. Trusting testimony means believing what's said.[19] However, "allies" are far too often unwilling to simply trust and accept a marginalized person's testimony at face value: they need to see the harm for themselves.

No More "Allies"[20]

I haven't yet said much about what's particularly wrong with gaslighting, above and beyond the harms that Fricker (2007) herself notes as the wrong of testimonial injustice. Fricker argues that the wrong of testimonial injustice is that a central feature of being human is being a knower, and testimonial injustice disrespects people qua knower. Thus, testimonial injustice disrespects people qua persons. One way to cash this out is that listeners fail to appropriately trust speakers.

However, I find that gaslighting produces possibly unique moral and epistemic harms. First, gaslighting, as a sub-species of testimonial injustice, creates all the same harms as the more generic forms of testimonial injustice. Second, consider the context in which gaslighting occurs: a disadvantaged person (say, a trans woman) reports an injustice to someone she considers an "ally," but the "ally" doesn't afford her testimony appropriate epistemic weight. But more than that, the "ally" responds by raising doubts viz. the speaker's perceptual (and perhaps reasoning) abilities. The claim of being harmed is dismissed or explicitly doubted. In an important sense, the speaker's moral trust of turning to an "ally" has been betrayed via the gaslighting. While generic testimonial injustice involves a listener's not appropriately trusting a speaker, gaslighting involves further betraying of a particular moral and epistemic trust of the speaker. This is particularly acute if the "ally" positively identifies themself as an ally (perhaps by proudly posting a "Safe Space" sign or some such on their office door).

This betrayal has a variety of consequences. The trans woman, in our case, will likely decrease her trust in the "ally" who gaslit her. One primary function of "allies" is to provide support, in a variety of forms. But if we don't trust our "allies," then we lose a critical source of epistemic and moral support. This can isolate those who are already vulnerable in our societies. Isolation can lead to a variety of harms, including mental health concerns such as depression, but also social harms of exclusion. For example, suppose that Victoria tends to eat lunch in a common room that both James and Susan frequent. If Victoria doesn't feel that she can sufficiently trust Susan to help her out when James, for example, mispronouns her, then Victoria may simply cease to eat lunch with her colleagues. She may even begin to avoid coming into the office when she can, which leads to missing out on important interpersonal interactions with colleagues. In a way, the workplace becomes increasingly toxic for Victoria merely through the betrayal of trust by her "ally," Susan. And these harms can be exacerbated if Victoria is structurally vulnerable by, for example, James and Susan being more senior and thus having institutional power over Victoria's career and economic well-being.[21]

But what should we make, epistemically speaking, of a speaker's claim that, for example, someone has harassed or mispronouned the speaker? While I advocate a default position of epistemic trust for such claims, I'm by no means arguing that one is epistemically required to believe the speaker. While one is epistemically positioned to form a justified belief or, in the case of true assertions, knowledge on the basis of the speaker's say-so, one is free to withhold belief. However, I do think that one ought not respond immediately by expressing doubt or doubt-raising the speaker's testimony.

Moreover, one ought not to respond by asking questions about details of events in a way that makes it seem like an interrogation of the victim.[22]

The epistemic and emotional harm of "allies," the people we ostensibly turn to in times of most need, responding to claims of harm by first expressing doubt or, worse, gaslighting can often be worse than the original harm that the person wishes to share. Simply put, those who aim to be a "good ally" ought both to afford appropriate epistemic weight to the testimony of the people for whom one wants to be an "ally" and to be responsive to criticism. I consistently and repeatedly find that "allies" fall far short in both respects. In recent empirical work on "allies," Brown and Ostrove (2013) found that "allies" tend to overestimate how good a job they're doing at being an "ally." Relatedly, I have noticed that "allies" are often insensitive to constructive criticism and, moreover, often react negatively (often going on the attack) to such criticism.

In the space that remains, I want to turn some attention to how we can move forward from many of the problems that I see with "allies" and "ally culture." In short, I argue that we should abandon the concept of "ally" and replace it with a focus on cultivating active bystanders. Active bystander training has been gaining steady momentum in recent years.[23] The idea is that if one develops strategies for how to respond to discrimination and harassment when one sees it happen, one will be more likely to (hopefully) appropriately intercede and assist the disadvantaged person. Importantly, active bystanders can be in-group or fellow out-group members of the disadvantaged person. A trans woman can thus act as an active bystander to another trans woman.

As noted above, one way that "allies" respond poorly to constructive criticism—particularly pointing out gaslighting or cases where they failed to adequately support the disadvantaged person—is by referencing their status as "really" an "ally." One relatively recent high-profile instance was Piers Morgan's misgendering Janet Mock (referring to her on his television show and in tweets as "formerly a man," which is often an offensive way to refer to trans women). In response to being called out, instead of contritely apologizing, Morgan went on the attack, demanding that Mock be the one to apologize to Morgan. To many, the identity of being an "ally"—whether or not one actually ever appropriately acts as an "ally"—is central to their overall identity.

One way to avoid the ability to point to one's identity as an "ally" as a defense from criticism is to focus on cultivating concrete actions in people, removing the label and—in a sense—certification as being an "ally." One cannot claim to be an active bystander unless one is actually appropriately active when one observes discrimination or harassment. Moreover, whether one has been an active bystander in the past isn't a laurel on which one can rest: in the context of a harm, did you act or not? When we observe harm, we're all bystanders (unless we're the one harmed). If you didn't act, then you were a passive bystander; if you did, then you were an active bystander. Active bystanders, by not being so explicitly an identity (no badges or signs), may well be more open to criticism on how to perform better in future instances.

I don't pretend to offer a fully fleshed-out argument for why we would do better with "active bystanders" than with "allies," partly because of space constraints. In an important sense, this is an empirical claim: one could conceivably measure whether people tend to act better with respect to a disadvantaged group as an "ally" or as an "active bystander." I conjecture that abandoning "ally" concepts and terminology—especially badges and certifications—and replacing it with "active bystander" would have better results. However, in this chapter I have identified a number of persistent and seriously harmful aspects of "allies" and their behavior. I suggest that this behavior is partially caused by the appeal to "ally" as an identity. When our identities—ones we strongly identify with—are under attack, it's predictable that we'll respond by counter-attacking. And "allies" tend to hit back with gaslighting and isolating the affected, disadvantaged person.

Notes

1. Some examples include Stone 1987; Namaste 2000 and 2009; Koyama 2003; Spade 2006; Stryker 2006; Hale 2007 and 2015; Serano 2007 and 2013; Bettcher 2009 and 2014; McKinnon 2014, 2015a, and 2016a; McKenzie 2014.

2. You'll note that I consistently use quotation marks for "ally" and its cognates. This is deliberate, for part of the purpose of this chapter is to argue for rejecting the concept and particularly its implementation as "ally culture" and its many attendant problems.

3. I note that "transgendered" is now a dispreferred term. "Transgender" is far better.

As I note in McKinnon 2014 and 2015a, I will generally use the language of "trans women" to refer only to transsexual women ("transsexual" is now strongly dispreferred by many trans people, though) and "trans* women," which is the current convention, to be the more inclusive term that refers to all forms of transgender women, including genderqueer, genderfuckers, bi-gender, and so on. The generic "trans*" denotes maximal inclusivity, including trans masculine people, agender people, and so on. The primary focus of this chapter, though, is on trans women's experiences. What I have to say applies, in varying degrees, to other trans* identities.

4. However, I am of the view that any biological feature, such as race, sex/gender, and so on, is also inherently socially constructed. For some of my thoughts on this, see McKinnon (forthcoming). What it means for someone to be black, mixed race, a man, or a woman (or neither!) inherently depends on social decisions, almost always implicit and undisclosed. For some useful discussions of Intersectionality, see Crenshaw (1991) and Garry (2008, 2012).

5. For some criticism of this view, though, and for a discussion of allies, see my blog post: www.metamorpho-sis.com/blog/2013/10/50-empirical-research-on-allies.html.

6. For example, see Abramson (2014) and Ruiz (2014).

7. I recognize that "crazy" is an ableist term, but I use it purposefully because the protagonist aims to have all the negative stigma of "crazy" attach to his wife.

8. This is based on a real case, but the names and some of the details have been changed.

9. For example, here is the Ontario Human Rights Commission 2000 "Policy on Discrimination and Harassment Because of Gender Identity": www.ohrc.on.ca/sites/default/files/Policy_on_discrimination_and_harassment_because_of_gender_identity.pdf.

10. For a review of recent developments in epistemic injustice, see McKinnon 2016b.

11. For a discussion of trans women stereotypes, see McKinnon (2014).

12. Indeed, this is at the heart of Fricker's discussion of Marge Sherwood in *The Talented Mr. Ripley*.

13. Another way to explain what's going on is that James is enjoying a credibility excess, if only implicitly based on Susan's perceptions of James's identity as an "ally." See Medina (2011).

14. I almost put "knowledge" in quotation marks, since it's likely that the hearer has some false beliefs about James.

15. Implicatures are things that are communicated, though not explicitly said. For the canonical view, see Grice (1989).

16. I raise this phenomenon in McKinnon 2012 and in Chapter 10 of McKinnon 2015b.

17. Pohlhaus Jr. 2012, 716.

18. I hesitate to say that Susan has misperceived things. She may well have never seen James mispronoun Victoria. She's simply giving her past experiences

of James too much epistemic weight: she should be giving Victoria's testimony much more weight than she is. Moreover, Susan might be privileging her own perceptions of James over Victoria's testimony, which would be doubly bad.

19. For a detailed treatment of the nature and implications of epistemic trust, see Zagzebski (2012).

20. This is the title of Mia McKenzie's blog post (and the associated chapter in her 2014 collection of blog posts and essays).

21. And the stress and harms that this creates can arise even if James and Susan never adversely affect Victoria's career (other than the harm created by the effects of the stress, of course). As I argue in McKinnon (2014), the mere possibility of the harm can create harm.

22. My thanks to Luke Barker for raising this point.

23. Here is one good resource: http://web.mit.edu/bystanders/strategies/.

Works Cited

Abramson, Kate. 2014. "Turning Up the Lights on Gaslighting." *Philosophical Perspectives* 28: 1–30.

Alcoff, Linda Martín. 2000. "On Judging Epistemic Credibility: Is Social Identity Relevant?" In *Women of Color and Philosophy*, edited by Naomi Zack, 235–62. Malden, MA: Blackwell.

Alcoff, Linda Martín. 2006. *Visible Identities: Race, Gender, and the Self*. New York: Oxford University Press.

Bettcher, Talia Mae. 2009. "Trans Identities and First-Person Authority." In *You've Changed: Sex-Reassignment and Personal Identity*, edited by Laurie Shrage, 98–120. Oxford: Oxford University Press.

———. 2014. "Trapped in the Wrong Theory: Re-Thinking Trans Oppression and Resistance." *Signs* 39 (2): 383–406.

Brown, Kendrick, and Ostrove, Joan. 2013. "What Does It Mean To Be an Ally?: The Perception of Allies From the Perspective of People of Color." *Journal of Applied Social Psychology* 43: 2211–22.

Collins, Patricia Hill. 2008. *Black Feminist Thought: Knowledge, Consciousness, and the Politics of Empowerment*. New York: Routledge.

Crenshaw, Kimberlé. 1991. "Mapping the Margins: Intersectionality, Identity Politics, and Violence Against Women of Color." *Stanford Law Review* 43: 1241–99.

Dotson, Kristie. 2011. "Tracking Epistemic Violence, Tracking Practices of Silencing." *Hypatia* 26 (2): 236–57.

Garry, Ann. 2008. "Intersections, Social Change, and "Engaged" Theories: Implications of North American Feminism." *Pacific and American Studies* 8: 99–111.

———. 2012. "Who Is Included? Intersectionality, Metaphors, and the Multiplicity of Gender." In *Out from the Shadows: Analytical Feminist Contributions*

to *Traditional Philosophy*, ed. Sharon L. Crasnow and Anita M. Superson, 493–530. Oxford: Oxford University Press.
Grice, Paul. 1989. *Studies in the Way of Words*. Cambridge, MA: Harvard University Press.
McKenzie, Mia. 2013. "No More Allies." *BGD*. www.bgdblog.org/2013/09/no-more-allies/.
———. 2014. *Black Girl Dangerous: On Race, Queerness, Class and Gender*. Oakland, CA: BGD Press.
McKinnon, Rachel. 2012. "What I Learned in the Lunch Room About Assertion and Practical Reasoning." *Logos and Episteme* 3 (4): 565–69.
———. 2014. "Stereotype Threat and Attributional Ambiguity for Trans Women." *Hypatia* 29 (1): 857–72.
———. 2015a. "Trans*formative Experiences." *Res Philosophica* 92 (2): 419–40.
———. 2015b. *The Norms of Assertion: Truth, Lies, and Warrant*. New York: Palgrave Macmillan.
———. 2016a. "Gender, Identity, and Society." In *Macmillan's Interdisciplinary Handbooks: Philosophy of Sex and Love*, edited by Arthur Zucker and James Petrik, 175–98. Farmington Hills, MI: Cengage Learning.
———. 2016b. "Epistemic Injustice." *Philosophy Compass* 11 (8): 437–46.
Medina, José. 2011. "The Relevance of Credibility Excess in a Proportional View of Epistemic Injustice: Differential Epistemic Authority and the Social Imaginary." *Social Epistemology* 25 (1): 15–25.
Namaste, Viviane. 2000. *Invisible Lives: The Erasure of Transsexual and Transgendered People*. Chicago, IL: University of Chicago Press.
———. 2009. "Undoing Theory: The "Transgender Question" and the Epistemic Violence of Anglo-American Feminist Theory." *Hypatia* 24 (3): 11–32.
Pohlhaus, Gaile, Jr. 2012. "Relational Knowing and Epistemic Injustice: Toward a Theory of Willful Hermeneutical Ignorance." *Hypatia* 27 (4): 715–35.
Ruíz, Elena Flores. 2014. "Spectral Phenomenologies: Dwelling Poetically in Professional Philosophy." *Hypatia* 29 (1): 196–204.
Spade, Dean. 2006. "Mutilating Gender." In *Transgender Studies Reader*, edited by Susan Stryker and Stephen Whittle, 315–32. New York: Routledge.
Stone, Sandy. 1987. *The Empire Strikes Back: A Posttranssexual Manifesto*. http://sandystone.com/empire-strikes-back.pdf.
Stryker, Susan. 2006. "(De)Subjugated Knowledges." In *Transgender Studies Reader*, edited by Susan Stryker and Stephen Whittle, 1–17. New York: Routledge.
———, and Stephen Whittle. 2006. *The Transgender Studies Reader*. New York: Routledge.
Zagzebski, Linda. 2012. *Epistemic Authority: A Theory of Trust, Authority, and Autonomy in Belief*. Oxford: Oxford University Press.

8

Racial Gaslighting

Angelique M. Davis and Rose Ernst

In the 1944 mystery-thriller film *Gaslight*, actor Charles Boyer manipulates his home environment in an attempt to control his wife, played by Ingrid Bergman. Unbeknownst to Bergman, Boyer is a murderer and a thief who has married her in order to return to the scene of his original crime, Bergman's house. His goal is to search the attic for the treasure of his original victim. As he must keep this a secret, he leaves his wife at home alone while he ostensibly socializes with friends in the evenings. In reality, he creeps up to the attic, makes ominous noises—dragging trunks and furniture across the floor—and turns on the lights in the attic, thus creating a flickering effect of the gaslights in the floors below. Night after night, Bergman becomes increasingly disturbed by these unexplained occurrences. She confesses this to her husband. He dismisses her experiences as flights of fancy; when she persists in telling him about them, he begins to question her sanity. She, in turn, begins to doubt her own perceptions. Boyer isolates her from friends and family on the pretext that she is unwell. Bergman's familial and social circle gradually disappears; Boyer is able to control her through this manipulation game for his own personal gain.

Conceptual Framework

The film *Gaslight* made the term popular, particularly among psychologists who used it to refer to a type of abusive relationship. Following the film, the *Oxford English Dictionary* defines "gaslighting" as "[t]he action or process of manipulating a person by psychological means into questioning his or her own sanity" (2016). In popular discourse, the gaslighting metaphor appears in entertainment, self-help, and, more recently, social justice and political arenas (Waltman 2016). In the field of psychology, it "describe[s] the effort of one person to undermine another person's confidence and stability by causing the victim to doubt [their] own senses and beliefs" (Kline 2006, 1148). In the area of family therapy, gaslighting describes a situation in which one partner attempts to control the other. A classic example is a philandering partner who tells their significant other that their perceptions of inappropriate or deceitful behavior are untrue. These scenarios often emerge in "male-female" relationships, though either partner may be the instigator. A typical pattern in the literature is a man's use of gendered stereotypes—such as the jealous or insecure woman—to not only deflect attention away from his activities but to also control her thoughts by causing her to doubt her perceptions (Gass and Nichols 1988).

Education scholars have used gaslighting to explain sociohistorical factors that led to the "disenfranchisement, marginalization, and overall invisibility of African American teachers writ large in the profession" (Roberts and Carter Andrews 2013, 70). They posit that the "normalized master narrative" about "the limited presence of Black teachers in teaching" has been used throughout US history as an "abuse tactic" to delude the US public into believing the Black community is solely at fault for the failure of the teaching profession to recruit and retain Black teachers. This normalized master narrative fails to address structural barriers and how the presence of Black teachers benefits all students (Roberts and Carter Andrews 2013, 70).

This manipulation of perception is powerful because our reality—how we perceive the world and our place in it—is socially constructed. In the context of race politics, scholars agree that race is not biological; instead, the construct of race and how it affects our perceptions is sociopolitical (Davis 2012). Interpretations of emotion can also be sociopolitical. Burrow (2005) posits that the dismissal of feminist anger is a key tool for leveraging women into their rightful place in society through subverting dominant ideologies. . . . Dismissing such anger does not then seem to be a matter of innocent oversight. Rather, dismissal silences one's political voice and, at the same time, compromises a valuable source of self-worth and self-trust (27).

Burrow discusses how this form of judgment is used to oppress others: emotional abusers often divert issues from legitimate targets by instead placing the focus on the way in which one expresses oneself. The implication is that the person raising the issue is herself inadequate to express that concern or she is to blame for how she has raised the issue. Diversion is a way of controlling the communication between the persons involved. This sort of abuse is common to women's lives. Restricting freedom of expression is a similar sort of abusive tactic used to oppress groups of persons (31).

An example of this type of diversion is the colloquial use of the phrase "tone policing." Dominant groups use tone policing to chastise the communication style of marginalized people who challenge their oppression. It focuses on the emotion behind a message rather than the message itself. By focusing on the manner in which the message is delivered, no matter the legitimacy of the content, tone policing prioritizes the comfort of the privileged (Hugs 2015) and minimizes marginalized peoples' experiences "by placing sanctions on how they will or will not be heard" (Zevallos 2017). For example, tone policing emerged in media coverage of the 2017 Women's March. Mainstream media chastised Women of Color who challenged white women to think about racial divides. The attempts by Women of Color to center race in dialogues about the march were criticized as "contentious." A *New York Times* article published before the march focused on the claims made by white women who felt "unwelcome," thereby prioritizing the comfort of white women (Stockman 2017). In what follows, we provide a sociopolitical contextualization of interpersonal relationships not only in individual-level interactions, but also in the maintenance of white supremacy.[1]

The Process of Racial Gaslighting

Omi and Winant's *Racial Formation in the United States* ([1986] 2014) became a classic text in race and ethnic politics, in part because these two sociologists provided an innovative framework for understanding why and how racial categorization changes. Racial formation, first and foremost, is a process: "the sociohistorical process by which racial identities are created, lived out, transformed, and destroyed" (109). Unlike a system, such as capitalism; an ideology, such as colorblind racism; an institution, such as a prison; or even a political era, such as the first Reconstruction, a process does not have particular content in and of itself; rather, it is a web of relationships, perceptions, and social control mechanisms.

In the vein of Omi and Winant's focus on process, racial gaslighting offers a way to understand how white supremacy is sustained over time. We define racial gaslighting as the political, social, economic, and cultural process that perpetuates and normalizes a white supremacist reality through pathologizing those who resist. Just as racial formation rests on the creation of racial projects, racial gaslighting, as a process, relies on the production of particular narratives. These narratives are called racial spectacles (Davis and Ernst 2011).[2] Racial spectacles are narratives that obfuscate the existence of a white supremacist state power structure. They are visual and textual displays that tell a particular story about the dynamics of race. For example, former President Bill Clinton gave a speech in 2012 (and again in 2016) in which he lamented the increasing number of deaths among white working-class people: "They could have said these people are dying of a broken heart. . . . Because they're the people that were raised to believe the American Dream would be theirs if they worked hard and their children will have a chance to do better—and their dreams were dashed disproportionally to the population as the whole" (Scheiner 2012).

This racial spectacle obfuscates how the white supremacist state power structure actively—since Bacon's Rebellion in 1676 and onward—has kept poor white people poor. If Clinton had said, "White people are dying of a broken heart because the pathology of whiteness is killing them," then this narrative would reveal the existence of white supremacy and call into question the role of the state as well.

Racial spectacles may be ongoing cultural narratives that generate media stories and private conversations and, in other cases, are momentary blips in the sea of media stories designed to elicit racial responses. They may become part of a larger, ongoing narrative, or they may fade from view, only to be resurrected fifty years later. Take, for example, the narratives surrounding anti–affirmative action initiative campaigns that began in the 1990s. They used the presumption of white innocence to frame the beneficiaries of affirmative action as undeserving. The synergy created between the public media campaigns and their solicitation of private "everyday opinion" formed a particularly virulent form of racial spectacle that informed voters and thereby created a direct link between the promulgation of these narratives and the creation of law (Davis and Ernst 2011).

Not all narratives about race are racial spectacles. One example of a narrative that is not a racial spectacle is the Black Lives Matter movement that emerged in response to the historical and ongoing dehumanization of Black lives in the United States. While this movement's narrative is not a racial spectacle, the colorblind narrative that appeared in response—All Lives Matter—is. The Black Lives Matter narrative illuminates the dehumanization of Black lives and is in no way suggesting other lives do not matter—instead, it shifts the focus away from whiteness by the assertion that Black lives matter, too. The Black Lives Matter movement exposes the white supremacist state power structure and how it dehumanizes Black life in the United States. The All Lives Matter colorblind narrative is a racial spectacle, however, because it disguises the prioritizing of white lives. The All Lives Matter movement achieves three core tasks: first, it co-opts Black social justice intellectual work; second, it pushes Black communities further to the margins of society by insisting that all lives in the United States are valued equally and treated as such. Consequently, it erases the centuries of brutalization and dehumanization of Black bodies. Finally, it obfuscates the role of the white supremacist state power structure by eliding the specific targeting of Black lives by state institutions and actors, such as prisons and police.

The process of racial gaslighting invites intersectional and multiplicative understandings of domination and resistance precisely because the process is a binary of normalization versus pathologization that can take place with or without individual agency. For those who are aware of racial gaslighting, it can be almost impossible to combat their pathologization by the dominant narrative because of the ubiquitous nature of white supremacy. Nevertheless, activists have challenged the white supremacist power structure, counted the cost, and still sacrificially engaged in acts of resistance. Some have resisted with less political motivation, but simply because they believed they were standing up for what was just. And others, like Bergman, were manipulated into believing their actions or mental state was problematic. Just as the process of white supremacy does not require those who are complicit to understand the racist nature of their actions, awareness is also not determinative of whether the process of racial gaslighting is taking place.

In the following sections, we provide examples of racial gaslighting, noting the role of racial spectacles in this process. We examine two historical court cases from Japanese American internment/incarceration and the Civil Rights Movement that highlight how micro-level individual actions are part of a larger, macro process of racial gaslighting. In both cases, *Korematsu v. United States* (1944) and *Commonwealth of Kentucky v. Braden* (1955), plaintiffs resisted white supremacist violence. As we delineate in more detail in each case discussion section, the process of racial gaslighting is markedly different for People of Color and white people who resist white supremacy in five ways: portrayal, exposure (or risk), pathologization, audience, and outcome.

Korematsu v. United States (1944): Criminalizing Resistance

> The two conflicting orders, one which commanded him to stay and the other which commanded him to go, were nothing but a cleverly devised trap to accomplish the real purpose of the military authority, which was to lock him up in a concentration camp.
>
> —Justice Owen Roberts, Dissent, *Korematsu v. United States*, 1944, 232

Background and Context

Although anti-Asian sentiment in the United States preceded the bombing of Pearl Harbor and World War II, these events resulted in the use of racial gaslighting to obfuscate state-sanctioned racism against those of Japanese ancestry. In 1942, President Roosevelt signed Executive Order 9066, which set into motion state forced removal of more than 110,000 persons of Japanese ancestry from their West Coast homes. Segregated schools, anti-miscegenation laws, alien land laws, and anti-Japanese wartime propaganda predated WWII, but the bombing of Pearl Harbor accelerated the level of concrete state action against them. The fact that two-thirds were US citizens by birth highlights the racism and xenophobia at play. The state did not file individual charges against them, nor was proof provided that they had engaged in acts of espionage or sabotage. Failure to comply was a federal crime (Bannai 2005).

Japanese Americans who challenged these laws did so at great personal cost.[3] One of these individuals, Fred Korematsu—a US citizen of Japanese ancestry—refused to report to a detention center in San Leandro, California. He was jailed for violation of a detention order and classified as an "enemy alien." Mr. Korematsu challenged the constitutionality of the order under the Fifth and Fourteenth Amendments. On December 18, 1944, the majority of the US Supreme Court upheld Executive Order 9066 and General DeWitt's orders. They acknowledged that racial discrimination should receive close scrutiny:[4] "all legal restrictions which curtail the civil rights of a single racial group are immediately suspect" (Korematsu 1944, 216). Yet, even with this acknowledgement, the majority denied the laws were a form of racial discrimination; instead, they provided a public-necessity justification: "To cast this case into outlines of racial prejudice, without reference to the real military dangers which were presented, merely confuses the issue. Korematsu was not excluded from the Military Area because of hostility to him or his race. He was excluded because we are at war with the Japanese Empire" (Korematsu 1944, 223–24).

Racial Spectacle

The US government used racial spectacles at the macro level to publicly justify its use of concrete state action against of those of Japanese ancestry during World War II. At the macro level, the federal government perpetuated and normalized its actions through the use of euphemistic language. The Supreme Court's decision and its objection to the characterization of the camps as concentration camps reflects this obfuscation: "Regardless of the true nature of the assembly and relocation centers—and we deem it unjustifiable to call them concentration camps, with all the ugly connotations that term implies—we are dealing specifically with nothing but an exclusion order" (Korematsu 1944, 223). The labels of assembly and relocation centers do not adequately explain their existence and serve to obscure reality: "Over time, researchers and scholars, studying historical artifacts, documents, and accounts of the period, have increasingly pointed out the euphemistic nature of the language employed by the US government during WWII in relation to the concentration camps in which Japanese American citizens were incarcerated" (National JACL 2013, 8). To authentically explain what happened to Japanese Americans requires accurate vocabulary: exclusion, or forced removal, not evacuation; incarceration, not relocation; US citizens of Japanese ancestry, not non-aliens; detention orders, not civilian exclusion orders; and American concentration camp, incarceration camp, or illegal detention center, not relocation center or internment camp (Ishizuka 2006).

Racial Gaslighting

The government's use of macro-level racial spectacles to obscure the existence of a white supremacist state power structure provided a narrative that set the stage for the racial gaslighting of Japanese Americans at a micro level. In this way, the political, social, economic, and cultural process of racial gaslighting used racial spectacles to perpetuate and normalize a white supremacist state by pathologizing those who resisted. The government's call to engage in acts of patriotism such as military service and loyalty questionnaires compelled compliance through manipulating the requirements for Japanese Americans to be seen as loyal to the United States: "the central loyalty question was phrased in such a way that an affirmative answer implied that internees were previously loyal to the Japanese Emperor" (Fong 2013, 242). White politicians as well as leaders within Japanese American communities called for voluntary compliance with the military orders and the attendant loss of personal liberty as well as land, businesses, homes, and the majority of personal possessions. Many also joined the military to defend the United States against Japan and became highly decorated war heroes. Those who refused to comply with detention orders, such as Mr. Korematsu, became convicted criminals who were ostracized by many in the Japanese American community (Bannai 2005).[5]

The use of racial spectacles and racial gaslighting by the government to hide white supremacist state action under the guise of national security continues after Japanese American incarceration, albeit in different sociopolitical contexts. For decades after incarceration, the convergence of the trauma and spectacle of incarceration resulted in silence by many Japanese Americans (Roxworthy 2008). The racial gaslighting of Japanese Americans did, however, eventually subside because of ongoing advocacy efforts of the Japanese American community. Almost forty years after Mr. Korematsu's conviction, a writ of *coram nobis* was filed to reverse his conviction based on newly discovered evidence that was not available at the time of his trial. It revealed that the government knowingly withheld evidence that undermined its assertions of disloyalty by those of Japanese ancestry. The US solicitor general's office did not challenge the petition. The incongruent result was the widely applauded reversal of Mr. Korematsu's individual conviction in 1983 by a federal district court—a micro-level legal action—while at the macro level the 1944 Supreme Court decision remained in effect.

In *Korematsu*, the racial gaslighting of People of Color is not only symbolic—sending a message to Japanese Americans in particular—but also linked to concrete state action. If, for example, the Supreme Court had decided to affirm Korematsu's argument, a concrete change to state action would have followed: incarceration/internment would have halted. If not halted, other state action would have needed to occur to maintain the camps.[6] In the case of *Commonwealth of Kentucky v. Braden* (1955), however, the outcome of the case did not stifle or enable a particular state action.

Commonwealth of Kentucky v. Braden (1955): Racial Sedition

The process of racially gaslighting white people fundamentally differs from that of People of Color for two reasons. First, white people may be pathologized like People of Color, but the narrative is distinctive: they are viewed as traitors to their race. Second, the purpose of gaslighting individual white people is largely symbolic or pedagogical. We do not mean these individuals do not suffer harm at the hands of the state or white society—as in the case of Anne and Carl Braden, discussed in this section. Instead, they are used symbolically as an example, or warning, *to other white people.*

Background and Context

On June 27, 1954, someone firebombed Andrew and Charlotte Wade's house near Louisville, Kentucky. Fortunately, the Wades were not at home when the explosion occurred; the perpetrators placed the dynamite underneath the bedroom of their child, Rosemary. This attack followed weeks of white neighbors' violent intimidation of the Wades (Braden 2001, 184, 186; Minter 2013, 362). The culprit, never brought to trial, was most likely an ex-policeman (Braden 2001, 187). We offer a brief overview of events linked to this racial terrorism and then discuss the case through the lens of racial gaslighting.

After facing institutional practices of redlining and outright intimidation, Andrew Wade approached a white activist couple, Carl and Anne Braden, about purchasing a home in an all-white suburb on his behalf in 1954 (1989). The Bradens agreed with alacrity. After the Wades moved into their new home, white people in the neighborhood reacted violently with threats and intimidation. The Wade Defense Committee formed as a result. After the bombing attack, prosecutors charged the Bradens with orchestrating the explosion themselves. Found guilty of "teaching or advocating sedition or Criminal Syndicalism," the state of Kentucky sentenced Carl Braden to fifteen years of hard labor at the State Penitentiary at LaGrange and fined him $5000 (Kentucky v. Braden). His $40,000 bond was the highest ever in the history of Kentucky as of 1955 (Fosl 2006). The lead prosecutor's case rested on demonstrating the Bradens were communists: "There is no question of white and colored in this case. There has been no colored man indicted. I don't know why [defense attorney] . . . wanted to harp on white supremacy and all that sort of thing. . . . The only question is whether or not Carl Braden advocated sedition, criminal syndicalism, or had material to circulate and display for that purpose of joint assemblages of persons for that purpose" (Braden transcript 1955, 161). During this period, Anne Braden described how the shape-shifting term communist was linked to fights against racism in the South: "To the white supremacist in the South, it means somebody fighting segregation" (Fosl 2006, 165). In the closing argument to the case, one of the prosecutors accused Braden of actually creating racial tension as a part of a communist plot: "[W]e should let this be a milestone in the historic fight of America today to stop this evil pitting race against race, white against black, Catholic against Protestants, Jew against the Gentile, rich against the poor. . . . We must ruthlessly cut out this cancer of communism, and here is the one place to start" (Braden transcript 1955, 2467–68). Unsurprisingly, the prosecutor's argument is contradictory: white supremacy is not at issue, but then it is because communists apparently instigate the "pitting" of "white against black." Though the Bradens never considered the legal ramifications of purchasing the Wades' home or anticipated what followed (Fosl 2006), prosecutors and other Kentucky officials decided to use the Braden case for their own purposes: "In my opinion, this is a test case for the white supremacists. . . . So far as I know, this is the first major case where an attempt has been made to place the blame for [anti-Negro] violence on the people fighting segregation" (Anne Braden, quoted in Fosl 2006, 165).

RACIAL SPECTACLES

The racial intimidation culminating in the bombing of the Wades' home represented the first of many racial spectacles[7] in this case. While state entities were complicit in setting the conditions for the bombing, the characterization of this act of racial terror as an isolated private action served to hide the existence of a white supremacist state power structure. The prosecutor laid forth two lines of inquiry in the grand jury hearing: "[e]ither it had been set by neighbors who resented the entry of blacks into a white neighborhood or it had been an 'inside job,' part of a communist plot to stir up racial friction in an otherwise contented community" (Fosl 2006, 156). Though the prosecutor chose not to actively pursue the first theory—though it is most likely what occurred—it still comports with a narrative of private action. The same is true for the second line of inquiry. Even if Kentucky tried the ostensible white perpetrator, the "backstage" white narrative (Feagin and Picca 2007) would have been one of justification or provocation. This is in contrast to the official "frontstage" state narrative of the bomber "going too far"—which would still leave the apartheid system undisturbed.

RACIAL GASLIGHTING

Individual white people may attempt to divest from or subvert their own power because they recognize what they have to gain by dismantling white supremacy (Jackson 2011). White society and the state will ignore or label them as obsessive, dangerous, or "crazy" people. Their whiteness may protect or cushion them from the violence visited upon People of Color, and sometimes it will not (table 8.1). The difference, regardless of

Table 8.1. Racial Gaslighting

	People of Color	White people who resist
Portrayal	The usual racist stereotypes	Race traitors and/or delusional
Exposure	Always collective and sometimes individual	Individual or small group
Pathologization	Always collective and sometimes individual	Individual or small group
Audience	People of Color and white people	White people
Outcome	Symbolic message Individual and collective co-optation, containment, or punishment State action against groups of People of Color	Symbolic message Individual co-optation, containment, or punishment

Source: Created by the author.

whether or not they are individually punished, is that they are singled out as subversive individuals, not as white subversive individuals. Ironically, though they are seen as dangerous individuals, their punishment is a collective message to white people as a whole. These messages feed into the macro-level process of racial gaslighting.

One of the most important points about the *Braden* case is that the possibility of a nonprosecution or acquittal would not have had any direct concrete effect on state action. This is the opposite of possible outcomes against People of Color. The decision in *Braden* might have provoked some additional policymaking attempts and spurred further cracks in the façade of the Southern "police state" (Anne Braden, quoted in Fosl 2006, 208), but it would not have halted enforcement of segregation. This is precisely because the charges were masked as ostensibly non-racial: sedition. Again, though the process appears targeted at individual action at a micro level, the messaging to all white people fuels macro-level narratives about white supremacy.

The final important contrast is that in the case of white people resisting, the effects of gaslighting only directly harm those individual white (and People of Color as in the case of the Wades) people involved. In the case of directly gaslighting People of Color, the opposite is true. The Wades' experience with racial gaslighting illuminates this point. Their house was bombed—and they would have been killed if at home—and they suffered a lifetime of consequences from the case. As Anne Braden herself noted, however, it became the Braden case, rather than the Wade case. The Wades' sacrifice was invisible, but if they had somehow been able to contest that fact, they would have been subject to ridicule and violence. Moreover, Kentucky charged the Bradens precisely because the official state version of the story was that Black people were satisfied with racial apartheid. This is the crux of racial gaslighting: to dismantle the racial spectacle that Black people were satisfied with racial apartheid, the Wades would have had to claim they bombed their own home to orchestrate a sedition campaign.

Bridging Past and Present

The process of racial gaslighting, as described in *Korematsu* and *Braden*, is markedly different for People of Color and white people in five ways: portrayal, exposure (or risk), pathologization, audience, and outcome.

Fred Korematsu, a person of Japanese ancestry, was portrayed by state and society in a racist light. In contrast, Anne and Carl Braden, a white couple, were labeled as communists and race traitors. Second, the exposure of Fred Korematsu was both individual (to him) and to the collective of Japanese Americans, though that collective exposure remains regardless of individual action. The Bradens' exposure was individual—white people as a whole had nothing to immediately gain or lose with the decision in the case. Third, the pathologization of Fred Korematsu, like his portrayal, was part of a process of projecting racist stereotypes on the entire group. Kentucky pathologized the Bradens as individual subversives, and also as subversives who made an active decision to become communists. Fourth, the audience for the racial spectacle of the *Korematsu* case was both People of Color and white people. In the case of the Bradens, white people were the primary audience, warned against the dangers of resisting white supremacy. Fifth, in terms of the outcome of racial gaslighting, *Korematsu* resulted in symbolic messages and concrete, racialized state-sanctioned action, in contrast to *Braden*, which resulted in individualized punishment and symbolic warnings to other white people.

The reader may be tempted to agree with our analysis of *Korematsu* and *Braden*, yet wonder how these examples are connected to the current state of white supremacy in the United States. Returning to *Korematsu*, we can see how the process of racial gaslighting continues, girded by the power of *stare decisis* and fueled by the narrative of national security. In 1988, the Civil Liberties Act provided an official apology and reparations to those individuals who were incarcerated. Mr. Korematsu's resistance was recognized, and he was widely considered a hero (Bannai 2005). In 1998, President Clinton awarded Fred Korematsu the Presidential Medal of Freedom.

Although the *Korematsu* decision has been undermined over time, the case has not been overturned and still has precedential value. It was used as precedent to support the Bush Administration's post-9/11 "War on Terror" (Green 2011) and the racialization of Muslims in the United States (Chon and Arzt 2005). In 2011, the Office of the Solicitor General issued a confession of error admitting it withheld reports on Japanese Americans' loyalty in the incarceration cases (Office of the Solicitor General 2011). Yet, in 2013, the Supreme Court denied certiorari to the *Hedges v. Obama* case, which challenged legislation permitting the US government to indefinitely detain people suspected of substantially supporting terrorist organizations. Review of this Second Circuit decision would have provided them the opportunity to formally overrule *Korematsu*. Add to this the plethora of state action focused on groups of People of Color, such as incarceration of immigrant families in camps in Texas and Pennsylvania (Hennessy-Fiske 2015), calls by politicians to incarcerate Syrian refugees (Varner 2015), as well as the executive order to temporarily ban travel from seven majority-Muslim countries in January 2017. These state actions underscore how the process of racial gaslighting ripples through time.

Racial gaslighting moves the ball forward in race politics scholarship in the tradition of both critical race and racial formation theories. Racial formation remains a touchstone for both theoretical and empirical scholarship (Pagliai 2009; HoSang, LaBennett, and Pulido 2012; Lawrence 2012; Feagin and Elias 2013; Golash-Boza 2013; Omi and Winant 2013; Wingfield 2013; Winant 2015), grappling with the persistence of racism in the United States. A rather heated series of exchanges in ethnic and racial studies (2013) underlines the continuing relevance of racial formation theory. Feagin and Elias critique racial formation theory as unable to conceptualize "the deep foundation, layered complexities, and institutionalized operations of systemic racism in the USA" (2013, 931). Omi and Winant respond that Feagin and Elias's account of systemic racism as a totalizing force and an alternative framework to racial formation theory has unintended consequences: "they dismiss the political agency of people of colour and of anti-racist whites. In Feagin/Elias's view, 'systemic racism' is like the Borg in the Star Trek series: a hive-mind phenomenon that assimilates all it touches. As the Borg announce in their collective audio message to intended targets, 'Resistance is futile'" (2013, 962). Our racial gaslighting framework addresses both concerns through a complementary analysis that addresses the primary critiques and rejoinders of racial formation theory. First, racial gaslighting emphasizes a structural and systemic analysis of white supremacy. Like racial formation theory, however, we view racial gaslighting as an iterative process. Second, while we agree with Feagin and Elias's emphasis on white supremacy, we also agree with Omi and Winant that resistance is not futile, but that certain types of resistance can be easily co-opted or have unintended consequences.[8]

Conclusion

Racial spectacles lurk everywhere, from our daily interpersonal interactions to the grotesque political theater of the presidency. These visual and textual narratives align in a process of racial gaslighting that not only targets micro-level players in the particular story, but also taps into broader historical white supremacist myths. Korematsu and Braden represent the often-catastrophic consequences of racial gaslighting for individuals who resist white supremacist violence and their subsequent effects on collectivities. While the individuals in these cases were pathologized and punished, the cases reflect the different "functions" of gaslighting People of Color versus white people in terms of portrayal, exposure, pathologization, audience, and outcome. Again, the process of racial gaslighting targets those who resist. By design, the survival, existence, resilience, and/or success of People of Color is an act of resistance on both macro and micro levels that results in racial gaslighting.

We contend that naming and clarifying this process of racial gaslighting enables us to build a common language in the struggle against white supremacy. Recognizing the process and developing narratives to resist the confines of gaslighting—or at the very least name it as what it is—automatically diminishes some of its power. At the close of the film *Gaslight*, Bergman regains her agency once she understands the manipulations of her husband and can clearly identify his attempts to discredit her. In the cases of Fred Korematsu and the Bradens, they exercised their individual agency to challenge white supremacy in their own ways, but were pathologized for noncompliance. And, in addition to the societal structures designed to punish their noncompliance, their pathologization was facilitated by the lack of language to name and expose this duplicitous tool of white supremacy. We do not suggest that naming and clarifying are enough; rather, we posit that recognizing our collective historical and contemporary patterns is a powerful step toward building movements equipped to stop fueling white supremacy's racial gaslight.

Notes

1. We use Ellinger and Martinas's definition of white supremacy: "White supremacy is an historically based, institutionally perpetuated system of exploitation and oppression of continents, nations and peoples of color by white peoples and nations of the European continent; for the purpose of establishing, maintaining and defending a system of wealth, power and privilege" (1994).

2. Our definition of racial spectacles builds on our previous work on the subject. The addition of the overarching process of racial gaslighting illustrates the specific role of racial spectacles in this context.

3. Others also resisted the incarceration through the court system, such as Yosh Kuromiya and Gene Akutsu (Bannai 2005).

4. While this is the first case to introduce the concept of strict scrutiny by the Supreme Court to equal protection analysis, it was not developed until later cases because of the majority's refusal to acknowledge the racism inherent in these orders.

5. Fred Korematsu's biography, *Enduring Conviction*, discusses his decision to resist: "Fred said he knew remaining in Oakland had been wrong and that he had intended to turn himself in. One might wonder now, over half a century later, why Fred didn't tell Mansfield that he had done nothing wrong—that he, as an American citizen, had a constitutional right to remain free. Maybe he was scared or intimidated or both. Maybe he wanted to protect his [girlfriend] Ida. Most importantly, however, he, as an American citizen, did not have to invoke his constitutional rights to be able to exercise them. While Fred may not have asserted his rights in words, he had asserted his right to liberty by choosing to stay. . . . while not quoting the Constitution, he was seeking the freedom it promised" (Bannai 2015, 42).

6. Concrete state action can also include state omission or delayed action. For example, during the 1921 Tulsa Race Riot, local public safety officials' complicity and failure to intervene allowed white mobs to injure and murder hundreds of African Americans and destroy more than 1000 Black-owned homes and businesses (Oklahoma 2001).

7. The other racial spectacles include multiple trials, arrests, hearings, press coverage, and the like.

8. Though racial gaslighting illustrates how white supremacy survives, we are aware of possible critiques of a single axis analysis along racial lines. Rather than view this framework as following a single axis analysis, however, racial gaslighting invites intersectional and multiplicative understandings of domination and resistance precisely because the process is a binary of normalization versus pathologization.

Works Cited

Bannai, Lorraine K. 2005. "Taking the Stand: The Lessons of the Three Men Who Took the Japanese American Internment to Court." *Seattle Journal for Social Justice* 4 (1): 1–57.

Bannai, Lorraine K. 2015. *Enduring Conviction: Fred Korematsu and His Quest for Justice*. Seattle: University of Washington Press.

Braden, Anne. 2001. "In the Midst of the Storm." In *The Price of Dissent: Testimonies to Political Repression in America*, edited by Bud Schultz and Ruth Schultz, 184–99. Berkeley: University of California Press.

Braden v. Commonwealth. 1955. 291 S.W.2d 843.
Burrow, Sylvia. 2005. "The Political Structure of Emotion: From Dismissal to Dialogue." *Hypatia* 20 (4): 27–43.
Chon, Margaret, and Donna E. Arzt. 2005. "Walking While Muslim." *Law and Contemporary Problems* 68: 215–54.
Commonwealth of Kentucky v. Braden. 1955. Court Transcript. Madison: Wisconsin Historical Society.
Cukor, George. 1944. *Gaslight*. Burbank, CA: Turner Entertainment (Warner Bros.).
Davis, Angelique M. 2012. "Political Blackness: A Sociopolitical Construction." In *Loving in a "Post-Racial" World: New Legal Approaches to Interracial Marriages and Relationships*, edited by Kevin Noble Maillard and Rose Cuison Villazor, 169–80. New York: Cambridge University Press.
———, and Rose Ernst. 2011. "Racial Spectacles: Promoting a Colorblind Agenda Through Direct Democracy." *Studies in Law, Politics and Society* 55: 133–71.
Ellinger, Mickey, and Sharon Martinas. 1994. "The Culture of White Supremacy." *Challenging White Supremacy Workshop*. http://whgbetc.com/mind/culture-white-sup.html.
Feagin, Joe, and Sean Elias. 2013. "Rethinking Racial Formation Theory: A Systemic Racism Critique." *Ethnic and Racial Studies* 36 (6): 931–60.
———, and Leslie H. Picca. 2007. *Two-faced Racism: Whites in the Backstage and Front Stage*. New York: Routledge.
Fong, Edmund. 2013. "Beyond the Racial Exceptionalism of the Japanese Internment." *Politics, Groups, and Identities* 1 (2): 239–44.
Fosl, Catherine. 2006. *Subversive Southerner: Anne Braden and the Struggle for Racial Justice in the Cold War South*. Lexington: University Press of Kentucky.
"Gaslighting, n.2." 2016. OED Online. Oxford University Press, March. http://www.oed.com/view/Entry/255555?rskey=qdZFWb&result=2&isAdvanced=false.
Gass, Gertrude Z., and William C. Nichols. 1988. "Gaslighting: A Marital Syndrome." *Contemporary Family Therapy* 10 (1): 3–16.
Golash-Boza, Tanya. 2013. "Does Racial Formation Theory Lack the Conceptual Tools to Understand Racism?" *Ethnic and Racial Studies* 36 (6): 994–99.
Green, Craig. 2011. "Ending the Korematsu Era: An Early View from the War on Terror Cases." *Northwestern University Law Review* 105 (3).
Hedges v. Obama. 2013. 724 F.3d 170, 173–74, cert. denied, 2014. 572 U.S. 5.
Hennessy-Fiske, Molly. 2015. "Immigrant Family Detention Centers Are Prison-Like, Critics Say, Despite Order to Improve." *Los Angeles Times*. http://www.latimes.com/nation/nationnow/lana-immigration-family-detention-20151020-story.html.
HoSang, Daniel Martinez, Oneka LaBennett, and Laura Pulido. 2012. *Racial Formation in the Twenty-First Century*. Berkeley: University of California Press.
Hugs, Robot. 2015. "No, We Won't Calm Down—Tone Policing Is Just Another Way to Protect Privilege." *Everyday Feminism*. http://everydayfeminism.com/2015/12/tone-policing-andprivilege/.

Ishizuka, Karen L. 2006. *Lost and Found: Reclaiming the Japanese American Incarceration*. Urbana: University of Illinois Press.

Jackson, Taharee Apirom. 2011. "Which Interests Are Served by the Principle of Interest Convergence? Whiteness, Collective Trauma, and the Case for Anti-racism." *Race Ethnicity and Education* 14 (4): 435–59.

Kline, Neal A. 2006. "Revisiting Once Upon a Time." *American Journal of Psychiatry* 163 (7): 1147–48.

Korematsu v. United States. 1944. 323 U.S. 214.

Lawrence, Charles. 2012. "Listening for Stories in All the Right Places: Narrative and Racial Formation Theory." *Law & Society Review* 46 (2): 247–58.

Minter, Patricia Hagler. 2013. "Race, Property, and Negotiated Space in the American South: A Reconsideration of Buchanan v. Warley." In *Signposts: New Directions in Southern Legal History*, edited by Sally E. Hadden and Patricia Hagler Minter, 345–68. Athens: University of Georgia Press.

National JACL (Japanese Americans Citizens League). 2013. *Power of Words Handbook: A Guide to Language about Japanese Americans in World War II*. National Japanese American Citizens League Power of Words II Committee. https://jacl.org/wordpress/wp-content/uploads/2015/08/Power-of-Words-Rev.-Term.-Handbook.pdf.

Office of the Solicitor General, U.S. Department of Justice. 2011. "Confession of Error: The Solicitor General's Mistakes During the Japanese-American Internment Cases." https://www.justice.gov/opa/blog/confession-error-solicitor-generals-mistakes-during-japanese-american-internmentcases.

Oklahoma Commission to Study the Tulsa Race Riot of 1921. 2001. *A Report by the Oklahoma Commission to Study the Tulsa Race Riot of 1921*. http://www.okhistory.org/research/forms/freport.pdf.

Omi, Michael, and Howard Winant. (1986) 2014. *Racial Formation in the United States*. 3rd ed. New York: Routledge.

———, and Howard Winant. 2013. "Resistance Is Futile?: A Response to Feagin and Elias." *Ethnic and Racial Studies* 36 (6): 961–73.

Pagliai, Valentina. 2009. "Conversational Agreement and Racial Formation Processes." *Language in Society* 38 (5): 549–79.

Roberts, Tuesda, and Dorinda J. Carter Andrews. 2013. "A Critical Race Analysis of the Gaslighting of African American Teachers: Considerations for Recruitment and Retention." In *Contesting the Myth of a Post Racial Era: The Continued Significance of Race in U.S. Education*, edited by Dorinda J. Carter Andrews and Franklin Tuitt, 69–94. New York: Peter Lang.

Roxworthy, Emily. 2008. *The Spectacle of Japanese American Trauma: Racial Performativity and World War II*. Honolulu: University of Hawai'i Press.

Scheiner, Eric. 2012. "Bill Clinton: White Americans Without H.S. Diplomas Are 'Dying of a Broken Heart.'" CNSnews.com. http://cnsnews.com/news/article/bill-clinton-white-americanswithout-hs-diplomas-are-dying-broken-heart.

Stockman, Farah. 2017. "Women's March on Washington Opens Contentious Dialogues About Race." *New York Times*. https://www.nytimes.com/2017/01/09/us/womens-march-on-washington-opens-contentious-dialogues-about-race.html.

Varner, Natasha. 2015. "Anti-refugee Rhetoric and Justifications for WWII-Era Mass Incarceration: Is History Repeating Itself?" Densho Blog. http://www.densho.org/5-alarming-similartiesbetween-anti-syrian-refugee-rhetoric-and-justifications-for-world-war-ii-era-mass-incarceration/.

Wade, Andrew. 1989. "Interview with Andrew Wade, November 8, 1989 [Catherine Fosl]." https://kentuckyoralhistory.org/catalog/xt7mcv4bpp1t.

Waltman, Katy. 2016. "From Theater to Therapy, the Eerie History of Gaslighting." *Slate*. http://www.slate.com/blogs/lexicon_valley/2016/04/18/the_history_of_gaslighting_from_films_to_psychoanalysis_to_politics.html.

Winant, Howard. 2015. "Race, Ethnicity and Social Science." *Ethnic and Racial Studies* 38 (13): 2176–85.

Wingfield, Adia Harvey. 2013. "Comment on Feagin and Elias." *Ethnic and Racial Studies* 36 (6): 989–93.

Zevallos, Zuleyka. 2017. "Intersectionality and the Women's March." *The Other Sociologist*. https://othersociologist.com/2017/01/25/intersectionality-womens-march/#more-5512.

9

Varieties of Gaslighting[1]

C%NTHIA A. STARK

Americans, it appears, are enduring an epidemic of gaslighting. Indeed "gaslighting" was Merriam-Webster's word of the year in 2022. A recent search for the word "gaslight" in the *Washington Post* returned 1,196 results. The same search in the *New York Times* yielded 2,047 results. The titles of the articles that turned up include "When Trump Says He Was Being Sarcastic, It's Just Part of His Gaslighting," "GOP Gaslighting on Infrastructure Has Begun," and "Kayleigh McEnany's Latest Briefing Is a Study in Gaslighting, Whataboutism and False Claims." Interpersonal gaslighting has also been much in the news. We are apprised of its warning signs, negative effects, and of techniques for avoiding it. All these news articles chronicle a troubling pattern of lying, misleading, willfully misinterpreting, deceiving, projecting, denying, and clinging to blatant falsehoods on the part of public officials, public figures, spouses, bosses, parents, or friends. It is not clear, however, what makes this constellation of behaviors gaslighting.

In what follows, I first describe, through examples, various ways in which someone can gaslight. I then identify five elements that place these somewhat disparate phenomena under the umbrella of gaslighting. Briefly, gaslighting, on my account, involves a person trying to get another to abandon her justified view in favor of his own unjustified view by claiming that she holds her view only because of a personal defect the existence of which he has no independent evidence for.[2] Next, I consider a possible counterexample to my characterization and explain that it in fact illustrates a phenomenon that is a cousin of gaslighting. Last, I examine two accounts of structural gaslighting, showing that these contain the unifying features I propose. My method is to build an account of gaslighting from the bottom up, as it were. I begin with paradigm cases, locate what they have in common, and then apply the resulting characterization to more controversial cases. This application then confirms the theoretical fruitfulness of the account I have constructed (Kirk-Giannini 2023, 746–47).

Cases of Gaslighting

Consider these instances of gaslighting:

> ***Classic:*** Gregory attempts to convince his wife, Paula, that she is insane by denying her credible reports of randomly dimming gaslights. He tells her that she is imagining this, even though he knows he is causing the dimming by secretly turning up the gaslights in the attic. Paula begins to believe that she is imagining the gaslights dimming and that she is therefore mentally unstable.

> ***Mispronoun:*** James, a cisgender man, mispronouns Victoria, a trans* woman colleague, repeatedly at a department function. Victoria relates this event to her cisgender colleague Susan, who rejects Victoria's testimony because she believes a stereotype of trans* women as overly emotional and hence unreliable interpreters of their own experiences. Susan insists that Victoria must have misheard James. Victoria becomes frustrated because she is certain of what she heard and, further, she feels betrayed by Susan. (Ivy [McKinnon] 2014, 168)[3]

> ***Crowd size:*** To foment political strife, former president Trump lies about the size of the crowd at his inauguration, claiming that it was larger than the crowd at his predecessor's inauguration, even though this is plainly false as shown by widely disseminated aerial photographs. Some of Trump's supporters believe, accept, or espouse this lie, and, taking a cue from Trump, explain away any perceptual evidence of the truth that they encounter. (Ford 2017; see also Sinha 2020)

These cases differ in various ways. In the first, the gaslighter lies to his target to get her to doubt her credible perceptions, and to, on that basis, adopt his competing point of view. He does this with the aim of psychologically destabilizing her. Furthermore, the target *does* doubt her perceptions and *does*, on that basis, adopt the gaslighter's point of view that she is imagining things and possibly losing her mind. In the second case, the gaslighter does not lie, but she nevertheless tries to get her target to doubt her own credible perceptions and to, on that basis, adopt her (the gaslighter's) competing point of view. The gaslighter is not aiming to psychologically harm her target; rather, she simply wants her target to see her own perception as mistaken. The target, however, does not doubt her perception and so does not adopt the gaslighter's point of view. Rather, she feels frustrated and betrayed. In the third case, the gaslighter lies to get people to adopt his erroneous point of view and, on that basis, to doubt any credible perceptions that contradict that point of view. Some people adopt his erroneous point of view and, on that basis, reject any credible perceptual evidence that counters it. The gaslighter, in this case, is arguably aiming to cause civic discord by making a shared reality among citizens extremely difficult to achieve.

On Holding a View and Lying

Before expanding on the differences among these examples, I will clarify the terms I use in my analysis. On my account, the phrase "hold a view" has a somewhat technical meaning. It means to *believe*, *accept*, or *espouse* a proposition or set of propositions. To believe a proposition is to feel that it is true (Cohen 1989, 368). To accept a proposition is to have a policy of going along with that proposition in the context of formulating arguments, deliberating, and so forth (Cohen 1989, 368), and to espouse a proposition is to simply to advocate it. A person may accept or espouse a proposition, then, without believing it and may espouse a proposition without accepting it.

Relatedly, what it is to lie, on my account, is to make a believed-false statement to another person with the intention that the other person believe that statement to be true, or that she accept it, or that she espouse it, or that she engage in some combination of those acts.[4] It follows that a gaslighter who lies does not believe the view he holds; he (merely) accepts or espouses it. For instance, Gregory, in the example above, holds the view that the gaslights are not dimming in the sense that he espouses it but does not accept or believe it. He merely advocates that view in his interactions with Paula. Similarly, Trump holds the view that his inaugural crowd was larger than his predecessor's in the sense that he accepts and espouses it but does not believe it. He has a policy deeming that proposition in his deliberations and arguments and he advocates it. Those whom he convinces to adopt that view—that is, to come to hold it—may believe it or accept it or espouse it or some combination of those acts.

Differentiating Factors

There are four factors that determine the differences among these cases. They are the *truthfulness* factor, the *success* factor, the *injury* factor, and the *method* factor. The first concerns whether or not the gaslighter lies to his target. The second concerns whether the gaslighter is successful in getting the target to abandon her point of view and adopt his. The third concerns whether the person uses gaslighting to hurt his target. The fourth concerns whether the gaslighter denies, in the first instance, another's perception, memory, or interpretation of the facts or whether he denies, in the first instance, the facts.

Truthfulness

In popular discourse, gaslighting is associated with lying (Duca 2016). However, as *Mispronoun* shows, a person can gaslight someone while being truthful: Susan believes that James did not mispronoun Victoria. Nevertheless, the assertion Susan makes is false. So it might seem that gaslighting requires confronting a target with a false claim, and indeed that is the case in the examples above. However, while gaslighters often make false claims, it seems clear that someone can gaslight another while making a true claim. Moreover, merely confronting someone's testimony with a false claim is not sufficient for gaslighting. This can be seen in these modified versions of *Mispronoun*.

Imagine that James did not in fact mispronoun Victoria, but Victoria believes he did, because she could not hear well over the din of conversation, James has mispronounced her in the past, and he has told her that he opposes people adopting their own pronouns. Susan is unaware of these facts about James, and she is in the grips of a stereotype of trans* women as unreliable testifiers. Susan's denial of Victoria's report is plausibly an instance of gaslighting, despite Susan's being correct about what happened.

This is because Susan's true belief that James did not mispronoun Victoria is unjustified.

Now imagine that James, as in the original case, *did* mispronoun Victoria, but Susan was part of the conversation in which James did this and she heard him use the correct pronoun several times, but missed the instances of mispronouning. Further, James believes that he did not mispronoun Victoria, having not realized he had done so, and he reported this to Susan. Assume, furthermore, that Susan does not harbor a stereotype of trans* women as unreliable interpreters of their own experiences. When Victoria reports the mispronouning incident to Susan, and Susan denies it, she is not gaslighting Victoria. She is simply disagreeing with her. This is because, although Susan is mistaken, she has grounds for her belief.[5]

SUCCESS

Gaslighters, as the examples above suggest, have a variety of aims and motives. Gregory, for example, aims to drive Paula insane and is motivated by a desire to locate some jewels, and Trump, let's say, seeks to wreak havoc. Susan, we might surmise, is motivated by a desire to see her colleague James in a good light. Despite this variety, all gaslighters are attempting to get their targets to abandon their view and to adopt the gaslighter's competing view on some matter. Gaslighting is successful when the gaslighter achieves the aim of recruiting his target to his view, regardless of his motives and regardless of whether he achieves his other aim(s).

INJURY

In some cases, gaslighters intend to injure their victims in some way. Gregory aims to damage Paula psychologically and Trump arguably seeks to damage the body politic. Susan, however, does not set out to injure Victoria, but rather to "set her straight," as it were. These injuries are separate from the harm or wrong of gaslighting itself. So, while gaslighting is wrong, and usually harmful, in itself, it may or may not be deployed in the service of further harm.[6]

METHOD

There are two ways that gaslighting, as such, can operate. In the first, which I call the "typical method," gaslighting is directed, in the first instance, at the perceptions, interpretations, or memories of the target. The gaslighter wants the target to doubt her own perceptions so that she will adopt his view. Gregory denies Paula's sensory perceptions so that she will believe or accept something that he knows to be false, namely that she is imagining things. Susan denies Victoria's sensory perceptions so that Victoria will adopt Susan's incorrect view that James did not mispronoun her.

In the second way, which I call the "reverse" method, gaslighting is directed, in the first instance, at the target's view. The gaslighter wants the target to adopt his view *so that* the target will subsequently doubt (or perhaps merely claim to doubt) his own perceptions. This is what is going on in *Crowd Size*. Trump announces that his inaugural crowd was bigger than Obama's so that people will hold the view that it was bigger. But because his claim is plainly contradicted by the evidence, for those who adopt his view to persist in this, they must doubt (or at least claim to doubt) their own perceptions.[7] This doubt insulates the view; only if the holder of the view questions his own perceptions is he apt to reject the evidence that contradicts this view. If he sees a photo showing that the crowd at Trump's inauguration was smaller than the crowd at Obama's, he will explain it away. He might claim that the photo was doctored or that the network broadcasting the photo is "out to get" Trump.

So, in the typical case, the gaslighter alleges that his target's perceptions are not credible and that they are therefore causing her to have an incorrect view. The gaslighter attempts to get the target to doubt the credibility of her perceptions so that she will abandon the view they caused in favor of the view the gaslighter wishes her to hold. In the reverse case, the gaslighter attempts to get targets to accept a particular view simply by asserting it. The targets may or may not be required to abandon their own contrary views in order to accept the gaslighter's belief. (Perhaps those assenting to Trump's claim that his inaugural crowd was larger than Obama's had no prior view about the relative size of Trump's inaugural crowd.) The gaslighter then insinuates that any perceptions that undermine the view he wants his targets to hold are not credible and that the targets should therefore doubt those perceptions.

Moral Judgments

Often gaslighting involves a challenge to someone's views about descriptive matters, and this is what is going on in the examples outlined above.

However, a gaslighter can also challenge a person's normative views, as is shown by this case:

> ***New Clothes:*** When [Mitchell] . . . wears [some] new clothes to Sunday dinner at his parents' home, his mother bursts out laughing. "Oh Mitchell, that outfit is all wrong for you—you look ridiculous," she says. "Please, dear, the next time you go shopping, let me help you." When Mitchell feels hurt and asks his mother to apologize, she shakes her head sadly. "I was only trying to help," she says. "And I'd like an apology from *you* for that tone of voice." (Stern, 2007, Kindle loc. 184)[8]

Gaslighting in response to people's plausible moral views is subject to the four differentiating factors identified above. The gaslighter may or may not be speaking truthfully, she may or may not be successful in getting the target to adopt or accept her view, she may or may not intend to harm the target, and she may, in the first instance, challenge the target's interpretation of events or she may, in the first instance, challenge the target's view.

This can be seen in *New Clothes*. Mitchell's mother denies that she was ridiculing Mitchell and maintains that she was, rather, offering help. This is plainly false, but Mitchell's mother may mistakenly believe that she was merely offering help because she is, say, self-deluded. Or, alternatively, she may be aware that she was ridiculing Mitchell and lie about this to avoid culpability. Furthermore, Mitchell's mother may or may not be successful in converting Mitchell to her point of view. Perhaps he concludes that he did in fact misread his mother's intentions and offers an apology. Or perhaps he stands his ground, insisting that her comments were disrespectful. Furthermore, it is reasonable to surmise that Mitchell's mother aimed to hurt him, as that is what ridicule is generally for. But insofar as she might believe that she was only helping, she likely did not intend to hurt her son.

With respect to method, *New Clothes* is typical: Mitchell's mother challenges Mitchell's interpretation of the event so as to get him to adopt the view that she was not disrespectful. However, she could gaslight him in a similar way using the reverse method. For instance, she might say to Mitchell at the start of dinner (under some pretext) that she would never condescend to him. If Mitchell believes or accepts this, then, when she later mocks his outfit and urges him to let her choose his clothing, Mitchell might conclude that she was only trying to help, despite his discomfort with her remarks. He might, in other words, question his interpretation of the event to preserve his view that his mother would never condescend to him.

Unifying Features

It is clear that there are a variety of ways to gaslight. Compare *Mispronoun* with *Crowd Size*. These two cases differ along all four dimensions discussed above: Susan is being truthful, she is not successful, she does not aim to harm Victoria, and she targets, in the first instance, Victoria's perceptions. In contrast, Trump is lying, he is successful, he aims to harm the public, and he targets, in the first instance, people's views. So what makes both *Mispronoun* and *Crowd Size* instances of gaslighting? I suggest that what unifies them is the following features:

1. The target of the gaslighting T holds a view V.

2. T's holding V is at least minimally justified.

3. The gaslighter G denies V and tries to get T to adopt his competing not even minimally justified view, typically ~V.[9]

4. G does this by stating or implying that T holds V only because of a personal defect that prevents T from seeing the truth.[10]

5. G is not even minimally justified in believing that T's holding V is explained by that non–truth-conducive defect.[11]

We can see the features 1 through 5 in all the cases discussed above. Start with *Classic*. Gregory tries to get Paula to believe or accept that the gaslights are not dimming by denying her testimony that they are. Her belief that they are is justified—she has seen them dim multiple times under circumstances conducive to normal perception. Gregory lacks grounds for holding that the gaslights are not dimming—indeed he has grounds for holding that they are—and he maintains that Paula believes that they are because of a psychological problem—she cannot distinguish between what is real and what she imagines. Moreover, Gregory has no independent evidence that Paula tends to imagine things; his only "evidence" for this is that she claims that the gaslights are dimming.

Now consider *Mispronoun*. Susan attempts to persuade Victoria that James did not mispronoun her by doubting Victoria's perception of the incident. Victoria's perception is likely correct—she heard James use the wrong pronoun under circumstances conducive to normal perception. Susan lacks grounds for holding that James did not mispronoun Victoria. She was not present when it happened, she has not heard reliable testimony from someone else that it did not happen, and Victoria's testimony in the past has been credible. Susan attributes Victoria's belief to Victoria's having defective hearing at the time of the incident, and Susan has no evidence that Victoria has difficulty hearing or that she tends to "hear" what she wants to hear or what she anticipates hearing. Susan's only "evidence" that Victoria misheard James is the fact that Victoria concluded that James mispronouned her.

In *Crowd Size*, Trump attempts to persuade the public that more people attended his inauguration than attended Obama's. The public's view that the crowd was bigger at Obama's inauguration is supported by strong perceptual evidence—photographs of the events produced by reliable sources. Trump has no grounds for holding that his inaugural crowd was the larger, and he intimates that those who deny this do so because they have a flaw of some sort—they are disloyal, or they are trying to undermine him, or they have been duped by "fake news." Again, his only "evidence" that they have one of these flaws is that they persist in their view that his inaugural crowd was smaller than Obama's.[12]

Finally, consider *New Clothes*. Mitchell's mother denies Mitchell's interpretation of her conduct in order to persuade him that she has not mistreated him. Mitchell has every reason to hold that she has—she tells him, in front of others, while laughing at him, that he looks ridiculous. Further, she lacks grounds for her view that she has done nothing wrong. Her claim that she was merely trying to help is not justified. And in making that claim and in demanding that Mitchell apologize, she attributes to him various flaws. She suggests that he has misunderstood her motives, that he doesn't appreciate her, and that he is impudent. Moreover, Mitchell's mother lacks independent evidence that Mitchell is bad at judging people's motives, and so forth. She draws these conclusions merely on the basis of the fact that Mitchell demanded an apology from her.

A Possible Counterexample

Below is a purported case of gaslighting that does not qualify as gaslighting on the account I have outlined. So it might serve as a counterexample to my view.

> *Miscarriage:* After a series of miscarriages, Sara begins to miscarry once again and goes to the hospital. The doctor who treats her does an ultrasound and discovers an approximately four-week-old embryo. She (the doctor) tells Sara that she is four weeks pregnant, that bleeding is common at this stage, and that she is not miscarrying. Sara states more than once that she is in fact *seven* weeks pregnant and that what the ultrasound shows is surely an embryo that stopped developing at four weeks. The doctor insists that Sara cannot be sure that she is seven weeks pregnant, and when Sara claims that she can be sure because she used an ovulation prediction kit, the doctor continues to deny Sara's belief, saying, "We cannot base a diagnosis on your intuitions, can we?" (Shabot, 2019, 15)

This looks a lot like gaslighting. However, on my view, Sara was not gaslighted because the doctor had grounds for her claim that Sara was four weeks pregnant: the ultrasound showed a four-week-old embryo and, furthermore, it is true that pregnant women cannot always be sure when they became pregnant.[13] The temptation to regard Sara's experience as gaslighting might reside in the fact that the doctor's treatment of Sara obviously was morally objectionable. But the doctor's conduct can be condemned on other grounds. First, Sara may have been a victim of testimonial injustice.[14] This type of injustice occurs when someone assigns a credibility deficit to a person because of an identity prejudice. Where the hearer thinks he is determining the credibility of a speaker's testimony on the basis of its content, he is in fact assessing it in terms of her social identity and downgrading it on that basis. This appears to be going on in *Miscarriage*. The doctor discounts Sara's testimony, claiming that it is merely a matter of "intuition," presumably because of a stereotype of women as irrational and emotional.

Second, even if Sara did not experience testimonial injustice—maybe the doctor was not beholden to a sexist stereotype—she was nevertheless wronged insofar as the doctor both patronized her and refused to give her the benefit of the doubt when she was owed that, and she was owed that because she had had experience with miscarriages; her pregnancy was planned, making it likely that she got pregnant when she thought she did; and miscarriages are common. The doctor had no grounds for refusing to take Sara's perspective seriously. So Sara's being wrongfully disbelieved can be accounted for without appeal to the notion of gaslighting.

Structural Gaslighting

In what follows, I consider two accounts of structural gaslighting and show that the features I identified above are present in these accounts.[15] This compatibility between my view and notions of structural gaslighting further supports my account.

Racial Gaslighting

Davis and Ernst identify a phenomenon they call "racial gaslighting." They define this as "the political, social, economic and cultural process that perpetuates and normalizes a white supremacist reality through pathologizing those who resist" (Davis and Ernst 2017, 3. See also Roberts et al. 2013, 70). Racial gaslighting is deployed through what they call "racial spectacles," which are "narratives that obfuscate the existence of a white supremacist state power structure" (Davis and Ernst, 2017, 3). To illustrate, the authors discuss the 1955 case of *Commonwealth of Kentucky v. Braden*. The background and outcome of the case are as follows: Andrew and Charlotte Wade enlisted a White couple, Carl and Ann Braden, to purchase them a home in an all-White neighborhood near Louisville, as they were unable to do so themselves because of practices of housing discrimination. As soon as they moved in, the Wades suffered violent intimidation at the hands of their White neighbors and then their house was firebombed. Fortunately, they were not home at the time. The prosecutor accused the Bradens of orchestrating the bombing. He rejected the idea that the bomb was set by White neighbors who opposed a Black family living in their neighborhood and argued instead that the bombing was part of a communist plot on the part of the Bradens to promote racial discord. Carl Braden was convicted of sedition, sentenced to fifteen years of hard labor, and fined $5000.

According to Davis and Ernst, the target in this case was White people generally. The gaslighter was arguably the local legal establishment. Here is why this case fits my account. The legal establishment attempted to get White citizens to adopt the view that racial strife is caused by White communists plotting to create political instability by fomenting racial strife. It advanced, then, a view for which it had no justification—indeed, one that it completely fabricated—denying the highly justified, and indeed obviously true, view that racial discord in the Jim Crow South was caused by White animus toward Blacks. The prosecutor in this case assigned a defect to the Bradens, whose willingness to purchase a house for a Black family expressed the justified belief that racial strife is caused by White racists. Specifically, he portrayed their anti-racist position as insincere—as a cover for their alleged adherence to communism, a political view he represented as diabolical: "[We] should let this be a milestone in the historic fight of America today to stop this evil pitting race against race, white against black, Catholic against Protestants, Jew against the gentile, rich against the poor. . . . We must ruthlessly cut out this cancer of communism and here is the one place to start" (Davis and Ernst, 2017, 8). Moreover, the prosecutor had no evidence that the Bradens were communists. This "defect" was manufactured.

Controlling Images and Gaslighting

Pohlhaus identifies a type of structural gaslighting whereby certain images circulating within a culture, which are created and embraced by dominant groups, pressure members of nondominant groups to question their accurate interpretations of events (Pohlhaus, 2020, 678). She offers this example. Imagine, she says, a lesbian student who attends a straight professor's office hours with a few other students. The professor has a "safe zone" sticker on her door, indicating that she has undergone training with regard to the needs of the LGBTQIA community and identifies as an ally of that community. Some of the students make homophobic remarks, which none of the others seem to notice, including the professor. The lesbian student, because of the professor's explicitly positioning herself as an ally, begins to doubt her interpretation of those remarks. The image of an ally acts, in this case, according to Pohlhaus, as a "controlling image of dominance," which encourages members of nondominant groups to question their experience of the world. Such images, Pohlhaus, explains, exert pressure on nondominant individuals to align their interpretations with those of dominant individuals, even though those interpretations conflict with their own experience. In so doing, controlling images induce members of nondominant groups to ignore or downplay injustices that they experience.

The gaslighter in this example is not a person, but rather a ubiquitous cultural image that places members of dominant groups in a positive light. Here is why this case also fits my account. These images function to persuade members of nondominant groups to reject their justified views—for instance, that fellow students are homophobic—and adopt, instead, the unjustified perspective of dominant groups—for instance, that homophobia is rare or "no big deal." In questioning their interpretations of events under the pressure of controlling images, targets are forced to find an alternative explanation for their sense of what happened, and the obvious option is to conclude that they are somehow defective. They are forced to wonder if they are oversensitive, unforgiving, or paranoid. But their suspicion that they are defective is not supported by independent evidence; they are led to that thought simply on the basis of the conflict between their interpretation and the one they are compelled to adopt.

Summary

Above I have proposed a way to unify various cases of gaslighting, explaining its relation to things it is commonly associated with, such as lies, falsehoods, deceit, and self-doubt. I have argued, further, that my unifying account can assist in understanding recent accounts of structural gaslighting.

Notes

1. Thanks to Ram Neta, Chris Weigel, and an anonymous referee for their helpful feedback on earlier drafts of this chapter.

2. As an account designed to unify many different cases of gaslighting, this characterization is slightly different from (but I believe largely compatible with) an account I defend elsewhere (Stark 2019, 2022). A main difference is that I have dropped the stipulation that a feature of gaslighting as such is "side-stepping." This is the phenomenon by which the gaslighter, using tactics such as turning the table, dismisses or avoids the target's evidence that his view is unjustified.

3. According to Ivy [McKinnon], the gaslighting perpetrated in this example is a species of testimonial injustice. In an earlier work (Stark 2019), I assumed that what made this a case of gaslighting is what, substantively, the gaslighter refused to believe, namely the target's testimony about a harm done to her. I now see that my interpretation was incorrect. What makes Susan's conduct gaslighting, on

Ivy's account, is that Susan, like Gregory in the film *Gaslight*, doubts her target's ability to perceive events accurately.

4. This is an adaptation of the tradition view of lying, modified to capture the psychological nuances of gaslighting (Mahon 2016).

5. I discuss this example in Stark (2019).

6. Works that canvas the wrongs and harms of gaslighting, which are multifarious, include Abramson (2014), Ahern (2017), Bagnoli (2023), Barton and Whitehead (1969), Benson (1994), Graves and Spencer (2022), Ivy [McKinnon] (2019), Johnson et al. (2021) Kurniawan and Limanta (2020), Manne (2023), Riggs and Bartholomaeus (2018), Stern (2007), Sweet (2019), and Tobias and Joseph (2018).

7. Those in power are uniquely positioned to do this; few people have the admiration or loyalty of others that allows them to persuade others to accept a patently false statement simply by making it.

8. I discuss the moral implications of this example in Stark (2022).

9. This feature makes my account an intentional view: the gaslighter intends to convert his target to his view, even if he is not aware of his intention. According to intentional views, conduct qualifies as gaslighting only if the gaslighter has a certain intention (or intentions). Notice that intentional views do not necessarily entail that gaslighters intend to gaslight. Indeed, that would make instances of gaslighting rather uncommon. For discussion, see Barnes (2023), Kirk-Giannini (2023), Manne (2023), Podosky (2021, 2023).

10. Thanks to an anonymous referee for pressing me to clarify this aspect of my view.

11. Immense thanks to Ram Neta for helping me formulate my account in a clear way. One clarification about this account: Suppose a target 1) actually has the defect the gaslighter alleges, 2) the gaslighter knows this, and 3) the defect is the cause of the target holding the belief the gaslighter challenges. This is still an instance of gaslighting if it is the case that in the absence of the defect, the target would have sufficient grounds for her view. That is, it is still gaslighting if the gaslighter is using the defect as an excuse to challenge the credibility of the target's point of view. For discussion, see Stark (2019).

12. An anonymous referee pointed out that Trump's aim was not merely to get people to hold against all evidence that his inaugural crowed was larger than his predecessor's. This incident was part of a larger strategy of "flooding the zone with bullshit," to use the words of Steve Bannon, Trump's chief advisor. The purpose of this flooding was to make it difficult for citizens to distinguish true from false, allowing that truth will be determined by power/Trump himself. I believe this observation may be compatible with my view: what the gaslighter does is try to convince his target that she is incapable of seeing the truth about some matter, causing her to turn to the gaslighter for the truth. Flooding the zone in essence creates a situation where it is hard for people to discern the truth

about politics, leading them to turn to Trump for the truth. For discussion, see Donzelli (2023) and Shane et al. (2022).

13. To be sure, this is not to deny the phenomenon of obstetric gaslighting. See Fielding-Singh and Dmowska (2022). See also Barnes (2023).

14. Some identify gaslighting as a species of testimonial injustice, so what I mean is that Sara may be a victim of a kind of testimonial injustice that is not gaslighting. See Ivy [McKinnon] (2017) and Spear (2017, 2023). The literature on testimonial injustice, and similar types of wrongs, is vast. A few influential works include Dotson (2011), Fricker (2009), Mendina (2013), and Pohlhaus Jr. (2012).

15. Other accounts of structural or other noninterpersonal types of gaslighting include Adkins (2019), Berebohm and Davis (2023), Berenstain (2020), Englehart (forthcoming), Rietdjk (2021), Ruiz (2020), Sinha (2020), and Wozolek (2018).

Works Cited

Abramson, Kate. 2015. "Turning Up the Lights on Gaslighting." *Philosophical Perspectives* 28: 1–30.

Adkins, Karen. 2019. "Gaslighting by Crowd." In *Health, Wellbeing and Society*, edited by Zachary Hoskins and Joan Woolfrey, 75–87. Charlottesville: Philosophy Documentation Center.

Ahern, Kathy. 2017. "Institutional Betrayal and Gaslighting." *Journal of Perinatal and Neonatal Nursing* 32 (1): 59–65.

Barnes, Elizabeth. 2023. "Trust, Distrust, and 'Medical Gaslighting.'" *Philosophical Quarterly* 73 (3): 649–76.

Bagnoli, Carla. 2023. "Normative Isolation: The Dynamics of Power and Authority in Gaslighting." *Aristotelian Society Supplementary Volume* 97 (1): 146–71.

Cohen, L. Jonathan. 1989. "Belief and Acceptance." *Mind* 98 (391): 367–89.

Barton, Russell, and J. A. Whitehead. 1969. "The Gas-light Phenomenon." *Lancet* 1258–60.

Davis, Angelique M., and Rose Ernst. 2017. "Racial Gaslighting." *Politics, Groups, and Identities* 7 (4): 761–44. https://doi.org/10.1080/21565503.2017.1403934.

Donzelli, Aurora. 2023. "On Metapragmatic Gaslighting: Truth and Trump's Epistemic Tactics in a Plague Year." *Signs and Society* 11 (2): 173–200.

Dotson, Kristie. 2011. "Tracking Epistemic Violence, Tracking Epistemic Silencing." *Hypatia* 26: 236–57.

Duca, Lauren. 2016. "Donald Trump Is Gaslighting America." *Teen Vogue*. https://www.teenvogue.com/story/donald-trump-is-gaslighting-america.

Beerbohm, Eric, and Ryan Davis. 2023. "Gaslighting Citizens." *American Journal of Political Science* 67 (4): 867–79.

Benson, Paul. 1994. "Free Agency and Self-Worth." *Journal of Philosophy* 91 (12): 650–68.

Berenstain, Nora. 2020. "White Feminist Gaslighting." *Hypatia* 35: 733–58.
Fielding-Singh, Priya, and Amelia Dmowska. 2022. "Obstetric Gaslighting and the Denial of Mother's Realities." *Social Science and Medicine* 301: 1–8.
Englehart, Jeff, forthcoming. "Some Reflections on Gaslighting and Language Games." *Feminist Philosophy Quarterly*.
Ford, Matt. 2017. "Trump's Press Secretary Falsely Claims: 'Largest Audience to Witness an Inauguration, Period.'" *Atlantic*. https://www.theatlantic.com/politics/archive/2017/01/inauguration-crowd-size/514058/.
Fricker, Miranda. 2007. *Epistemic Injustice: Power and the Ethics of Knowing*. Oxford: Oxford University Press.
Graves, Clint G., and Leland G. Spencer. 2022. "Rethinking the Rhetorical Epistemics of Gaslighting." *Communication Theory* 32 (1): 48–67.
Johnson, Vernica E., Kevin L. Nadal, D. R. Gina Sissoko, and Rukia King. 2021. "'It's Not in Your Head': Gaslighting, 'Splaining, Victim-Blaming and Other Harmful Reactions to Micro-Aggressions." *Perspectives on Psychological Science* 16 (5): 1024–36.
Kirk-Giannini, Cameron Domenico. 2023. "Dilemmatic Gaslighting." *Philosophical Studies* 180: 745–72.
Kurniawan, Licia, and Liem Satya Limanta. 2020. "Unwritten Scars: Gaslighting in Relationships." *Kata Kita* 9 (2): 253–58.
Ivy, Veronica [McKinnon, Rachel]. 2017. "Allies Behaving Badly: Gaslighting as Epistemic Injustice." *The Routledge Companion to Epistemic Injustice*, edited by Ian James Kidd, José Medina, and Gail Pohlhaus Jr., 167–74. New York: Routledge.
———. 2019. "Gaslighting As Epistemic Violence: 'Allies,' Mobbing, and Complex Posttraumatic Stress Disorder, Including a Case Study of Harassment of Transgender Women in Sport." In *Overcoming Epistemic Injustice*, edited by Benjamin R. Sherman and Stacey Goguen, 285–302. New York: Rowman and Littlefield.
Mahon, James Edwin. 2016. "The Definition of Lying and Deception." In *The Stanford Encyclopedia of Philosophy*, edited by Edward N. Zalta. https://plato.stanford.edu/archives/win2016/entries/lying-definition/.
Manne, K. 2023. "Moral Gaslighting." *Proceedings of the Aristotelian Society* 97 (1): 122–45.
Mendina, José. 2013. *The Epistemology of Resistance: Gender and Racial Oppression, Epistemic Injustice and the Social Imagination*. Oxford: Oxford University Press.
Podosky, Paul-Mikhail Catapang. 2021. "Gaslighting First and Second Order." *Hypatia* 36: 207–27.
Podosky, Paul-Mikhail Catapang, forthcoming. "Manne, Moral Gaslighting and the Politics of Methodology." *Logos and Episteme*.
Pohlhaus, Gaile, Jr. 2012. "Relational Knowing and Epistemic Injustice: Toward a Theory of 'Willful Hermeneutical Ignorance.'" *Hypatia* 27 (4): 715–35.

———. 2020. "Gaslighting and Echoing, or Why Collective Epistemic Resistance Is Not a 'Witch Hunt.'" *Hypatia* 35 (4): 674–86.

Rietdyk, Natascha. 2024. "Post-Truth Politics and Collective Gaslighting." *Episteme* 21 (1): 229–45: 1–17. https://doi.org/10.1017/epi.2021.24.

Riggs, Damien W., and Clare Bartholomaeus. 2018. "Gaslighting in the Context of Clinical Interactions with Parents of Transgender Children." *Sexual and Relationship Therapy* 33 (4): 382–94. https://doi.org/10.1080/14681994.2018.1444274.

Roberts, Tuesda, and Dorinda J. Carter Andrews. 2013. "A Critical Race Analysis of the Gaslighting Against African American Teachers." In *Contesting the Myth of a Post-Racial Era: The Continued Significance of Race in U.S. Education*, edited by Dorinda J. Carter Andrews and Frank Tuitt, 69–94. New York: Peter Lang.

Ruíz, Elena. 2020: "Cultural Gaslighting." *Hypatia* 35 (4): 687–713.

Shabot, Sara Cohen. 2019. "'Sisters, Amigas, We're Being Gaslighted.'" In *Childbirth, Vulnerability and the Law: Exploring Issues of Violence and Control*, edited by Camilla Pickles and Jonathan Herring, 14–29. London: Routledge.

Shane, Tommie, Tom Willaert, and Marc Tutors. 2022. "The Rise of 'Gaslighting': Debates About Disinformation on Twitter and 4chan, and the Possibility of a 'Good Echo Chamber.'" *Popular Communication* 20 (3): 178–92.

Sinha, Alex G. 2020. "Lies, Gaslighting and Propaganda." *Buffalo Law Review* 68 (4): 1037–116.

Spear, Andrew D. 2020. "Gaslighting, Confabulation and Epistemic Innocence." *Topoi* 29: 229–41.

———. 2023. "Epistemic Dimensions of Gaslighting: Peer Disagreement, Self-Trust and Epistemic Injustice." *Inquiry* 66: 868–91.

Stark, Cynthia A. 2019. "Gaslighting, Misogyny and Psychological Oppression." *The Monist* 102: 221–35.

———. 2022. "Gaslighting, Self-Respect, and the Kingdom of Ends." In *Human Dignity and the Kingdom of Ends*, edited by Jan-Willem van der Rijt and Adam Cureton, 266–82. New York: Routledge.

Stern, Robin. 2007. *The Gaslight Effect: How to Spot and Survive the Hidden Manipulation Others Use to Control Your Life*. New York: Doubleday.

Sweet, Paige L. 2019. "The Sociology of Gaslighting." *American Sociological Review* 84 (5): 851–75.

Tobias, Heston, and Ameil Joseph. 2018. "Sustaining Systemic Racism Through Psychological Gaslighting: Denials of Racial Profiling and Justifications of Carding by Police Using Local News Media." *Race and Justice* 10 (4): 424–55. https://doi.org/10.1177/2153368718760969.

Wozolek, Boni. 2018. "Gaslighting Queerness: Schooling as a Place of Violent Assemblages." *Journal of LGBT Youth* 15 (4): 319–38.

10

Giving an Account of the Harms of Medical Gaslighting

Lilyana Levy

Medical Gaslighting as Epistemic Injustice

WHAT IS MEDICAL GASLIGHTING?

The term "gaslighting" has gained traction in recent years to describe both acute forms of psychological abuse and more subtle forms of denial that members of marginalized groups face as they attempt to articulate the violence they experience. The term comes from the 1938 play by Patrick Hamilton and the 1944 film adaptation, *Gaslight*, in which the main character, Gregory, manipulates his wife, Paula, into believing she is delusional as part of an elaborate ploy to steal her family's jewels. Feminist theorists have gravitated toward the term to explain a number of diverse phenomena ranging from abusive interpersonal dynamics in romantic relationships to workplace microaggressions to more subtle forms of denial about the existence of structural and systemic racist and sexist oppression. More recently, Elena Ruíz and Nora Berenstain have given accounts of cultural and structural gaslighting that name the ways in which the connections between interlocking forms of systemic oppression and their consequences are masked by discourses that shift blame to individual actions or character traits (Ruíz 2020, 687–713; Berenstain 2020, 733–58). Giving an account of medical gaslighting requires elements of both approaches to theorizing gaslighting: the interpersonal and the structural. Medical gaslighting appears as one-on-one encounters between patients and healthcare providers and is driven by systemic biases in medical knowledge that map onto other forms of structural oppression: sexism, racism, and ableism.

Before turning to the mechanisms of medical gaslighting, there are several features I want to highlight about gaslighting in general: 1) Gaslighting is a form of epistemic injustice because it harms a person in their capacity as a knower by casting doubt on their ability to accurately perceive situations. 2) This injury is cumulative and occurs over time through many iterations. 3) Gaslighting is easier to identify when it takes the form of acute psychological abuse. In more subtle modalities it may be harder to recognize, especially if the gaslighter occupies a position of epistemic authority or social power over the victim, such as an expert physician. 4) Gaslighting is not always intentional, and indeed, as Veronica Ivy [Rachel McKinnon] stresses, it often results from the operation of unconscious bias among individuals seeking to help (Ivy 2017, 167–74). This is especially true of medical gaslighting. 5) At its core, gaslighting involves blame shifting to an intrinsic quality of the victim that is used to discredit or devalue the individual's testimony.

It is useful to begin our discussion of medical gaslighting by way of a recent high-profile example. In the January 2018 issue of *Vogue* magazine, champion professional tennis player Serena Williams recounts her experience of medical gaslighting following the birth of her daughter via emergency C-section. Williams describes how the day after giving birth she began to experience shortness of breath and immediately became concerned that she was developing a pulmonary embolism. As an elite athlete with a history of blood clots, Williams has developed a high level of bodily vigilance and awareness. She requested a CT scan but was refused by a nurse who attributed her concern to confusion caused by pain medication. Williams persisted in her self-advocacy and was eventually given the scan, which revealed several small clots in her lungs (Haskell 2018). She experienced medical gaslighting when the nurse downplayed her symptoms. This kind of dismissal and denial is incredibly common among women, especially Black women, who face a general credibility deficit.

Just as with gaslighting in general, medical gaslighting should be understood as a form of epistemic injustice, specifically testimonial injustice, because it harms a person precisely in their capacity as a knower. This is an epistemic and moral harm. The person who faces persistent medical gaslighting is damaged as a knower when they lose confidence in their ability to accurately perceive things about themselves and their embodied and sensory experiences. Whereas the victim of gaslighting tends to doubt their own sanity and the reliability of their faculties to perceive the world in common, the victim of medical gaslighting tends to doubt their own bodily sensations. They might wonder if they are indeed just "oversensitive" or if their symptoms really are "all in their head." This can produce immense feelings of shame, self-doubt, self-loathing, and bodily alienation. Medical gaslighting is almost always accompanied by significant corollary material harms such as delayed diagnosis, disease progression, financial burden, and even death. Understanding the harms of medical gaslighting requires tracking both the epistemic and material consequences of these clinical encounters.

Medical Gaslighting as Testimonial Injustice

Medical gaslighting occurs when a patient's illness testimony is dismissed, denied, or otherwise downgraded in a healthcare context. It involves the refusal of the clinician to take the patient's symptoms seriously instead offering a non-medical explanation for the patient's experience. Medical gaslighting shifts the blame for the patient's bodily distress from a legitimate medical issue to something that is deemed medically illegitimate such as anxiety, hypochondria, or stress. The message behind these dynamics is that the person is an unreliable perceiver of their own body, that they cannot be trusted to accurately interpret symptoms, that they are prone to overreacting such that they cannot determine when they have truly fallen ill. In short, that their illness is "all in their head."

The way medical gaslighting plays out in clinical contexts ranges from the very subtle microaggression to the belligerent accusation. Women's healthcare advocate and independent journalist Sarah Graham collects stories from women who have been gaslit in medical contexts and anonymously republishes them on her blog "Hysterical Women" and the associated Instagram account. I replicate some of the things doctors have said here to illustrate the range of medical gaslighting tactics women and people assigned female at birth (AFAB) tend to encounter.[1] On the topic of pelvic pain and endometriosis, Graham reports women have been told: "You're a woman, deal with it." "Period pain is normal, you're just really sensitive." "Just get pregnant." "Everything has come back as normal, so there's nothing wrong." "I was taught in medical school that endometriosis isn't painful and women talk themselves into pain" (@sarahgraham7writer, March 19, 2021). On the topic of side effects from the controversial surgical pelvic mesh, women were told:[2] "The pain is all in your head and you need to see a psychiatrist." "Are you sure you have a UTI or are you imagining the symptoms?" "Your pain is nothing to do with the mesh. It's due to your flat shoes." "Many young women are quite highly strung. I'm not sure what you want me to do for you." "You're obese. Lose weight and your symptoms will go away." "Stop jumping on the mesh bandwagon. You women believe everything you read" (@Sarahgraham7writer, January 25, 2021).

These quotes reveal how negative identity prejudicial bias against women is used to dismiss medical concerns. The clinicians' comments are nasty, pointed, and cruel. They use gendered stereotypes to discount symptoms, effacing the singularity of each patient's experience. Hearing some of these statements while seeking medical care can rightly provoke a range of emotions: anger, fear, sadness, rage, shame, and despair. However, expressing these emotions often only fuels the gaslighting dynamic by providing "evidence" of "oversensitivity" and "over-emotionality," which are then taken as further proof that the patient is "less than rational." This is what Veronica Ivy refers to as the "epistemic injustice circle of hell" (Ivy 2017, 169). In the presence of medical gaslighting, the ill person is prompted to give an account of themselves, as if they were on trial, accused of causing their own suffering. The mechanism of self-injury can take many forms: being "crazy," being over-emotional, being fat, being anxious, being stressed out, being a hypochondriac, and so forth. Any of these charges amounts to a moralizing of illness in which the sick person is to blame.

Medical gaslighting occurs when ontological claims about the nonexistence or epistemic claims about medical irrelevance of a patient's illness are made on the basis of negative identity prejudicial stereotypes rather than thorough differential diagnosis. Havi Carell and Ian James Kidd argue that ill persons are especially vulnerable to testimonial injustice because they are likely to be coded as "cognitively unreliable, emotionally compromised, and existentially unstable" such that their testimonies and bodily interpretations are rendered "suspect simply by virtue of their status as an ill person with little sensitivity to their factual condition and state of mind" (Carel and Kidd 2014, 530). However, this fails to account for the other identity markers that tend to be operative in cases of medical gaslighting such as disability, gender, race, size, and history of psychiatric diagnosis. A more robust intersectional analysis is needed.

Medical Gaslighting as Hermeneutical Injustice

Understanding how medical gaslighting is enacted in one-on-one interactions between patients and clinicians is helpful; however, a robust account of how these practices harm individuals requires an investigation of what Miranda Fricker initially termed hermeneutical injustice, or the ways in which gaps in collective interpretive resources render certain experiences unintelligible. Hermeneutical injustice can be approached at the structural level by examining the ways in which knowledge is produced in specific domains, such as medicine, and how dominant ways of knowing within these fields work to uphold existing oppressive structures.

Individual instances of medical gaslighting occur against a backdrop of medical knowledge that is fraught with racist, sexist, and ableist bias that might reliably be termed hermeneutical injustice. This occurs at the structural level in terms of how medical knowledge is produced: what is and is not studied, who is studied and whether consent is given, how research funding is allocated, how diagnostic criteria are written, and how medical research can be used to reinforce existing stereotypes about certain groups.

In her book *Doing Harm: The Truth about How Bad Medicine and Lazy Science Leave Women Dismissed, Misdiagnosed, and Sick*, Maya Dusenberry presents a thorough analysis of how clinical research practices and legacies of hysteria come together to create vast gendered inequality in medicine. She intertwines illness narratives with a litany of facts about funding decisions, disease profiles, exclusionary research practices, and gendered patterns of normalization (pelvic pain) and medicalization (pregnancy).

Indeed, the gender gap and knowledge gap are noncoincidental. Women were excluded from participating in clinical trials from 1977 until June 10, 1993, when President Bill Clinton signed the NIH Revitalization Act, mandating that all NIH-funded studies include both women and racial minorities such that a "valid analysis of whether the variables being studied in the trial affect women or members of minority groups, as the case may be, differently than other subjects in the trial" (NIH Guidelines on the Inclusion of Women and Minorities in Clinical Research). The medical model is deeply androcentric, built on the hypothetical "average" patient who is male, white, and able-bodied. For example, the majority of research about cardiovascular disease was conducted exclusively on men even though heart attacks tend to present differently in women. Heart disease in women remains understudied, underdiagnosed, and undertreated

(Wenger 2012, 604–11). Women experiencing early signs of heart attacks are often gaslit about their symptoms and denied critical care (Dusenberry 2018, 116–19). Diseases that primarily afflict women are disproportionally underfunded. For example in 2020 the NIH allocated $285 million for schizophrenia research, a condition that affects 1.1% of the population, while endometriosis research was given $14 million though it is estimated to affect 10% to 20% of women.

Unsurprisingly, racism is also embedded within the very "objective" metrics by which physicians evaluate, diagnose, and allocate treatments. In August 2020, the *New England Journal of Medicine* published an article titled "Hidden in Plain Sight—Reconsidering the Use of Race Correction in Clinical Algorithms." The article included a three-page table of race-corrective clinical formulas commonly used in nearly all medical specialties that unfairly disadvantage Black patients (Vyas et al. 2020, 876–78). Clinicians use these algorithms to make diagnoses, assess risk, and create treatment plans. As the authors explain, "many of these race-adjusted algorithms guide decisions in ways that may direct more attention and more resources to white patients than to members of racial and ethnic minorities" (Vyas et al. 2020, 874). Tracking health disparities at the population level helps illuminate how biased medical resources differentially affect already marginalized and precarious groups.

Racial and gendered bias in medical research and clinical algorithms constitutes gaps in the collective hermeneutic resources clinicians rely on to make diagnoses and prescribe treatments. This unfair hermeneutical landscape underlies many individual instances of medical gaslighting.[3]

On the Harms of Medical Gaslighting

Delayed Diagnosis and Other Measurable Harms

The harms suffered by those who face persistent medical gaslighting may seem obvious—delayed diagnosis, misdiagnosis, disease progression, increased morbidity, increased suffering, and decreased access to medical resources and treatment. Diagnostic delays—the time between symptom onset and diagnosis—are a particularly useful metric for demonstrating the measurable harms incurred by persistent medical gaslighting. An Anglo-American study found a mean delay of 11.73 ± 9.05 years from onset of pain to endometriosis diagnosis in the United States (Hadfield et al. 1996,

879). A European study on diagnostic delay in patients with Ehlers-Danlos syndrome in several European countries found a fourteen-year average delay for 50 percent of respondents and a twenty-eight-year delay for 75 percent of respondents (Kole and Faurisson 2009, 43). During that time a patient will continue suffering, spend unnecessary resources seeking healthcare, and likely experience worsening disease. However, simply tracking the number of years until diagnosis is insufficient to account for the depth of the epistemic harm incurred by those facing persistent medical gaslighting while they wait for medical recognition and treatment.

Consider Abby Norman's journey toward endometriosis diagnosis as chronicled in her memoir, *Ask Me about My Uterus*. When she was nineteen years old, Abby fell ill and her body changed forever. She began to experience such intense pelvic pain that she could not leave her bed for a full week. Having grown up with a challenging family life, Abby excelled in school and secured a full scholarship to Sarah Lawrence college, one contingent on her continued academic success. After a week of missed class, her roommate dragged her to the ER, where the doctor normalized her pain as a combination of stress and a UTI. As she recounts:

> By the time the doctor came in to examine me, I was even more exhausted than when I'd arrived. I was aware that I was still crying and worried that while crying I couldn't possibly present my situation rationally. The doctor seemed completely unsurprised by my distress. I was a Sarah Lawrence girl—historically what you might call "bright and wound tight" . . . He also seemed uncomfortable, which made me feel worse. I was suddenly flooded by memories of being warned not to be "difficult" as a child. I stopped talking after several futile attempts to explain, discharged without so much as a CT scan, prescribed a hefty dose of antibiotics and encouraged to drink my weight in cranberry juice. (Norman 2018, 14–15)

Abby's initial ER experience reveals the complex intersection of social meanings that determine how her illness testimony is taken up. She cannot simply be sick and in pain and cry freely in reaction to her situation. Instead she is preoccupied with how her display of emotions interferes with her being read as a rational person, able to accurately describe her experience. Her status as a young woman casts her as emotionally unstable, "high-strung," and "wound up" from the start, delegitimizing the wrenching pain that has ruled her life and inviting easy explanations from her physician: stress and a urinary tract infection.

Reacting to her display of emotion, the doctor "seems uncomfortable" and rushes her out without performing any tests to verify his diagnosis. She recounts messaging she received as a child not to be difficult, as if being sick and being difficult were equivalent such that she might will her pain away. In her description of this initial medical encounter, Abby captures the various intersecting horizons of intelligibility that mold her experience of illness within the contemporary medical establishment. They constitute what Lisa Guenther names "quasi-transcendentals" or "the social structures that shape experience" (Guenther 2019, 12). These social structures do not uniformly determine experience, because individuals are differentially affected based on their social positions, but, at the same time, they form certain patterns that contour the very experience of illness.

Abby seeks out a second and then a third opinion and receives several scans that reveal no abnormalities and are used to reinforce the clinician's opinion that her pain is normal. This scene is repeated for several months while her pain worsens. Having used the customary two allowed absences per semester in all her college courses, Abby's grades drop rapidly as attendance policies are enforced. She meets with a dean who suggests a medical leave of absence, which she has no choice but to accept. She never returns to school.

After leaving Sarah Lawrence, Abby returns home to and sees an OB-GYN who finally believes her enough to perform an exploratory laparoscopic surgery. The surgeon discovers a large ovarian cyst filled with old blood and a torqued fallopian tube, the ostensible source of her suffering. However, the surgeon opts to only partially remove the cyst, preserving her fertility over minimizing her pain against her stated wishes.[4] Shortly after, the pain returns.

Filled with self-doubt yet consumed by worsening pain, Abby begins researching her symptoms and eventually finds an endometriosis specialist who is able to surgically excise the adhesions that have been knitting her internal organs together and scarring her abdominal wall, causing her incredible pain. Before she receives the endometriosis diagnosis, her suffering is considered largely medically unexplained, and she is viewed as a malingerer and hypochondriac. This message is communicated to her countless times in clinical settings, both directly and indirectly. She has begun to doubt herself and her own bodily perceptions such that she wonders if she is somehow inventing the debilitating pain that rules her life.

The harms Abby has suffered are both calculable and incalculable, material and epistemic. During the many years between symptom onset and diagnosis, her uterus became so badly scarred that she will likely experience permanent pain. She has spent unnecessary years suffering, and the financial burden of seeking treatment has been significant both in terms of lost wages due to sick days and out-of-pocket expenses to see her specialist. What is far less calculable, and, I argue, far more detrimental, is the epistemic harm to her sense of self and her relationship to her body. How should we understand the harm she endures?

Embodied Epistemic Harm

I am interested in elucidating the kind of wounding that occurs when an individual's lived experience of illness is persistently denied and dismissed by medical authorities. Building on Miranda Fricker's account of epistemic harm as objectification and loss of confidence, I develop an understanding of the harm of medical gaslighting as the emergence of radical bodily self-doubt that erodes a person's ability to interpret their bodily sensations. Phenomenological insights following the tradition of Merleau-Ponty can deepen our understanding of how this kind of epistemic harm is disclosed through sensory experiences.

Fricker identifies two harms of testimonial injustice that are particularly relevant to the case of medical gaslighting: 1) epistemic objectification and 2) loss of intellectual confidence, or self-doubt. Taking feminist critiques of sexual objectification as her model, she understands epistemic objectification as the intrinsic harm of testimonial injustice. As she explains, "testimonial injustice demotes the speaker from informant to source of information, from subject to object" (Fricker 2007, 133). In medical contexts, this distinction is especially slippery and complicated. Contemporary medicine requires treating patients as both sources of information and informants. Philosophers of medicine make a distinction between illness as the subjective lived experience of being sick and disease as the objective pathology to which the science of medicine can be applied. While individuals have privileged, private, subjective knowledge of bodily experiences and sensations, this is matched by an opacity with regard to the objective qualities of one's body such as white blood cell count or cholesterol level that are used to diagnose diseases.

There is not always a clear correspondence between the feeling of illness and measurable biomarkers of disease. As we have learned during the global pandemic, a person can feel absolutely fine while being infected with the SARS-COV-2 virus and spreading it to others. A cancerous tumor can grow for years before symptoms arise. There is a limit to what I can know about my body through bodily sensations, and there is a limit to what others can know about my body through scientific measurement. Subjective symptoms like pain, fatigue, and nausea cannot be easily verified through diagnostic testing. The practice of medicine thus necessitates treating patients as both informants and sources of information.

It is important to note that objectification in medical practice is not uniform across all specialties. The way in which the pathologist objectifies a tissue sample is different from the way the sonographer peers into the pained abdomen. The way a primary care clinician might make prejudicial judgments about a patient based on surface characteristics like gender, weight, and race is different from the objectification of a surgeon who may detach themselves from the humanity of the patient in order to better perform their craft. Objectification in medicine is neither uniform nor necessarily problematic.

For Fricker, epistemic objectification becomes morally problematic when a person is treated as a mere object in a way that "signifies a more general denial of their subjectivity" (Fricker 2007, 133). In cases of persistent medical gaslighting, certain modes of objectification can be particularly pernicious, especially those that involve using information gleaned from the body to discount the seriousness of subjective symptoms for which no biomarkers exist. Recall Abby Norman's experience with pelvic imaging before her endometriosis diagnosis. Imaging technologies such as ultrasound, MRI, and CT are unable to detect endometriosis, one of the most common causes of symptoms like Abby's. While these limitations are known, the objective yet inaccurate measurement of Abby's body was used to normalize her pain. Receiving this message again and again planted a seed distrust in her body, reinforcing the already precarious relationship she has to her ailing flesh.

This makes an enemy of the flesh, effectively splitting the ill person into the sick objective body that reliably provides information to the clinician and casting the gaslit person as a "crazy" and unreliable perceiver of their own bodily sensations. This form of objectification distorts the signals of the body, the songs and cries of the flesh, and sows doubt at that very ownmost level of sensory perception. It effectively makes an enemy of the body, intensifying feelings of bodily alienation and betrayal. This injury is cumulative; it is the result of repeated instances of medical gaslighting that slowly erode self-trust.

According to Fricker, what is at stake in this kind of epistemic harm is that a person is being treated "as if she were a lesser rational being" or "in a way that denies or undermines their status as a rational agent" (Fricker 2007, 136). This understanding is helpful in articulating why the charge of psychogenic illness is so deeply troubling to many who face medical gaslighting. However, Fricker's commitment to a Cartesian account of the rational self-transparent subject omits something important about how this kind of epistemic injury appears within bodily sensations themselves, how it is felt, experienced, and lived out. Key insights from the phenomenological tradition help clarify and deepen our understanding of this injury as a distortion and disruption of embodied self-relation.

Phenomenologists of medicine, disability, and embodiment often turn to the classical distinction between the objective body (Körper) and the lived body (Leib) to explicate various forms of objectification that take place in contemporary medical practice. This distinction was first made by Husserl in *Ideas II* and later developed by Merleau-Ponty as the foundation of his phenomenology of the body in *The Phenomenology of Perception*.

Körper refers to the body as a thing or object that appears to others and is available for observation, measurement, and analysis. Körper is extended in space and fundamentally public, open to the scrutiny of others. My body cannot occupy the same space of as the body of another, and vice-versa. This objective quality of the body differs significantly from an individual's experience of their own body through which the world is experienced. Leib signifies this other, more primordial sense of the body as it is lived out. It is this sense of the body, as lived body, that is typically prioritized by phenomenologists of illness in critiques of objectifying or instrumentalist medical practices. On this account, Körper names the public, objective, and material body, and Leib signifies my ownmost inner experience of my body.

While the distinction between Korper and Leib appears to map onto illness/disease, public/private, and subject/object distinctions, upon deeper interrogation, it does not easily form such a strict binary. There is dimension to the lived body that is inherently ambiguous and conditioned by the way it appears to others. In other words, even though our embodied experiences feel private and subjective, there is a dimension in which they are also intersubjective. As Jenny Slatman has compellingly argued, when contemporary phenomenologists of medicine employ the Körper/Leib distinction, they risk reestablishing the very dualism intended for critique (Slatman 2019, 204).

Slatman argues for a more ambiguous and nuanced understanding of Leib as a "conditioned condition." That is, on her account, the double ontology of the body is inherently social insofar as the social meanings that are attached to one's objective body affect the lived experience of that body. For Slatman, as for Merleau-Ponty in his later work, the double ontology of the body as both Körper and Leib is central to understanding how medical encounters affect the experience of illness. As she explains, "the way in which 'the world' conditions subjectivity and agency should be directly related to the social meaning of the body, which is given with the fact that the body is not just a *Leib* but also, and equally primordial, a *Körper*" (Slatman 2014, 533).

This tension appears in bodily sensations that we typically take to be private and subjective such as pain. Despite Elaine Scarry's famous assertion that having pain may be thought of as "the most vibrant example of what it is to have certainty," phenomenological accounts of pain reveal it to be a fundamentally paradoxical, ambiguous, and mediated sensation (Scarry 1985, 4). As Drew Leder explains:

> Pain manifests as both sensation and interpretation, certain and yet uncertain to the sufferer and others. It unfolds in both a present and projective time, exhibiting a never-changing and yet ever-changing pattern. It is seemingly located simultaneously in body and mind, self and other, the here and everywhere. Presenting as both in-control and out-of-control, pain unleashes productive and destructive forces in the realm of meaning. . . . Pain is more than an aversive physical sensation. It can trigger a series of experiential paradoxes that shock and destabilize one's world. (Leder 2016, 459)

Pain is not static, and being-in-pain is not a simple matter of truth or falsity, certainty or doubt. Pain, through its many paradoxes and ambiguities, reveals how we are caught up in various horizons of meaning that register in the very experience of pain itself. Though we colloquially take pain to be a private, subjective experience, the feeling of pain, its intensity and tenacity, is modulated by context. Various horizons of meaning inform how pain is interpreted and felt: religious, medical, familial, interpersonal, cultural, and historical. Leder writes of how his chronic leg pain morphed as different diagnoses were suggested:

> With each new interpretive perspective, the sensed pain itself changed in quality, intensity, meaning, and affective content.

> The pain of a possible stress fracture felt sharp, as if something inside was indeed broken. As "inflammation," it exuded warmth; when varicose veins seemed the cause I felt heaviness in the leg; the ultimate diagnosis of a peripheral neuropathy highlighted the pain's stinging and burning qualities. Also, based on the shifting prognoses, these pains felt at times more serious or less so, on the way to recovery or depressingly untreatable. (Leder 2016, 446)

For Leder, pain is far from a clear and immediate experience marked by certainty. Rather, the very feeling of pain, its intensity, sharpness, temporality, meaning, and affectivity shift with different explanations. His phenomenological account reveals that the experience of pain is never pure or immediate and never fully certain. Pain demands explanation and interpretation, pushing him to seek out diagnoses, prognoses, and treatments. As he encounters different horizons of meaning, the sensory experience itself changes.

The presence of one diagnosis over another can change the very lived experience of pain. Inversely, the refusal of diagnosis—the denial of pain and its clinical significance—has the capacity to mediate sensory experience as well, inspiring distrust, self-doubt, and confusion about the many and varied cries of the flesh.

We can see this kind of doubt play out in Abby Norman's testimony: "Maybe all of this was in my head. . . . What if I was lying to everyone—even myself? What if the pain wasn't real at all, what if it never had been?" (Norman 2018, 181–82). After being persistently gaslit about her symptoms, Abby's experience of her own body is infused with an additional layer of self-doubt. She feels pain and doubts whether that pain is real. She feels bloated, observes her distended stomach, but wonders if that bloating is imaginary. Every sensation is disrupted by this extra layer of skepticism and scrutiny. What is at stake is not just whether she is ill and if she can find relief, but also if she is sane and if she can reliably read her body's messages. Was the charge of hypochondria a self-fulfilling prophecy, or is she still sick?

According to the medical perspective and paradigm she has internalized, the "reality" of her illness hinges on it being fully physiological and therefore legitimate. She worries that her symptoms flow from her unresolved childhood trauma, which somehow makes them less real and less worthy of care:

> Had the trauma from my childhood, which I had diligently worked to resolve, which I had taken copious antidepressants to dull the ache of, somehow escaped my brain and taken up residence in my bones. . . . Had my brain succeeded in convincing my body that it had no right to live? Could emotional pain actually cause your physical body to slowly rot away, like some sort of dramatic, psychological consumption? Was I really losing my mind rather than my body? Was I a Freudian hysteric with an iPhone? (Norman 2018, 182)

The charge of madness, present at nearly all of Abby's clinical encounters, has infused a deep sense of self-doubt and conflicting self-narratives. She is gripped by an internal restless dialectic. On the one hand, her illness is "real," there is something wrong with her body that impacts her daily life severely and causes her to feel pain almost constantly. It is legitimate and medically relevant, something that has befallen her for which she is not responsible. On the other hand, she wonders if this pain is imaginary, it's all in her head, the result of some unresolved childhood trauma. For this she feels blameworthy and underserving of medical attention. The voice of doubt mirrors the messaging she receives from the medical practitioners she encounters. It fractures her sense of self such that she does not fully trust herself to know if she is sick, despite the persistence of her symptoms.

I want to suggest that experiencing persistent medical gaslighting can thrust an individual into this kind of restless dialectic between the lived reality of chronic illness, of living with pain, of being unwell, of being unable to partake in regular activities, of knowing that "I am suffering," and the internalized voice infused with medical authority that "nothing's wrong," that "it's all in my head." This compounds the struggles an ill person faces and produces a sense of despair and hopelessness with regard to the possibility of relief. The erosion of confidence in bodily knowledge creates an additional level of doubt, insecurity, and mistrust in oneself that can grow and overtake other areas of life.

It is the nature of pain as ambiguous and paradoxical, characterized by both certainty and doubt, mediated by shifting hermeneutic frames, that makes it so vulnerable to medical gaslighting and enables medical gaslighting to be so damaging. Bodily knowledge and awareness are a primordial part of human subjectivity, and living in a state of perpetual doubt and anxiety about bodily sensations is a deeply precarious form of embodiment. Thoughts like "Is this serious?" "Is this real?" "Am I just crazy?" interrupt the easy sense of fidelity that typically accompanies physical sensations as we move through the world engaged in projects. To distrust one's bodily sensations is an extreme form of fractured subjectivity and dispossession. And it is one of the most profound harms medical gaslighting can inflict.

Notes

1. I do not intend to use the term women here in a gender-exclusionary way. I acknowledge that many of the conditions I discuss, especially those related to female reproductive anatomy, also affect trans men and nonbinary people, and that they likely face additional layers of gender discrimination and other barriers when seeking healthcare. Transwomen also face different mechanisms of medical gaslighting such as the reduction of symptoms to hormonal therapies.

2. Many women have reported severe side effects, including intense pain, bleeding, and autoimmune disease onset from the use of transvaginal surgical pelvic mesh used to treat pelvic organ prolapse and urinary stress incontinence. For more information on the recent legal settlement about this medical device, see Keown 2021.

3. The structural gaslighting framework proposed by Elena Ruíz (2020) helps elucidate the connections between this hermeneutic backdrop and individual instances of medical gaslighting in more depth; however, this analysis exceeds the scope of the current chapter.

4. Women, particularly young women, are frequently gaslit about their desire not to have children. Fertility is often prioritized over pain or other forms of suffering related to reproductive illnesses. It is incredibly difficult for young women to find a surgeon willing to perform a hysterectomy, even if it would bring immense relief. Similarly, women who are not ill but simply do not wish to procreate are denied tubal ligation surgeries under the paternalistic assumption they will later change their minds.

Works Cited

Carel, Havi, and Ian James Kidd. 2017. "Epistemic Injustice in Medicine and Healthcare." In *The Routledge Handbook of Epistemic Injustice*, edited by Ian James Kidd, José Medina, and Gaile M. Pohlhaus. 336–46. New York: Routledge.

Darshali A. Vyas, Leo G. Eisenstein, and David S. Jones. 2020. "Hidden in Plain Sight—Reconsidering the Use of Race Correction in Clinical Algorithms." *New England Journal of Medicine* 383 (9): 774–82.

Dusenbery, Maya. 2018. *Doing Harm: The Truth about How Bad Medicine and Lazy Science Leave Women Dismissed, Misdiagnosed, and Sick*. New York: HarperOne.

Fricker, Miranda. 2007. *Epistemic Injustice: Power and the Ethics of Knowing*. New York: Oxford University Press.

Graham, Sarah. n.d. "About." *Hysterical Women Blog*. https://hystericalwomen.co.uk/about/.

———. 2021. (@sarhargraham7writer). "In Honour of #EndoMonth, This Week's #Shitmydoctorsays Is All About the Shit That Doctors Say to People with #Endometriosis. (And My God Is There a Lot of It.)" *Instagram*, March 19, 2021. https://www.instagram.com/p/CMmNqMrjL2I/.

———. 2021. (@sarhargraham7writer). "#ShitMyDoctorSays Is Back. Today's Horrifying Quotes Were Kindly Shared with Me by @Slingthemesh, The Game-Changing Campaign Against What Has Become the Defining Women's Health Scandal of Recent Years: The Use of Pelvic Mesh Implants." *Instagram*, January 25, 2021. https://www.instagram.com/p/CMmNqMrjL2I/.

Guenther, Lisa. 2020. "Critical Phenomenology." In *50 Concepts for a Critical Phenomenology*, edited by Gail Weiss, Ann V. Murphy, and Gayle Salamon, 11–16. Evanston, IL: Northwestern University Press.

Hadfield, Ruth, Helen Mardon, David Barlow, and Stephen Kennedy. 1996. "Delay in the Diagnosis of Endometriosis: A Survey of Women from the USA and the UK." *Human Reproduction* 11 (4): 878–80.

Haskell, Rob. "Serena Williams on Motherhood, Marriage, and Making Her Comeback." *Vogue*, January 10, 2018. https://www.vogue.com/article/serena-williams-vogue-cover-interview-february-2018.

Ivy, Veronica [McKinnon, Rachel]. 2017. "Allies Behaving Badly: Gaslighting as Epistemic Injustice." In *The Routledge Handbook of Epistemic Injustice*, edited by Ian James Kidd, José Medina, and Gaile M. Pohlhaus, 167–74. New York: Routledge.

Keown, Alex. 2021. "Boston Scientific to Pay $189 Million in Vaginal Mesh Lawsuit." *BioSpace*, March 24, 2021. https://www.biospace.com/article/boston-scientific-settles-multistate-vaginal-mesh-lawsuit-for-189-million/.

Kole, Anna, and François Faurisson. 2009. *The Voice of 12,000 Patients: Experiences and Expectations of Rare Disease Patients on Diagnosis and Care in Europe*. Paris: European Rare Disease Council (EURODIS). https://www.eurordis.org/IMG/pdf/voice_12000_patients/EURORDISCARE_FULLBOOKr.pdf.

Leder, Drew. 2016. "The Experiential Paradoxes of Pain." *Journal of Medicine and Philosophy* 41: 444–60. https://doi.org/10.1093/jmp/jhw020.

National Institutes of Health. 2001. "NIH Policy and Guidelines on The Inclusion of Women and Minorities as Subjects in Clinical Research." October 9, 2001. https://grants.nih.gov/policy/inclusion/women-and-minorities/guidelines.htm.

National Institutes of Health. 2024. "Estimates of Funding for Various Research, Condition, and Disease Categories (RCDC)." May 14, 2024. https://report.nih.gov/funding/categorical-spending#/.

Norman, Abby. 2018. *Ask Me about My Uterus: A Quest to Make Doctors Believe in Women's Pain*. New York: Nation Books.

Ruiz, Elena. 2020. "Cultural Gaslighting." *Hypatia* 35 (4): 687–713. https://doi.org/10.107/hyp.2020.33.

Scarry, Elaine. 1985. *The Body in Pain: The Making and Unmaking of the World*. New York: Oxford University Press.

Slatman, Jenny. 2014. "Multiple Dimensions of Embodiment in Medical Practices." *Medicine, Healthcare, and Philosophy* 17: 549–57. https://doi.org/10.1007/s11019-014-9544-2.

———. 2019. "The Körper/Leib Distinction." In *50 Concepts for a Critical Phenomenology*, edited by Gail Weiss, Ann V. Murphy, and Gayle Salamon, 203–9. Evanston, IL: Northwestern University Press.

Wenger, N. K. 2012. "Women and Coronary Heart Disease: A Century after Herrick: Understudied, Underdiagnosed, and Undertreated." *Circulation* 126 (5): 604–11.

11

Structural Gaslighting

Hurricane María and Recovery in Puerto Rico

Taína M. Figueroa

¡Techo seguro ya!

Secure roof, already!

—2021 campaign slogan by Taller Salud for dignified housing, including secure roofs still unrepaired from Hurricane María.[1]

In October 2017, three weeks after Hurricane María hit the Caribbean, I traveled to Puerto Rico. My extended family, living in the interior mountainous region of Ciales, had described a situation in which access to filtered water and power was going to be a long time coming. We brought medical supplies, water filtration systems, solar lights, and solar panels. Upon arrival, driving from San Juan to Ciales, I was struck by the lack of any "official personnel" on the ground—no visible presence of military aid or the Federal Emergency Management Agency (FEMA) or the national guard.

When we reached Ciales, we saw that the mayor and community members had turned the Cancha Angel Rafael "Chucho" Figueroa (outdoor basketball court with roof) into a makeshift headquarters.[2] It was three weeks after a Category IV storm, and I did not see a single power-line worker in Ciales during that first of many trips. My first sighting of a federal/military vehicle was at the closest functioning Walmart, fifteen miles from Ciales, where an armed HMMVV sat by the entrance with its barrel aimed at the long line of us waiting to get inside.

Four months following the landfall of Hurricane María in Puerto Rico, my grandparents were still without power. Neighbors were dying because they couldn't store insulin, and family members who could, fled to the continental United States. Three years later, as my plane prepared to land in Puerto Rico, blue tarps on houses still waiting to be repaired dotted the horizon. This chapter emerged out of my need to understand what happened—or didn't—in Puerto Rico after María. Because of the archipelago's colonial status with the United States, for those with ties to Puerto Rico, what happened wasn't a surprise. However, as anthropologist Yarimar Bonilla, who has written extensively on the aftermath of Hurricane María, writes, "[Local residents] were forced into an affective reckoning with the kinds of structural violence they had been enduring for decades" (Bonilla 2020, 1). What were the federal policies and practices at play that determined how Puerto Ricans experienced the weeks, months, and years following the storm, especially compared with the US response to other 2017 natural disasters? And how were these policies related to the official narratives the federal government circulated about the hurricane recovery?

The year 2017 was difficult for many across the United States. Hurricane Harvey devastated Texas and Louisiana, and Hurricane Irma left its mark on the US Virgin Islands, Puerto Rico, Florida, and Georgia just a few weeks before Hurricane María. Those on the West Coast of the country battled wildfires across California. Emergency declarations were issued for all these disasters. However, there was a marked difference in how disaster response and recovery were mobilized following Hurricane María versus Hurricanes Harvey and Irma.

When a major disaster occurs in the United States, there are both short- and long-term recovery and response efforts that are activated. Hurricane María should have triggered a massive and coordinated response from FEMA and the US Department of Housing and Urban Development (HUD) as witnessed in Texas after Hurricane Harvey. It did not. The scale and scope of damage wrought by Hurricane María was massive (Willison et al. 2019). All communications, power, and clean water for many were lost across the archipelagos of Puerto Rico and the US Virgin Islands. Close to 3.5 million people were affected, living without clean water or power for weeks, months, up to a year in some parts of Puerto Rico. Hospitals ran on generators for months.

As this chapter demonstrates, the federal government increased oversight and added delay tactics in granting Puerto Rico access to aid resources and monies, which continues to stall recovery to this day. Simultaneously, they circulated a narrative about María recovery that took two forms: denial (e.g., only sixty-four people died) or a recognition of the harms and delays in the recovery that placed blame on Puerto Ricans themselves (Straub 2021, 1617). How were Puerto Ricans to blame? Puerto Rico's debt.

The municipal debt Puerto Rico had been grappling with for years before Hurricane María was of primary concern and used as an indication of Puerto Rican corruption and "financial malfeasance" (US Department of Housing and Urban Development 2019c). This invocation of debt signaled Puerto Ricans as culpable and disposable. This process, in which institutions mask actual policies and practices that produce harms and violences against certain populations through the circulation of interpretive frameworks that either deny and shift focus from the harm and/or place blame for the harm on the violated community itself, is *structural gaslighting*. This chapter discusses the development of structural gaslighting in recent literature on gaslighting in racist legal practices, white feminism, and white settler colonialism. Puerto Rico then serves as an example of structural gaslighting at work. Finally, I turn to what structural gaslighting in the case of Puerto Rico reveals about the relationship between structural gaslighting and colonialism.

Structural Gaslighting

Recent critical scholarship on gaslighting as developed by Nora Berenstain, Elena Ruíz, Angelique Davis, and Rose Ernst move beyond gaslighting as an interpersonal phenomenon to reveal the cultural and structural forms of gaslighting that are foundational to *racio-colonial capitalism* (Bonilla 2020, 2). These structural gaslighting theorists are concerned with different but interrelated political, social, and economic systems that structural gaslighting seeks to uphold, from white supremacy (Davis and Ernst 2019) to oppression more generally (Berenstain 2020) to white settler colonialism (Ruiz 2020). White settler colonialism and white supremacy are forms of oppression, and white settler colonialism and white supremacist state structures can be understood as parts of the same process: one that seeks white wealth accumulation. Developed by Yarimar Bonilla, who expands on Cedric Robinson's concept of racial capitalism, *racio-colonial capitalism* captures the interrelated political, social, and economic systems these structural gaslighting theorists are concerned with. But Bonilla's concept also makes room for practices that are often referred to as "disaster-capitalism" and the unique social/economic/political history of Puerto Rico. For Bonilla, *racio-colonial capitalism* describes this political and economic landscape:

> [Hurricane] Maria reveals the insufficiencies of certain theories of "disaster capitalism" that fail to show how it is the "slow violence" of colonial and racial governance which sets the stage for the accelerated dispossession made evident in a state of emergency. That is, the accelerated forms of extraction and dispossession evident in the wake of modern disasters are conditioned by the subjectivities and technologies of the colonial encounter. For this reason, I argue that disaster capitalism needs to be understood as foundationally a form of *racio-colonial capitalism*, that emerges directly out of the capitalist incubator of plantation slavery. (Bonilla 2020, 2)[3]

This framing allows for the response and policies used by the United States in Puerto Rico after the storm to be situated within a history of colonial political and economic policies that in fact are not exceptional but common. Racio-colonial capitalism as developed by Bonilla also places what happened in Puerto Rico within a "broad US archipelago of racialized neglect" that includes the deaths and displacement of Black Americans after Hurricane Katrina in New Orleans, water poisoning in Flint, Michigan, and what she terms "urban ruin and social neglect like Detroit" (2020, 2). This framing allows for thinking about Puerto Rico as a part of the racial-imperial governance structure of the United States that arises out of a 400-year colonial history of Indigenous genocide and land theft alongside plantation slavery that preceded the arrival of the United States in 1898 in Puerto Rico but is still very much with us.[4]

Theorists of structural gaslighting identify gaslighting as a process at the level of structures that impact whole communities and populations. They identify patterns of structural gaslighting as central to how racio-colonial capitalist structures operate to control resistant narratives or epistemologies that may undermine or reveal oppressive structures and how they are maintained. Structural gaslighting serves to eliminate resistance so that the project of racio-colonial capitalism can continue. This structure of racio-colonial capitalism is aimed at extraction: land, wealth, and labor through a coloniality of power that operates on a racialized gendered hierarchy. Within this framework, structural gaslighting serves to obscure the existence and functioning mechanisms of a racio-colonial capitalist power.

Angelique Davis and Rose Ernst's scholarship focus on a particular type of structural gaslighting—racial gaslighting—which obscures white supremacist structures by "pathologizing those who resist" (2019, 761). Racial gaslighting happens through the development of what Davis and Ernst call racial spectacles or "narratives that obfuscate the existence of a white supremacist state power structure" (2019, 763). They demonstrate how these racial spectacles pathologize those who resist through two court cases, *Korematsu v. United States* (1944) and the *Commonwealth of Kentucky v. Braden* (1955). In both cases, individuals were criminalized for attempting to disrupt state-sanctioned racist policies or practices. Fred Korematsu, a US citizen, did not comply with Executive Order 9066, which forced Japanese Americans into concentration camps and detention centers during WWII, and he was therefore criminalized as an "enemy alien." Carl and Anne Braden attempted to resist institutional redlining by purchasing a home in an all-white neighborhood for Andrew and Charlotte Wade, who were Black. The Wades' home was subsequently bombed, and the Bradens were charged with sedition—not the ex-policeman who most likely planted the bomb (Davis and Ernst 2019, 765–68).

In both cases, the US government not only denied that racist practices were at work, gaslighting both Korematsu and the Bradens, but in pathologizing Korematsu's and the Braden's attempts to resist and expose racist structures, they sent a broader warning to all Japanese Americans in the case of Korematsu and to both white and Black Americans who might consider similar acts or even interpret these practices as racist in the case of the Bradens. This is racial gaslighting—structural gaslighting that is operating both on a micro level to the individuals Fred Korematsu, the Bradens, and the Wades, but with much broader impact. It functions through structures and institutions and impacts communities. Davis and Ernst emphasize that structural gaslighting here is aimed at neutralizing resistance to existing state structures of oppression.[5]

Nora Berenstain expands on the concept of structural gaslighting through a critique of the discipline of white feminism. White feminism, which never announces itself as such, lays claim to a universal feminism.

White feminism then is itself constituted through a process of structural gaslighting as it denies the particular and contextual structures that inform the creation of white feminist theory. This leads those whose lived experience differs from white feminists to doubt their own experiences or how they understand and interpret their experiences. Berenstain sees structural gaslighting then as:

> any conceptual work that functions to obscure the nonaccidental connections between structures of oppression and the patterns of harm that they produce and license. Individuals engage in structural gaslighting when they invoke epistemologies and ideologies of domination that actively disappear and obscure the actual causes, mechanisms, and effects of oppression. Structural oppressions are maintained in part through systems of justification that locate the causes of pervasive inequalities in flaws of the oppressed groups themselves while obscuring the social systems and mechanisms of power that uphold them. (Berenstain 2020, 734)

Berenstain illustrates this definition through an analysis of Miranda Fricker's development of the concept of hermeneutical injustice now taught as foundational work in feminist epistemology. Fricker assigns "epistemic bad luck" to experiences of sexual violence that are direct impacts of oppressive structures of domination and erases the long history of any women of color theorizing of and resistance to workplace sexual violence or what has come to be called sexual harassment. Berenstain agrees with Davis and Ernst, who also recognize that structural gaslighting can occur regardless of a perpetrator's intent, but Berenstain goes farther by repeatedly reminding readers that this process of structural gaslighting is *non-accidental*. Elena Ruiz, whom I turn to next, also emphasizes that the differential harms that certain populations experience are by design and not random.[6]

Ruiz and Berenstain's pieces on structural gaslighting appear as part of a cluster series in *Hypatia* on gaslighting and epistemic injustice. Both authors focus on examples that illustrate how structural gaslighting functions through the realm of the epistemic—through the theoretical tools and narratives employed and circulated for interpreting the harms and violence people experience. Berenstain examines Fricker's concept of "hermeneutic injustice" and Ruiz the concept of "medical gaslighting" (among others). What Ruiz's complex analysis of medical gaslighting makes clear is the relationship between the epistemic injustice that lies at the heart of structural gaslighting and the very real material outcomes these seemingly abstract epistemic injustices are designed to elicit.[7] "Medical gaslighting" is described as an interpersonal phenomenon in which a clinical professional doubts or minimizes the reported illness of a patient or attributes symptoms to psychological factors. When medical gaslighting is deployed in relation to Black maternal health outcomes, it fails to account for the long-standing structures and practices built into medical care in the United States: everything from histories of medical exploitation of Black Americans from the days of slavery to current-day researchers blaming Black infertility on STI rates (i.e., infertility is blamed on risk-inducing personal choice applied to whole populations as opposed to histories of forced sterilization, higher exposure to toxins, etc.). "Medical gaslighting" as it pertains to Black maternal health outcomes must acknowledge the institutional policies and practices that structure the experiences of Black women and how Black maternal health outcomes are researched. Ruiz writes: "A structural approach to medical gaslighting is helpful here because it illustrates that the gaslighting in question is not simply from the presiding clinical provider: a tightly woven net of policies, training manuals, advisory boards, disciplinary and institutional procedures—even medical equipment—upholds the *structured inattention* to the productive health needs of . . . Black women who continue to have the highest maternal mortality rates of any group for which metrics are kept" (Ruiz 2020, 693). A narrative that focuses on the individual clinician serves to mask the oppressive racist structures that continue to exact deadly outcomes for Black mothers, keeping those structures in place; in other words, this epistemic process can impact life outcomes of whole populations. In her critique of gaslighting as interpersonal phenomenon, Ruiz clarifies that "the notion of gaslighting as interpersonal, emotive harm works to foreclose awareness of ongoing cultural processes through organized failures of understanding. These failures are functionalized through vast networks of settler institutions, social policies, and publicly licensed resources of interpretation" (Ruiz 2020, 688–89). Cultural gaslighting, for Ruiz, then, "shows how rhetorical strategies that name a public grievance yet actively *abate relief or remedy of that grievance* are some of the most commonly taught and preserved interpretive resources in settler epistemic systems" (2020, 705).

The fundamentals of structural gaslighting that emerge from these theorists, which I apply to the case of Puerto Rico, are as follows:

1. The What: Structural gaslighting is an epistemological phenomenon and is deployed through particular narratives or "publicly licensed resources of interpretation" that have material impact (at its most severe—death) by design on whole populations and communities.

2. The How: Structural gaslighting masks the oppressive systems, policies, and practices that are actually functioning through:

   a. Structured inattention (ignoring or denying the grievance/harm), and/or

   b. Recognizing the grievance or harm that is happening and

      i. Locating the cause of the grievance or harm in the oppressed group themselves

      ii. And/or pathologizing those who resist[8]

The case of Puerto Rico in the wake of Hurricane María offers us an example of how this structural gaslighting functions in a blunt way in public spheres (outside the specialized language of the courtroom or feminist epistemology texts or public health datasets). At its most basic, in this case, structural gaslighting takes the following form: the government offers a particular interpretive framework, a narrative, that acknowledges a public grievance/harm but masks the actual structural systems of domination and oppression at work in the creation of that public grievance/harm/violence. It masks the public grievance or harm by denying/ignoring it or recognizing it and blaming those being harmed. In the case of Puerto Rico and the federal government's response to Hurricane María, the harms include the deaths of at minimum 2,975 to upwards of 4,645 people and the permanent displacement of more than 130,000 people.[9] What were the actual systems, policies, and practices that contributed to these deaths and displacements? How did they differ from the recovery efforts of the 2017 natural disasters on the US mainland?

Federal Policies and Practices[10]

Disaster response, at the federal level in the United States, comes in two general phases—short and long term—via different but related and collaborative agencies—FEMA, SBA, and HUD. Here I argue that the federal government employed a deliberate and differential strategy intended to delay and limit the federal response to Hurricane María through FEMA, HUD, and the entire chain of aid and services. Both FEMA (DHS Office of the Inspector General 2020) and HUD (HUD Office of Inspector General 2021) have produced documentation on the severe delays and oversight added to the accessing of aid for Puerto Rico, as has Puerto Rico's Centro de Periodismo Investigativo/Center for Investigative Journalism (2021a) and Charley Willison et al. in *BMJ Global Health* (2019).

When disaster declarations are made, FEMA is the agency tasked with handling short-term disaster recovery. Through FEMA, federal monies and logistical resources are engaged when a state or local area cannot manage response to disasters via existing resources and logistics. FEMA can be used to help with everything from organizing search and rescue missions, to providing food and shelter, to engaging government agencies to help with distribution of aid, to debris removal, to medical care, and so forth. FEMA funds aid to areas impacted by natural disasters through its Disaster Relief Fund following congressional allocation of adequate funding.

Longer-term recovery from disasters then shifts to HUD. This longer-term recovery funding is accessed through Community Development Block Grants for Disaster Recovery. Because of the plethora of natural disasters in 2017, these grants are now divided into two types:

- Community Development Block Grants for Disaster Recovery (**CDBG-DR**): Funding focused on "un-met" needs not covered by FEMA and shorter-term funding

- Community Development Block Grants for Mitigation (**CDBG-MIT**): Funding focused on longer-term mitigation projects intended to "increase resilience to and lessen impact of future disasters" (Bipartisan Budget Act of 2018)

Congress passed multiple bills in fall 2017 and spring 2018 to fund disaster aid, allocating more than $50 billion for FEMA and $35 billion for HUD.[11] Of the $35 billion allocated to HUD for the 2017 disasters, $12 billion was specifically for the CDBG-MIT programs. Puerto Rico was one of sixteen grantees (which included states like Texas, Florida, Georgia, and California) that were to be granted access to this funding.

Access to all disaster aid (FEMA and HUD monies) granted to Puerto Rico in 2017 and 2018 had two additional requirements versus other states and towns receiving aid. First, access to aid was dependent on approval by the PROMESA Board (or Junta, as it is known in Puerto Rico). PROMESA, or the Puerto Rico Oversight, Management, and Economic Stability Act of 2016, created a seven-member board appointed by Congress after Puerto Rico was denied access to federal bankruptcy laws to oversee the restructuring of Puerto Rico's debt.[12] The second requirement was that the governor of Puerto Rico would have to submit monthly reports to FEMA on the progress of disaster recovery plans. Other grantees were not saddled with these requirements to receive disaster aid funds.

SHORT-TERM RECOVERY EFFORTS

One simple way to help deliver aid and supplies more quickly immediately following Hurricane María's landfall would have been by repealing the Jones Act. Also known as the Merchant Marine Act of 1920, this act requires that all goods shipped to Puerto Rico come from vessels built, owned, and operated by Americans. It was not until ten days after the storm that the Jones Act was suspended—for a period of ten days only (Chokshi 2017).[13] This is indicative of the major lags, delays, and added oversight that would also come to characterize FEMA's response in the short term (see DHS Office of Inspector General 2019, 2020).

The scope of damage caused by Hurricane María was historic, yet FEMA failed to effectively provide Puerto Ricans with short-term basic needs like food and shelter. Granted, getting supplies like water, food, and tarps to Puerto Rico and the US Virgin Islands quickly was a challenge given their location. FEMA supplies had not been replenished after Hurricane Irma. In Puerto Rico, all ports and the airport were damaged, and Puerto Rico and the US Virgin Islands are archipelagos more than 1000 miles from the continental United States. However, FEMA reports reveal multiple canceled contracts: $70 million for 30 million meals that were never delivered, $30 million in blue tarps that also never arrived (just two examples of many). What is significant about these representative canceled contracts is that FEMA realized too late—weeks into the recovery—that the contractors could not deliver during those critical few months after the storm. Nine days after Hurricane Harvey made landfall, FEMA had 30,000 employees in Texas compared to only 10,000 who made it to Puerto Rico in the same time frame. The most on-site FEMA employees ever posted in Puerto Rico was 19,000 over thirty days after the storm (Willison et al. 2019).

To make matters worse, families (more than 40 percent of whom live below the federal poverty line in Puerto Rico) were told to apply for FEMA aid monies online at a time when power and most forms of communication were down. Six months after the storm for those who had managed to submit an application, more than 60 percent of applicants from Puerto Rico were deemed ineligible for FEMA aid (Panditharatne 2018).[14] As of September 2021 (four years after the storm), 81 percent of FEMA monies that were obligated to Texas from the 2017 disasters had been paid out versus Puerto Rico, where only 41 percent of obligated FEMA funds had been paid out (see table 11.1).

LONG-TERM RECOVERY EFFORTS

In the long term, a closer look at the HUD process for CDBG-MIT funding and how and when Puerto Rico was allowed to apply for these funds versus other grantees paints a very clear picture of the kind of delay tactics and additional strictures Puerto Rico had to contend with in accessing disaster monies (beyond what has already been described).

Table 11.1. Percentage of Obligated FEMA & HUD Monies Spent in Texas vs. Puerto Rico as of Sept., 2021

Table 11.1a. Texas

Aid Type	Obligated (in Billions)	Outlaid (in Billions)	Percentage Outlaid
FEMA	$8.05	$6.54	81%
HUD	$10.06	$1.71	17%
Total	$18.1	$8.25	46%

Table 11.1b. Puerto Rico

Aid Type	Obligated (in Billions)	Outlaid (in Billions)	Percentage Outlaid
FEMA	$35.63	$14.56	41%
HUD	$18.01	$0.46	3%
Total	$53.64	$15.02	28%

Source: Data from Recovery Support Function Leadership Group (2021).

Once Congress allocates funds for the CDBG-DR/MIT grants, HUD requests the funds from the Office of Management and Budget (OMB) housed within the Executive Office of the President. OMB creates a schedule for releasing the funds, known as an apportionment schedule. With this information, HUD releases a Federal Register notice outlining the specifics for applying for CDBG-DR/MIT grants. Until a Federal Register notice is released, this funding cannot be applied for.

Housed within OMB is the Office of Information and Regulatory Affairs (OIRA). OIRA "develops and oversees the implementation of government-wide policies in the area of information policy, privacy, and statistical policy" (White House 2021). If an OIRA review is invoked, the Federal Register notices cannot be released until the OIRA review either has been waived or completed, or a ninety-day review process has expired. OIRA reviews have never been invoked in the past for CDBG DR/MIT Federal Register notices.

Figure 11.1 below shows when Federal Register Notices were released for the 2017 CDBG-DR and CDBG-MIT grants. Puerto Rico and the US Virgin Islands were separated out from the original sixteen grantees for the CDBG-MIT monies, and the delay tactics described below meant Puerto Rico couldn't even begin the application process for CDBG-MIT funds until five months after the other states had been granted access to the funding.

A HUD investigation revealed that from the time the appropriations were made for the 2017 disasters, the OMB consistently intervened in relation to Puerto Rico's access to funding. For example, at the end of 2018 there was a government shutdown. OMB instructed HUD to stop working on Puerto Rico's CDBG-DR grant, which was already in process, further delaying the application (HUD Office of the Inspector General 2021).

The HUD investigation also revealed that as with FEMA monies the Office of Management and Budget (OMB) indicated early on that they wanted to separate out Puerto Rico and the USVI from the other grantees by releasing separate Federal Register Notices so that they could "allow monies to flow to the other states" (HUD Office of the Inspector General 2021, 32). The president's office wanted to place additional oversight and requirements, particularly around property title and management records, as well as suspend the federal minimum wage on federal contracts in the guidelines for Puerto Rico. HUD didn't actually think this was legal, nor were they sure that separating out Puerto Rico and the USVI from the original sixteen grantees to create a different mitigation notice was legal (HUD Office of the Inspector General 2021, 25–27). Days before HUD's

May 1, 2019, deadline to release the CDBG-MIT notices, the president's office via OMB intervened by instituting an OIRA Review Process for the mitigation notices. As indicated above, an OIRA Review had never been initiated for CDBG-DR/MIT notices. In August 2019, HUD issued a press release indicating that Puerto Rico and the USVI would receive separate mitigation notices from the other fourteen grantees for the CDBG-MIT funding.[15] The conditions that OMB wanted about property records and suspending the federal minimum wage ultimately were included in the CDBG-MIT Federal Register notice for Puerto Rico, which was finally released at the end of January 2020. Figure 11.1 is a timeline showing all CDBG-DR and CDBG-MIT Federal Register notice release dates related to HUD aid allocated for all 2017 natural disasters. This figure shows the resultant delay added to Puerto Rico's ability to access CDBG-MIT funding that the invocation of the OIRA review process created.

The distribution of aid to Puerto Rico following a catastrophic natural disaster was met with an orchestrated disaster on the part of the federal government.[16]

Federal Narrative Used to Explain Delay

In a review of statements regarding Puerto Rico from official US Federal government channels—Trump tweets, White House news conferences, and HUD press releases—beginning immediately after the storm, two consistent themes emerged. There was denial and rejection of reported deaths and denial that Puerto Rico was getting less assistance (Straub 2021, 1616). However, the narrative often deployed *did* recognize the slow recovery response in Puerto Rico in comparison to other states that experienced massive destruction following Hurricanes in 2017. At times, the reason given was the location and topography of Puerto Rico, poor maintenance of infrastructure, or political corruption; however, Puerto Rico's debt, often cast as fiscal mismanagement, malfeasance, or financial irregularities, became the most frequently deployed reason for the slow recovery response (1616). Ultimately, the Puerto Rican people were to blame, incapable of fiscal, structural, or political self-management. The use of these references, especially that of fiscal mismanagement or Puerto Rico's debt, became the strategy for the US response.

Presidential tweets might be seen as less officious in crafting an epistemological framework for interpreting the events in Puerto Rico, but the same language was used by the secretary of housing to introduce

Figure 11.1. Timeline of the release of HUD Federal Register Notices pertaining to Disaster Recovery (CDBG-DR) and Mitigation (CDBG-MIT) for all 2017 disasters. Note that this is the first step in the process allowing for grantees to apply. It can take months, even years, for the applications to be approved and longer for the monies to be outlaid (US Department of Housing and Urban Development 2018a, 2018b, 2019a, 2019b, 2020).

Timeline of HUD Federal Register Notice Release Dates For 2017 CDBG-DR/MIT Funding

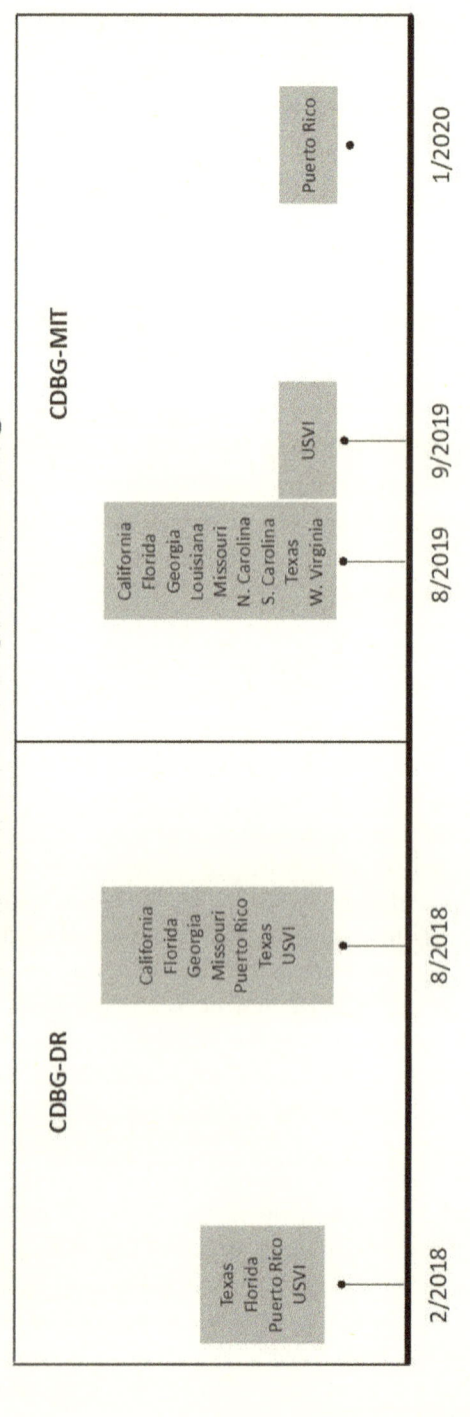

CDBG-DR

- 2/2018: Texas, Florida, Puerto Rico, USVI
- 8/2018: California, Florida, Georgia, Missouri, Puerto Rico, Texas, USVI

CDBG-MIT

- 8/2019: California, Florida, Georgia, Louisiana, Missouri, N. Carolina, S. Carolina, Texas, W. Virginia
- 9/2019: USVI
- 1/2020: Puerto Rico

new restrictions for Puerto Rico to access CDBG-DR/MIT funding. These tweets became the framing for federal policy. They signaled to US agencies and departments how the Executive Branch would approach recovery for Puerto Rico.

The president's first tweet regarding Puerto Rico after Hurricane María made landfall was filled with sentiment:

> Governor @RicardoRosello We are with you and the Puerto Rican people. Stay safe! #PRStrong (Donald Trump 2017a)

However, the president's next tweet in relation to Hurricane María and Puerto Rico came five days later when he publicly admitted a distinction between the recovery efforts in Texas and Florida and the response in Puerto Rico. Because all electricity and nearly 100 percent of communications had been destroyed, it had taken time for information regarding the extent of the damage to be relayed, particularly from regions beyond the San Juan metropolitan area. The tweets read:

> Texas & Florida are doing great but Puerto Rico which was already suffering from broken infrastructure & massive debt is in deep trouble . . . (Donald Trump 2017b)

> . . . It's old electrical grid, which was in terrible shape, was devastated. Much of the Island was destroyed, with billions of dollars . . . (Donald Trump 2017c)

> . . . owed to Wall Street and the banks which, sadly, must be dealt with. Food, water and medical are top priorities—and doing well. #FEMA (Donald Trump 2017d)

Even before most funds were requested and/or allocated, the responsibility for the delays in Puerto Rico points to its own inadequacy managing its finances. This quickly became the dominant narrative the US government would employ in reference to the response and recovery from Hurricane María in Puerto Rico. Looking back on this tweet, it is disturbingly predictive of what would follow.

Applying the framework of structural gaslighting, the president acknowledged that harm was happening and that public grievances were beginning to surface. He recognized that Puerto Rico had been devastated but that its possibility for recovery would be different from the experiences in Texas and Florida. The president was signaling to his followers and government staff that the response and recovery in Puerto Rico would be handled by first ensuring that the banking industry's interests would be addressed. Recovery would be dependent on responding to the "billions of dollars owed to Wall Street."

The tweets then provide a rationale, narrative framing, or, as theorist Elena Ruiz terms it, a "publicly licensed resource of interpretation" for both the magnitude of the destruction and the differential treatment in response and recovery. Puerto Ricans as a people—not even Hurricane María—were to blame for the suffering that had occurred and the suffering that was to come. This narrative was deployed to foreclose the possibility that delays in releasing disaster resources or aid monies to Puerto Rico would be seen as direct and deliberate. Puerto Rican fiscal mismanagement would be blamed for how the recovery would unfold. This is structural gaslighting at work.

This narrative masks the long history of both the differential and inequitable treatment of Puerto Rico as a colony of the United States over the past 120-plus years *and* the differential and inequitable treatment that would be applied to Puerto Rico in recovery from Hurricane María. Whatever the actual response by the federal government, Puerto Ricans were at fault five days after the storm hit.

In 2019, then-secretary of HUD Ben Carson would use the same narrative in approving Puerto Rico's disaster recovery action plan for accessing $8.2 billion of CDBG-DR funding that had been allocated to Puerto Rico by Congress more than a year earlier. Secretary Carson is quoted as saying, "This is an unprecedented investment and since Puerto Rico has a history of fiscal malfeasance, we are putting additional financial controls in place to ensure this disaster recovery money is spent properly" (US Department of Housing and Urban Development 2019c). This same language was used to explain the differential requirements and oversight added by OMB and HUD for Puerto Rico to access aid (HUD Office of Inspector General 2021, 32). To explain inequities like tying the funding to approval by PROMESA or creating a separate process for applying for CDBG-MIT funding from the original fourteen other grantees, HUD wrote: "As a result of the Administration's serious concerns over Puerto Rico's past fiscal irregularities, and to ensure that all disaster relief funds will be spent in a manner that helps the citizens of Puerto Rico, HUD will impose strict conditions and financial controls on the use of the funds. This heightened scrutiny will include enhanced monitoring of expenditures and other measures designed to ensure Puerto Rico's legal and prudent use of the funds" (US Department of Housing and Urban Development 2019c).

Recent analysis by Adam Straub of more than 400 news reports from the *New York Times* and the *Wall Street Journal* regarding Puerto Rico and the response to Hurricane María in the year following the storm confirms the frequent invocation of Puerto Rican debt as responsible for problems with the recovery (Straub 2021, 1617). As part of the project, Straub analyzed the discourse coming from the federal government. Straub found that:

> [r]hetoric from the spokespeople for the federal government closely mirrored that of President Trump. Here PREPA [Puerto Rican Power Authority] and the Puerto Rican government were targeted as negligent, mismanaged, and ill-prepared for Hurricanes Irma and Maria. Federal officials defended FEMA's delayed and poor response to the disaster on the basis of the geographic location and the topography of the islands. *However, the most common and widely deployed narrative adopted by the federal government to defend the catastrophe was Puerto Rico's financial debt.* (Straub 2021, 1616, my emphasis)

Structural Gaslighting, Debt, and Colonialism

This chapter has examined how structural gaslighting functions within racio-colonial capitalism to maintain the structures (policies, practices, and institutions) that uphold this system. The federal government engaged in structural gaslighting in two ways relating to Puerto Rico during the Hurricane María recovery. First, by denying harms that were clearly visible—for example, by claiming that only sixty-four people died as a result of Hurricane María while refrigerated trucks stacked with bodies had to be used as makeshift morgues because there were so many dead (Schwartz 2017). But it is the second way in which Puerto Ricans were structurally gaslit that interests me. Racio-colonial capitalism is dependent on harms and violences that are meted out differently across different populations, and structural gaslighting allows for these differential harms to be recognized. That recognition comes in the form of circulating a narrative that places blame on those experiencing the violence and harms, thereby capturing resistance. The narrative in this second type of structural gaslighting witnessed in relation to Hurricane María recovery centered on Puerto Rican debt. Here I want to examine more closely why invoking Puerto Rican debt worked so well in this process of structural gaslighting and what it tells us about the relationship between colonialism, debt, and structural gaslighting.

In *Colonial Debts*, Rocío Zambrana argues that debt in the case of Puerto Rico reinstalls the colonial condition. Zambrana writes:

> debt is an apparatus of capture, one that functions as a form of coloniality. Debt captures land, coasts, body, time, the future itself. It actualizes a race/gender/class hierarchy by marking populations as culpable, hence, disposable. Debt is a product of a colonial history. It is materially indexed to the emergence, expansion, and mutations of capitalism. As a mode of coloniality, however, debt exceeds its origins, organizing material conditions in light of colonial/racial violence anew. It does so by updating forms of dispossession essential to the creation and capture of value in a capitalist economy. (Zambrana 2021a, 143)

Zambrana details how the municipal debt—the same debt the federal government so often invoked as the reason for delays and added oversight in Puerto Rico following the storm—is itself a mechanism of what I am here calling racio-colonial capitalism, which Zambrana develops as "neoliberal coloniality." Zambrana tracks the development of debt as a financial instrument alongside the transition to large neoliberal states. Through this development, debt becomes a form of economic and political control that forecloses future possibilities and is indexed to race/gender/class hierarchies that arise out of the history of colonialism and slavery (2021a, 21–52). The force of what Zambrana suggests, which we must take seriously, is how debt and its deployment reference and signal colonial interpretive frameworks that uphold and reinscribe racio-colonial capitalism.

Debt reinscribes coloniality because it doesn't simply describe a financial instrument but is also a moral determinant. As Zambrana writes, "Debt actualizes race/gender in positing anew certain bodies and populations as disposable, amenable to more than political control but rather violence, expulsion, precarity, outright death. Debt marks disposability by establishing culpability" (Zambrana 2021a, 43). Being in debt can mark one as culpable and incapable of fiscal self-management.[17]

If we unpack the meaning of actualizing race/gender anew—signaling who is culpable and disposable—debt then functions differently for President Trump than for the Puerto Rican people. Debt doesn't *only* signal disposability and culpability. For the president of the United States, corporate debt and multiple bankruptcies were not negative moral determinants, as he had been elected to run the largest economy in the world. Good debt, American middle-class mortgages, "healthy" credit scores, and the federal deficit are all central to the functioning of racio-colonial capitalism. That is, debt (including Puerto Rico's debt) is a financial instrument on which American prosperity depends. For certain people, it is a positive moral determinant. For President Trump, debt and bankruptcies were shrewd financial instruments. For Puerto Rico, debt was "fiscal malfeasance." It is not cancellable or eligible for a "bailout" and indicates Puerto Ricans are culpable and disposable. Puerto Rican debt isn't white debt.[18]

Debt, as emerging out of the racio-colonial histories of the Americas, was and continues to be an effective vehicle through which the federal government gaslights Puerto Ricans and why it was chosen as the "publicly licensed resource of interpretation." When structural gaslighting is deployed in a racio-colonial capitalist system like the United States, debt provides a racialized rationale while never invoking race. Debt references and signals justifications for colonialism, narrative frameworks that are centuries old, while never referencing colonialism. Debt in racio-colonial capitalism, when indexed to Puerto Rican bodies, names a moral difference that is insurmountable. No amount of "tutelage" can redeem them. This racio-colonial historical framework locates the problem with Puerto Rican debt in who Puerto Ricans are—their very being—not what they do. Debt will only have a negative meaning when referencing Puerto Rico, while debt for others remains a vehicle for prosperity. In fact, racio-colonial capitalist prosperity depends on it.[19]

Structural gaslighting has been a part of the colonial system since its inception. In deploying debt as the narrative framework for interpreting delays in recovery from Hurricane María, the federal government signaled that Puerto Ricans are disposable. This allowed for these delays and added oversight to have their intended consequence: Puerto Ricans died, Puerto Ricans fled the archipelago in massive numbers, and more groundwork has been laid for the further extraction of Puerto Rican land and resources to wealthy American non–Puerto Ricans (Villamena 2020; Negron-Muntaner 2019).

Notes

1. This chapter is written in honor of *la gente de La Calle Morovis*—those who continue to *subir la cuesta* and those who walk with us in spirit. This epigraph is a reminder that while I treat Puerto Ricans as a monolith in this piece, the impacts described were not experienced equally by all. That is, racial, gender, class, and urban/rural hierarchies played a significant role in who bore the brunt of the delays and violences the federal policies and practices I describe created after Hurricane María. Taller Salud, a feminist women's health organization that has been around for more than forty years, bases its work in Loíza, Puerto Rico, a historically Black town. Black families, rural families, women, and all the intersections therein have disproportionately experienced the harms of María. See Ayuda Legal Puerto Rico (2020) for how different communities in Puerto Rico have fared in recovery. See also Lloréns (2019) for unique ways in which Puerto Rico's Black communities approach and survive times of "disaster."

2. This basketball court is named after my eighty-six-year-old great uncle, who played basketball there daily from the 1970s to 2020. He can make more than seventy three-point shots in a row.

3. Bonilla also writes of the concept: "I use the term racio-*colonial* capitalism to stress the co-constitutive nature of race and colonialism and foreground the importance of conquest and colonial outposts for the development of modern capitalism" (2020, 2).

4. Bonilla grounds the concept of racio-colonial capitalism in Quijano's notion of coloniality, situating it within a much longer history of colonial—including white settler colonial—practices. See Zambrana (2021a, 55) for coloniality as emergency; Maldonado-Torres (2019) for colonialism and Hurricane María as catastrophe; Rivera (2020) for colonialism as disaster.

5. In focusing on pathologizing resistance, Davis and Ernst's work highlights that while structural gaslighting might in part be aimed at getting people to doubt their own experience, it seems fundamentally about capturing and neutralizing resistance. Gaslighting is about power and control, and in all instances structural and interpersonal gaslighting is an attempt to eliminate resistance to the gaslighters' (a government's or an individual's) oppressive and abusive relation to whoever is gaslit. Elena Ruiz recognizes this but frames it differently: "While it may be strategically helpful to understand gaslighting as placing a special focus on the power relations that can affect a person's trust in their own judgements, what is at stake is not just the existential and ontological spectrum of emotional abuse sustained but the *asymmetrical death toll of some populations over others*, consistently predictively, and from one generation to the next" (2020, 705).

6. See Ruíz 2020, 690, 692, 704–5. Ruiz writes of design that it "does not simply refer to the pattern of distribution, *but intent of distribution effects*, as in a grand design or master plan" (2020; 706n7, my emphasis).

7. Ruiz is demonstrating not simply a general example of how structural gaslighting occurs with a theoretical tool (as Berenstain does with "hermeneutic injustice"), but that structural gaslighting occurs in the very development and use of the concept "gaslighting" itself. This was exactly my experience when first attempting to use gaslighting as it is described in psychological literature to explain what was happening in Puerto Rico. Ruiz then is expanding the meaning of the term gaslighting itself—to incorporate structural aspects into its deployment—the structures, institutions, and histories that prefigure any interpersonal interactions, beginning with the white settler colonialism, which makes possible all interpersonal interactions in North and South America. Gaslighting is always also structural gaslighting. Ruiz then focuses on this process as cultural gaslighting, as she identifies instances of both structural and prestructural hermeneutic violences.

8. While the limited scope of this chapter does not allow for a discussion of resistance in Puerto Rico (of which there was plenty), I include it here because it is an important part of the development of the scholarship on structural gaslighting.

9. The Puerto Rican government's official death toll from a study it commissioned by the Milken Institute School of Public Health at George Washington University on excess deaths in Puerto Rico in the three months following the storm is 2,975 (Milken Institute of Public Health 2018). The number of excess deaths from an independent group of researchers from the Harvard T.H. Chan School of Public Health at Harvard University attributed to Hurricane María in the same time frame is 4,645 (Kishore et al. 2018). Permanent outmigration from Puerto Rico following Hurricane María is very difficult to estimate, but 130,000 permanent migrations in the year following the storm is on the low end (See Hinojosa, Meléndez, and Maria 2018; Acosta et al. 2020; *El Nuevo Dia* 2019).

10. For further scholarship on federal responses to the storm, see Molinari (2019); Ficek (2018); Murray (2018); and Joseph et al. (2020).

11. The Continuing Appropriations Act 2018 and Supplemental Appropriations for Disaster Relief Requirements Act, 2017, was in response to Hurricanes Harvey and Irma and designates $7.4 billion for HUD's CDBG-DR. The Additional Supplemental Appropriations for Disaster Relief Requirements Act, 2017, designates funding for FEMA (none for HUD). The Bipartisan Budget Act of 2018 designated $16 billion for HUD CDBG-DR and $12 billion for HUD CDBG-MIT.

12. PROMESA was created by a US Congress in which Puerto Rico has no voting representation. It should also be noted that residents of Puerto Rico cannot vote in US presidential elections.

13. The Jones Act substantially raises the prices of all goods coming onto the island and limits what ports ships bringing goods can come from.

14. The denial of FEMA assistance to families to repair properties after the storm was often based on the inability of applicants to prove ownership of their homes. For an in-depth discussion of the title restrictions FEMA and HUD

created for accessing disaster aid in Puerto Rico, see Garcia (2020, 2021); Ayuda Legal Puerto Rico (2019).

15. The HUD press release said: "Recovery efforts in jurisdictions prepared to do their part should not be held back due to the alleged corruption, fiscal irregularities and financial mismanagement occurring in Puerto Rico and capacity issues in the US Virgin Islands, which is why HUD will award disaster mitigation funds in two separate tranches" (HUD Office of Inspector General 2021, 33).

16. This is not to suggest there were not also mistakes made by local Puerto Rican government and agencies. Part of what sparked SoVerano 2019 (massive public protests across Puerto Rico) was corruption and clear disregard for Puerto Rican suffering by government officials, including then-governor of Puerto Rico, Ricardo Roselló. Here again, Centro de Periodismo Investigativo (CPI) was key, as it first published the leaked chats that would result in Roselló being forced to resign (see Centro de Periodismo Investigativo 2021b).

17. One is reminded here of the Valladolid debates in sixteenth-century Spain meant to determine who could be enslaved, in which Sepulveda argued that Indigenous people in what we now call the Americas could be enslaved because they were incapable of self-governance.

18. This does not imply that many Puerto Ricans are not also white. On the complicated racialization of Puerto Ricans, see recent work by Godreau and Bonilla (2021).

19. See cluster in issue of *Critical Times* for more on Puerto Rico, the effects of the municipal debt, and Puerto Rican resistance to the debt (Zambrana 2021b; Contreras Capó and Delgado 2021; Godreau-Aubert and Phillips 2021; Prados Rodríguez and Delgado 2021; Santory Jorge and Delgado 2021).

Works Cited

Acosta, Rolando J., Nishant Kishore, Rafael A. Irizarry, and Caroline O. Buckee. 2020. "Quantifying the Dynamics of Migration after Hurricane Maria in Puerto Rico." *Proceedings of the National Academy of Sciences of the United States of America* 117 (51): 32772–78. https://doi.org/10.1073/pnas.2001671117.

Ayuda Legal Puerto Rico. 2019. "Hacia Una Recuperación Justa." https://www.ayudalegalpuertorico.org/wp-content/uploads/2019/06/reporte-recuperacion-justa-junio-2019-esp-3-flattened.pdf.

———. 2020. "¿Quiénes Se Quedan Atrás?" https://www.ayudalegalpuertorico.org/wp-content/uploads/2020/12/informe-mesa-de-investigación.pdf?utm_source=pub&utm_medium=alpr-blog&utm_campaign=informe-mesa&utm_content=informe.

Berenstain, Nora. 2020. "White Feminist Gaslighting." *Hypatia* 35 (4): 733–58. https://doi.org/10.1017/hyp.2020.31.
Bonilla, Yarimar. 2020. "The Coloniality of Disaster: Race, Empire, and the Temporal Logics of Emergency in Puerto Rico, USA." *Political Geography* 78: 102181. https://doi.org/10.1016/j.polgeo.2020.102181.
Centro de Periodismo Investigativo. 2021a. "María: The Money Trail." https://periodismoinvestigativo.com/en-los-chavos-de-maria/.
———. 2021b. "#RickyLeaks." https://periodismoinvestigativo.com/series/rickyleaks/.
Chokshi, Niraj. 2017. "Trump Waives Jones Act for Puerto Rico, Easing Hurricane Aid Shipments." *New York Times*. https://www.nytimes.com/2017/09/28/us/jones-act-waived.html.
Contreras Capó, Vanessa, and Nicole Delgado. 2021. "Debt and Structural Gender Violence." *Critical Times* 4 (1): 167–69. https://doi.org/10.1215/26410478-8855299.
Davis, Angelique M., and Rose Ernst. 2019. "Racial Gaslighting." *Politics, Groups, and Identities* 7 (4): 761–74. https://doi.org/10.1080/21565503.2017.1403934.
DHS Office of Inspector General. 2019. "FEMA Should Not Have Awarded Two Contracts to Bronze Star LLC." https://www.oig.dhs.gov/sites/default/files/assets/2019-05/OIG-19-38-May19.pdf.
———. 2020. "FEMA Mismanaged the Commodity Distribution Process in Response to Hurricanes Irma and Maria." https://www.oig.dhs.gov/sites/default/files/assets/2020-09/OIG-20-76-Sep20.pdf.
El Nuevo Dia. 2019. "La Emigración Registrada En 2018 En La Isla Fue La Más Alta Desde 2006." October 4, 2019. https://www.elnuevodia.com/noticias/locales/notas/la-emigracion-registrada-en-2018-en-la-isla-fue-la-mas-alta-desde-2006/?r=93705.
Ficek, Rosa E. 2018. "Infrastructure and Colonial Difference in Puerto Rico after Hurricane María." *Transforming Anthropology* 26 (2): 102–17. https://doi.org/10.1111/traa.12129.
Garcia, Ivis. 2020. "The Lack of Proof of Ownership in Puerto Rico Is Crippling Repairs in the Aftermath of Hurricane Maria Housing in Puerto Rico." *American Bar Association*. https://www.americanbar.org/groups/crsj/publications/human_rights_magazine_home/vol--44--no-2--housing/the-lack-of-proof-of-ownership-in-puerto-rico-is-crippling-repai/.
———. 2021. "Deemed Ineligible: Reasons Homeowners in Puerto Rico Were Denied Aid After Hurricane María." *Housing Policy Debate*. https://doi.org/10.1080/10511482.2021.1890633.
Godreau-Aubert, Ariadna Michelle, and Tara Philips. 2021. "We Women Who Don't Owe Anyone: *Las Propias* in Times of Public Debt and Austerity." *Critical Times* 4 (1): 130–47. doi: https://doi.org/10.1215/26410478-8855283.
Godreau, Isar, and Yarimar Bonilla. 2021. "Nonsovereign Racecraft: How Colonialism, Debt, and Disaster Are Transforming Puerto Rican Racial

Subjectivities." *American Anthropologist* 123 (3): 509–25. https://doi.org/10.1111/AMAN.13601.

Hinojosa, Jennifer, and Edwin Meléndez. 2018. "Puerto Rican Exodus: One Year Since Hurricane Maria." Center for Puerto Rican Studies, Hunter College, City University of New York. https://centropr.hunter.cuny.edu/sites/default/files/RB2018-05_SEPT2018 %281%29.pdf.

HUD Office of Inspector General. 2021. "Review of HUD's Disbursement of Grant Funds Appropriated for Disaster Recovery and Mitigation Activities in Puerto Rico." Washington, DC.

Joseph, Samantha Rivera, Caroline Voyles, Kimberly D. Williams, Erica Smith, and Mariana Chilton. 2020. "Colonial Neglect and the Right to Health in Puerto Rico after Hurricane Maria." *American Journal of Public Health* 110 (10): 1512–18. https://doi.org/10.2105/AJPH.2020.305814.

Kishore, Nishant, Domingo Marqués, Ayesha Mahmud, Mathew V. Kiang, Irmary Rodriguez, Arlan Fuller, Peggy Ebner, Cecilia Sorensen, Fabio Racy, Jay Lemery, Leslie Maas, Jennifer Leaning, Rafael A. Irizarry, Satchit Balsari, and Caroline O. Buckee. 2018. "Mortality in Puerto Rico after Hurricane Maria." *New England Journal of Medicine* 379 (2): 162–70. https://doi.org/10.1056/NEJMsa1803972.

Lloréns, Hilda. 2019. "The Race of Disaster: Black Communities and the Crisis in Puerto Rico." *Black Perspectives*. https://www.aaihs.org/the-race-of-disaster-black-communities-and-the-crisis-in-puerto-rico/.

Maldonado-Torres, Nelson. 2019. "Afterword: Critique of Decoloniality in the Face of Crisis, Disaster, and Catastrophe." In *Aftershocks of Disaster*, edited by Yarimar Bonilla and Marisol Lebrón. Chicago: Haymarket Books.

Milken Institute of Public Health. 2018. "Ascertainment of the Estimated Excess Mortality from Hurricane María in Puerto Rico." George Washington University. https://publichealth.gwu.edu/sites/g/files/zaxdzs4586/files/2023-06/acertainment-of-the-estimated-excess-mortality-from-hurricane-maria-in-puerto-rico.pdf.

Molinari, Sarah. 2019. "Authenticating Loss and Contesting Recovery." In *Aftershocks of Disaster*, edited by Yarimar Bonilla and Marisol Lebrón. Chicago: Haymarket Books.

Murray, Yxta Maya. 2018. "FEMA Has Been a Nightmare: Epistemic Injustice in Puerto Rico." *Willamette Law Review* 55. https://heinonline.org/HOL/Page?handle=hein.journals/willr55&id=335&div=15&collection=journals.

Negron-Muntaner, Frances. 2019. "The Emptying Island: Puerto Rican Expulsion in Post-Maria Time." *Hemispheric Institute*. https://hemisphericinstitute.org/en/emisferica-14-1-expulsion/14-1-essays/the-emptying-island-puerto-rican-expulsion-in-post-maria-time.html.

Panditharatne, Mekela. 2018. "Hurricane Maria Aftermath: FEMA Rejects 60 Percent of Assistance Requests." *Slate*. https://slate.com/technology/2018/06/

hurricane-maria-aftermath-fema-rejects-60-percent-of-assistance-requests.html.

Prados Rodríguez, Eva, and Nicole Delgado. 2021. "Gender Violence and Debt Auditing." *Critical Times* 4 (1): 170–73. https://doi.org/10.1215/26410478-8855307.

Recovery Support Function Leadership Group. 2021. "RSFLG—State Profiles." RSFLG Financial Data. September 30, 2021. https://recovery.fema.gov/state-profiles.

Rivera, Danielle Zoe. 2020. "Disaster Colonialism: A Commentary on Disasters beyond Singular Events to Structural Violence." *International Journal of Urban and Regional Research*. https://doi.org/10.1111/1468-2427.12950.

Ruíz, Elena. 2020. "Cultural Gaslighting." *Hypatia* 35 (4): 687–713. https://doi.org/10.1017/hyp.2020.33.

Santory Jorge, Anayra, and Nicole Delgado. 2021. "Destroying a Country Is Men's Business." *Critical Times* 4 (1): 148–66. https://doi.org/10.1215/26410478-8855291.

Schwartz, Mattathias. 2017. "Maria's Bodies: The Hurricane in Puerto Rico Has Become a Man-Made Disaster, With a Death Toll Threatening to Eclipse Katrina." *New York Magazine*. https://nymag.com/intelligencer/2017/12/hurricane-maria-man-made-disaster.html.

Straub, Adam M. 2021. "'Natural Disasters Don't Kill People, Governments Kill People:' Hurricane Maria, Puerto Rico-Recreancy, and 'Risk Society.'" *Natural Hazards* 105: 1603–21. https://doi.org/10.1007/s11069-020-04368-z.

The White House. 2021. "Information and Regulatory Affairs—The White House." https://www.whitehouse.gov/omb/information-regulatory-affairs/.

Trump, Donald. 2017a. (@realDonaldTrump). "Governor @RicardoRossello-We are with you and the people of Puerto Rico. Stay safe! #PRStrong," Twitter (now X), September 20, 2017, 11:13 p.m. https://twitter.com/realdonaldtrump/status/910703407555600386.

———. 2017b. (@realDonaldTrump). "Texas & Florida are doing great but Puerto Rico which was already suffering from broken infrastructure & massive debt is in deep trouble," Twitter (now X), September 25, 2017, 8:45 p.m. https://twitter.com/realdonaldtrump/status/912478274508423168.

———. 2017c. (@realDonaldTrump). ". . . It's old electrical grid, which was in terrible shape, was devastated. Much of the Island was destroyed, with billions of dollars," Twitter (now X), September 25, 2017, 8:50 p.m. https://twitter.com/realdonaldtrump/status/912479500511965184.

———. 2017d. (@realDonaldTrump). ". . . owed to Wall Street and the banks which, sadly, must be dealt with. Food, water and medical are top priorities—and doing well. #FEMA," Twitter (now X), September 25, 2017, 8:58 p.m. https://twitter.com/realdonaldtrump/status/912481556127780865.

US Department of Housing and Urban Development. 2018a. "Allocations, Common Application, Waivers, and Alternative Requirements for 2017 Disaster

Community Development Block Grant Disaster Recovery Grantees." *Federal Register* 83 (28): 5844. https://www.govinfo.gov/content/pkg/FR-2018-02-09/pdf/2018-02693.pdf.

———. 2018b. "Allocations, Common Application, Waivers, and Alternative Requirements for Community Development Block Grant Disaster Recovery Grantees." *Federal Register* 83 (157): 40314. https://www.govinfo.gov/content/pkg/FR-2018-08-14/pdf/2018-17365.pdf.

———. 2019a. "Allocations, Common Application, Waivers, and Alternative Requirements for Community Development Block Grant Mitigation Grantees." *Federal Register* 84 (169): 45838. https://www.govinfo.gov/content/pkg/FR-2019-08-30/pdf/2019-18607.pdf.

———. 2019b. "Allocations, Common Application, Waivers, and Alternative Requirements for Community Development Block Grant Mitigation Grantees; U.S. Virgin Islands Allocation." *Federal Register* 84 (175): 47528. https://www.govinfo.gov/content/pkg/FR-2019-09-10/pdf/2019-19506.pdf.

———. 2019c. "HUD Approves Puerto Rico's Latest Disaster Recovery Action Plan; Approval Comes With Tight Fiscal Controls." News release no. 19-017, March 1, 2019. https://archives.hud.gov/news/2019/pr19-017.cfm.

———. 2020. "Allocations, Common Application, Waivers, and Alternative Requirements for Community Development Block Grant Mitigation Grantees; Commonwealth of Puerto Rico Allocation." *Federal Register* 85 (17): 4676. https://www.govinfo.gov/content/pkg/FR-2020-01-27/pdf/2020-01334.pdf.

Villamena, Vicenzo. 2020. "How Entrepreneurs Can Save on Taxes in Puerto Rico." *Forbes*. https://www.forbes.com/sites/theyec/2020/06/08/how-entrepreneurs-can-save-on-taxes-in-puerto-rico/?sh=734811f04cfc.

Willison, Charley E., Phillip M. Singer, Melissa S. Creary, and Scott L. Greer. 2019. "Quantifying Inequities in US Federal Response to Hurricane Disaster in Texas and Florida Compared with Puerto Rico Analysis." *BMJ Global Health* 4: 1191. https://doi.org/10.1136/bmjgh-2018-001191.

Zambrana, Rocío. 2021a. *Colonial Debts: The Case of Puerto Rico*. Durham: Duke University Press.

———. 2021b. "Introduction: On Debt, Blame, and Responsibility: Feminist Resistance in the Colony of Puerto Rico." *Critical Times* 4 (1): 125–29. https://doi.org/10.1215/26410478-8855275.

Contributors

Nora Berenstain, PhD, is professor of philosophy and chair of the Women, Gender, and Sexuality Program at the University of Tennessee-Knoxville, where she specializes in metaphysics of science and intersectional feminist epistemology. Her current research explores the stability of structures of oppression and their non-accidental connections to the population-level harms they produce and license. Her work has appeared in *Ergo, Hypatia, Synthese, Contemporary Political Theory, Mind, Australasian Journal of Philosophy*, and various collections with Oxford University Press. Dr. Berenstain also co-directs the University of Tennessee's Intersectionality Community of Scholars, an interdisciplinary group of researchers oriented toward transformative social change.

Angelique M. Davis, PhD, is a professor of political science and African and African American studies at Seattle University. Her research concentrates on racial gaslighting, dehumanization, apologies and reparations, the sociolegal construction of race, and the reinvention of white supremacy in the twenty-first century. Her published articles are in several journals, including the *Journal of Black Studies, The Black Scholar, Berkeley La Raza Law Journal,* and *Studies in Law, Politics, and Society*. She published a book chapter, "Political Blackness: A Sociopolitical Construction of Blackness Post-Loving v. Virginia," in Loving in a "Post–Racial" World: New Legal Approaches to Interracial Marriages and Relationships (Cambridge University Press, 2012). She published a co-authored article with Rose Ernst titled "Racial Gaslighting" in *Politics, Groups, and Identities* that won the 1999 Best Article Award from the Western Political Science Association. She is in the process of writing a book, *Racial Gaslighting*, with Rose Ernst. She received her Juris Doctor from the University of Washington in 1999. She served as a federal law clerk and subsequently practiced law until she joined the faculty at Seattle University in 2005. In addition to her academic pursuits, Professor Davis served as a commissioner on the Seattle Civil Service Commission (2013–2022), owns Exhale Academic Writing Retreats, and is a coach and campus workshop facilitator for the National Center for Faculty Development and Diversity (NCFDD) (available at https://angeliquedavis1.academia.edu/).

Rose Ernst, PhD, is an honorary research fellow at the Centre for the Study of Women and Gender at the University of Warwick as well as former chair and associate professor of political science at Seattle University. She received her PhD from the University of Washington and her BA from Cornell University. Her research empirically investigates and theorizes political phenomena traditionally ignored or hidden in public policy debates. Such subjects include welfare politics, street-level bureaucracy, race, gender, class inequality, antiracist social movement organizing, pedagogies of intersectionality, processes of racialization, and racial gaslighting in the United States. She is the author of a book, twelve peer-reviewed and law journal articles, and has a book (*Colonial Moods*) under review. NYU Press published her first book, *The Price of Progressive Politics: The Welfare Rights Movement in an Era of Colorblind Racism*. She has also published articles in the *Annual Review of Law & Social Science*; *Journal of Gender, Race & Justice*; *The Oxford Handbook of U.S. Women's Social Movement Activism*; *Perspectives on Politics*; *Politics, Groups, and Identities*; *Race and Justice*; *The Politics of Protest: Readings on the Black Lives Matter Movement*; *Race and Pedagogy Journal*; *Social Movement Studies*; *Social Science Quarterly*; *Studies in Law, Politics, and Society*; and *Whose Welfare? Marginalized Groups, Inequalities, and the Post-War Welfare State*. Her most recent collaboration with Professor Angelique M. Davis is titled *Racial Gaslighting: An Antiracist Guide*. They also have a forthcoming podcast on the subject.

Taina Figueroa, PhD, is a postdoctoral fellow in philosophy and the Latin American, Latinx, and Caribbean Studies Program (LALCS) at Emory University, where she teaches and is working to build out a new Latinx Studies minor. Through her institutional work she creates space, programming, and coursework for Latine students to learn about their histories, explore the complexity of their identities, practice creating change/new futures, and celebrate who they are. Her research areas center on Latinx and Caribbean Feminisms. Her most recent work focuses on strategies of survival and community building in Puerto Rico post Hurricane María.

Hanna Kiri Gunn, PhD, is assistant professor of philosophy in the Department of Philosophy at the University of California, Merced, where she teaches epistemology, applied ethics (in particular technology ethics and bioethics), and feminist philosophy. Her current research focuses on content moderation, social cohesion and resilience, and political epistemology. Recent publications include "Can Retributivism and Risk Assessment Be Reconciled?" in *Criminal Justice Ethics* (2024), co-authored with Toby Napoletano; "Listening for Epistemic Community" (2023) in *The Epistemology of Democracy*, edited by Quassim Cassam and Hana Samaržija; and "Is There a Duty to Disclose Epistemic Risk?" (2022) in *Online Manipulation*, edited by Michael Klenk and Fleur Jongepier.

Sabrina L. Hom, PhD, is an associate professor of philosophy and an affiliate of the Women's and Gender Studies Program at Georgia College and State University in Milledgeville, Georgia. She is a founder and co-director of the Luce Irigaray Circle. Her research focuses on continental feminist theory and critical mixed race studies.

Veronica Ivy, PhD, is an interdisciplinary scholar who has published widely on topics of knowledge, language, gender, and issues of equity (particularly in sport). She is a world-leading expert on trans and intersex athlete rights and offers institutional diversity and inclusion training workshops. Veronica has penned articles for the *New York Times, Washington Post, Economist, NBC News, VICE,* and many more. She has appeared on major TV, radio, and podcast interviews to discuss trans issues and particularly trans and intersex athlete rights, including CNN, BBC, Sky News, and *The Daily Show*. In addition to her academic work, she is a two-time masters track cycling world champion and previous masters world-record holder. Dr. Ivy also happens to be a queer trans woman. She is the first known trans woman to win a track cycling world championship. Veronica also engages in advocacy and activism for trans and intersex athletes. Her message is that #SportIsAHumanRight. Ivy brings a unique perspective of being an academic, athlete, and activist to her work. She advises various national and international organizations including the International Olympic Committee, World Triathlon, and others.

Lilyana Levy, PhD, received her doctorate in philosophy from Emory University in 2021. Her dissertation, "Contested Illness and Embodied Knowing: On Medical Gaslighting as Epistemic Injustice," foregrounds patient perspectives on medical error, diagnostic delay, and illness dismissal to give an account of medical gaslighting as a systemic and pervasive form of epistemic injustice. She is currently a postdoctoral scholar at UCLA's David Geffen School of Medicine. As a postdoc, her work focuses on the ethics of brain computer interfaces (BCI), especially in relation to issues of disability justice.

Holly Longair, PhD, is a full-time regular instructor in the Philosophy Department at Kwantlen Polytechnic University in Surrey, BC, Canada. She specializes in feminist political philosophy and social epistemology, with particular interests in egalitarian theories of justice and epistemic oppression. She received her PhD in philosophy from Vanderbilt University in 2022, with a dissertation titled "Cooperative Systems: Characterizing the Requirements of Relational Egalitarian Justice."

Kate Manne, PhD, is an associate professor in the Sage School of Philosophy at Cornell University, where she's been teaching since 2013. Before that, she was a junior fellow at the Harvard Society of Fellows and completed her graduate work in philosophy at MIT. Manne specializes in moral philosophy (especially metaethics and moral psychology), feminist philosophy, and social philosophy. She is the author of three books, *Down Girl*, *Entitled*, and *Unshrinking*, which was nominated for the 2024 National Book Award. She also often writes opinion pieces, essays, and reviews for a wide audience.

Kelly Oliver, PhD, is W. Alton Jones Distinguished Professor of Philosophy Emerita at Vanderbilt University. She is the author of sixteen scholarly books, including *Response Ethics* (Rowman & Littlefield), *Carceral Humanitarianism* (Minnesota University Press), *Earth and World*, *Philosophy After the Apollo Missions* (Columbia University Press), and *Animal Lessons, How They Teach Us to Be Human* (Columbia University Press); the editor of another thirteen books, Including *Refugees Now* (Rowman & Littlefield); and the author of more than one hundred scholarly articles on a variety of topics including refugee detention, capital punishment, animal ethics, sexual violence, images of women and war, feminism, psychoanalysis, and film. Her work has been translated into eight languages. She has been interviewed on *ABC News*, appeared on C-SPAN *BookTV*, and published in the *New York Times* and *Los Angeles Times*, among other appearances and publications in popular media. Kelly is also the bestselling author of three award-winning mystery series.

Cynthia Stark, PhD, is professor of philosophy at the University of Utah specializing in feminist, political and moral philosophy. She received her PhD in philosophy from the University of North Carolina in 1993. She also holds a master's degree in political science (specializing in political theory) from the University of Pittsburgh. Her articles are published in the *Journal of Philosophy, Hypatia, Nous*, and the *Journal of Political Philosophy*, among others. She has been a co-editor of the *Feminist Philosophy Quarterly* since 2023 and is the recipient of the David Eccles School of Business Daniels Fund Leadership in Ethics Education Teaching Award.

Shiloh Whitney, PhD, is a critical phenomenologist and feminist philosopher leading efforts to theorize affective injustice and emotional labor. An associate professor of philosophy at Fordham University, she was a fellow at the University of Connecticut's Humanities Institute while doing the initial research for her contribution to this volume. Her current book project theorizes uniquely affective varieties of injustice: just as epistemic injustices concern knowledge and credibility, affective injustices concern emotions and affective influence. Her work can be found in *Philosophical Topics, Phenomenology and the Cognitive Sciences, Hypatia, Philosophy and Social Criticism, Chiasmi International, Journal of Phenomenological Psychology, Southern Journal of Philosophy, Journal of Speculative Philosophy*, and *PhaenEx*, among others. Look for her contribution in the Northwestern University Press edited collection *50 Concepts for a Critical Phenomenology*, as well as *Thinking the US South: Contemporary Philosophy from Southern Perspectives*.

Index

1619 Project, 92

ableism: agency and, 5; medical gaslighting and, 232, 235; naturalization of disability and, 25, 26, 44–55
Abramson, Kate: definition of gaslighting by, 66–67, 104, 128–30; on dismissal, 169n7; on epistemic injustice, 69, 127–28; on *Gaslight* (1944 film), 135; on gaslighters, 13–14, 98, 110–13; on gaslighting as interpersonal phenomenon, 66–68, 117, 118, 130–31; on misogyny, 81; on projective identification, 4, 12
Abu-Laban, Yasmeen, 24
accomplices, 177, 178–79
"Accomplices Not Allies: Abolishing the Ally Industrial Complex" (Indigenous Action Media), 178–79
Adkins, Karen C., 97
affect, 3, 4, 5–6
affective exploitation, 168n2
affective gaslighting: concept of, 127, 133–41; rape culture and, 141–43; shame and, 137–39, 141–43
affective injustice: concept of, 140–41, 147–49; anger gaslighting as, 162–68; epistemic injustice and, 166–67

affective marginalization, 168n2
affective powerlessness, 168n2
affective smothering, 165
affective violence, 168n2
African American Heart Failure Trial (A-HeFT), 39
agency: ableism and, 5; anger and, 154; in *Gaslight* (1944 film), 207; shame and, 138; social imaginary and, 96, 98, 100; testimonial injustice and, 11
Akutsu, Gene, 208n3
Alexander, Marissa, 56n9
All Lives Matter, 197
allies and ally culture, 177, 178–88
"Allies Behaving Badly" (McKinnon), 130–31, 177–88
American Psychological Association (APA), 57n21
Anderson, Elizabeth, 66, 72–74
Anderson, Ellie, 160
Angel Street (*Gas Light*) (Hamilton), 2–3, 105–6, 134–36, 181, 231
anger backfiring, 164
anger gaslighting: concept of, 147–51; as affective injustice, 162–68; functions of anger and, 151–56; moral gaslighting and, 161–62; uptake and, 148–49, 153–55, 156–60, 162–67

anger muting, 164
anger smothering, 171n27
anti-Asian sentiment. See *Korematsu v. United States* (1944)
Applied Behavior Analysis (ABA), 46–48
Archer, Alfred, 168n2
Aristotle, 169n9
Ask Me about My Uterus (Norman), 237–39, 240, 243–44
asthma, 42
Augmentative and Alternative Communication (AAC), 57n23
Austin, J. L., 11, 153, 169n4
autism spectrum disorder, 46–48, 54

Bagnoli, Carla, 13
Bailey, Alison, 12, 165, 168–69n3, 171n27
Bakan, Abigail B., 24
Bannon, Steve, 226–27n12
Bartky, Sandra, 160
Bauer, Ida (Dora), 96–98
Beerbohm, Eric, 135–36
Berenstain, Nora: on epistemic gaslighting, 66; on epistemic injustice, 9–10, 88; on hermeneutical injustice, 83n7; on narrative complicity, 24, 32–34, 36, 48, 51; on naturalization of disability, 24, 25, 26, 36–37, 43–55; on structural gaslighting, 12, 14, 23–55, 65, 72, 231, 251; on white feminism, 253–54; on white ignorance, 74–75
Bergman, Ingrid, 2. See also *Gaslight* (1944 film)
Bettcher, Talia Mae, 184
BiDil, 38–42
Bierria, Alisa, 32–34
Black Lives Matter movement, 158, 197

Black respectability politics, 33
Bonilla, Yarimar, 250, 252
Bouie, Jamelle, 98–99
Bouson, J. Brooks, 138–39
Boyer, Charles, 2. See also *Gaslight* (1944 film)
Braden, Anne and Carl. See *Commonwealth of Kentucky v. Braden* (1955)
Brennan, Teresa, 170n14
British Social Model (BSM), 45
Brown, Chris, 32–33
Brown, Cyntoia, 56n9
Brown, Kendrick, 180, 187
Burchard, Esteban, 42–43
Burke, Tarana, 6, 103, 118
Burrow, Sylvia, 194–95
Buss, David, 57n12

Calef, Victor, 3–4
Callow, Ella, 52–53, 54
Campbell, Sue, 147, 149, 159–60
Canton Indian Insane Asylum (Hiawatha Insane Asylum), 52–53
capitalism, 26, 28–30, 45. See also racial capitalism; racio-colonial capitalism
Carby, Hazel, 28
Carell, Havi, 234
Carson, Ben, 264
Carter Andrews, Dorinda J., 194
Cartwright, Samuel, 38
Centro de Periodismo Investigativo (CPI), 257, 270n16
Chalupa, Andrea, 116–17
Chavis, Lakeidra, 46
Chemaly, Soraya, 148, 151, 155
Cherry, Myisha, 168–69n3
cisheterosexism, 26, 28–30, 45
Civil Liberties Act (1988), 205
Clinton, Bill, 196, 235
Code, Lorraine, 90

cognitive bias, 91–92
Cohen, Jodi S., 46
Collins, Patricia Hill, 28–30, 89
Collins, Randall, 170n14
Colonial Debts (Zambrana), 266
colonialism, 72. *See also* white settler colonialism
coloniality, 268n4
colonization of psychic space, 129–30, 132–33
common knowledge (common sense), 35
Commonwealth of Kentucky v. Braden (1955), 197–98, 201–5, **203**, 207, 223–24, 253
Community Development Block Grants for Disaster Recovery (CDBG-DR), 257–58, 260, 264
Community Development Block Grants for Mitigation (CDBG-MIT), 257–58, 259–61, 264
confabulation, 12
confirmation bias, 91–92
Cooper, Brittany, 161
Cotten, Joseph, 2
countertransference, 97–98
COVID-19 pandemic, 24
craniometry, 37–38
credibility: anger gaslighting and, 149, 163–64; epistemic injustice and, 130; power and, 128–29; social imaginary and, 93–95, 100–101; testimonial injustice and, 9, 178, 182–88; Trump and, 218
critical race theory, 8, 9, 206
Cross, Christina, 56n6
Cukor, George. See *Gaslight* (1944 film)
cultural gaslighting: concept of, 12–13, 24–25, 231, 255; white settler colonialism and, 12–13, 24–25, 77–78, 81–82, 117, 118

cultural imperialism, 168n2

Danforth, Scott, 46
Davidson, Donald, 171n22
Davis, Angela Y., 101n2
Davis, Angelique M.. *See* racial gaslighting
Davis, Ryan, 135–36
diagnostic delays, 236–37
Dirty John (podcast), 107–10
disability, 24, 25, 26, 36–37, 43–55
disableization, 52–55
disaster capitalism, 252
Disaster Relief Fund, 257–58
disaster response. *See* María (hurricane)
distributive justice, 73
Doing Harm (Dusenberry), 235
"Donald Trump is Gaslighting America" (Duca), 116–17
Dora (Ida Bauer), 96–98
Dorpat, Theo, 168–69n3
Dotson, Kristie: on epistemic injustice, 56n9, 88; on epistemic oppression, 10, 56n9; on legitimating narratives, 77; on testimonial quieting, 109, 183; on testimonial smothering, 171n27
Duca, Lauren, 116–17
Dusenberry, Maya, 235

Elias, Sean, 206
Ellinger, Mickey, 207n1
emotional labor, 160
Enduring Conviction (Korematsu), 208n5
Entitled (Manne), 131–33
environmental racism, 42–43
epistemic apartheid, 41
epistemic gaslighting: affective gaslighting and, 130–38, 143; Ivy on, 65–66, 68–70, 74; vs.

epistemic gaslighting *(continued)*
  manipulative gaslighting, 70–71; as structural gaslighting, 74–79. *See also* epistemic injustice
epistemic harm, 239–45
epistemic injustice: concept of, 1, 4, 8–10, 66, 87, 127–28, 150–51; Abramson on, 69, 127–28; affective injustice and, 166–67; Anderson on, 72–74; credibility and, 149, 163–64; Fricker on, 9–10, 69–70, 87–89, 127–28, 130, 163–64; Ivy on, 68–70, 74, 177–78, 180–88; medical gaslighting as, 232–36, 255; Medina's epistemology of resistance and, 88–89. *See also* testimonial injustice
epistemic objectification, 239–41
epistemic oppression, 10, 56n9, 93
epistemic violence: concept of, 4, 24–25; Dotson on, 10; Ivy on, 177, 178; Ruíz on, 72
epistemological crisis, 4, 6–7, 8–9
epistemology of resistance, 88–89
Ernst, Rose. *See* racial gaslighting
evolutionary psychology, 35

facilitated communication, 50
Fanon, Frantz, 139
FDA (Food and Drug Administration), 38–42
Feagin, Joe, 206
Federal Emergency Management Agency (FEMA), 250, 256–60, **259**
feminist epistemic phenomenology, 1–2. *See also* epistemic injustice
feminist social epistemology, 1–2, 7–8, 9–12
Fields, Barbara, 30–32. *See also* racecraft
Fields, Karen, 30–32. *See also* racecraft

first-person authority, 184–88
Flint, Michigan, 252
Food and Drug Administration (FDA), 38–42
forced institutionalization, 45–46, 52–54
forced sterilization, 45–46, 53
Foucault, Michel, 91
Fragments of an Analysis of a Case of Hysteria (Freud), 96–98
fraternity culture, 141–42
Freud, Sigmund, 95–98
Fricker, Miranda: on epistemic harm, 239–41; on epistemic injustice, 9–10, 69–70, 87–89, 127–28, 130, 163–64; on hermeneutical injustice, 235, 254; on social imaginary, 90–91, 92; on testimonial injustice, 9–10, 73, 83n5, 88–89, 109, 128, 166, 178, 182–83, 185, 239–41
Frye, Marilyn, 147, 148–49, 152–54, 156–57, 162, 166

Garza, Alicia, 157
Gas Light (*Angel Street*) (Hamilton), 2–3, 105–6, 134–36, 181, 231
Gaslight (1940 film), 2, 134–35
Gaslight (1944 film): affective gaslighting and, 134–37; agency in, 207; as example of classic gaslighting, 68, 214–16, 217, 218, 220–21; origins of term and, 2–3, 181, 193–94, 231; testimonial injustice and, 9
gaslighting: cases and examples of, 213–23; counterexample of, 222–23; definitions of, 104, 128–30, 193–94; epistemic injustice as (*see* epistemic injustice); necessary conditions for, 71; origins and use of term, 2–3, 65, 82, 181, 193–94, 213, 231; philosophical approaches

to, 1–3, 4–8; post-truth and, 4, 6–7; psychological and psychiatric treatments of, 3–4, 5, 8, 12 (*see also* Abramson, Kate); theoretical context and approaches to, 8–13. *See also* affective gaslighting; anger gaslighting; cultural gaslighting; interpersonal gaslighting; manipulative gaslighting; medical gaslighting; moral gaslighting; racial gaslighting; structural gaslighting
gaslighting by crowd, 97
Gaslit Nation (podcast), 116–17
gay conversion therapy, 57n21
Goodwill, 46–47
Graham, Sarah, 233–34
Grossberg, Michael, 94
Guenther, Lisa, 238

Hamilton, Patrick, 2–3, 105–6, 134–36, 181, 231
Harvey (hurricane), 250, 258–59, **259**
Hatch, Anthony R., 24
Hedges v. Obama (2013), 205–6
Heil, John, 120–21n6
hermeneutic labor, 160
hermeneutical injustice: Anderson on, 73–74; anger gaslighting and, 155, 167; Fricker on, 9, 83n7, 89, 128, 254; medical gaslighting as, 235–36; white ignorance as, 77, 92
hermeneutical violence, 77–78
Hiawatha Insane Asylum (Canton Indian Insane Asylum), 52–53
Highsmith, Patricia. See *The Talented Mr. Ripley* (Highsmith)
himpathy, 142
Hochchild, Arlie Russell, 140
Hornsby, Jennifer, 11
HUD (US Department of Housing and Urban Development), 250, 256–58, 260–61, 264–65

The Hunting Ground (2015 film), 142
hurricanes. *See* María (hurricane)
Husserl, Edmund, 241–42
Hypatia (journal), 12, 65, 254–55
hysteria, 95–101
Hysterical Women (blog), 233–34

Ideas II (Husserl), 241–42
identity power, 88–89, 94, 100
ignorance, 8–9, 10–11
illegitimacy, 93–95
incarceration, 45–46, 52–53
Indigenous Action Media, 178–79
Indigenous populations, 52–55, 78
interpersonal gaslighting: Abramson on, 66–68, 117, 118, 130–31; Fricker on, 128; medical gaslighting and, 231–32; narrative complicity and, 32–34; in the news, 213; structural gaslighting and, 23–24, 65–66, 71–82, 251; theories of, 66–71. *See also* manipulative gaslighting
intersectionality, 7–8
introjection, 3–4
Irigaray, Luce, 95–96, 97–98
Irma (hurricane), 250
Ivy, Veronica (Rachel McKinnon): on allies and ally culture, 177, 178–88; definition of gaslighting by, 104; on epistemic injustice, 65–66, 68–70, 74, 127–28, 177–78, 180–88, 234; on epistemic violence, 177, 178; on gaslighting as interpersonal phenomenon, 130–31; gaslighting as not always intentional, 232; on testimonial injustice, 177–78, 180, 182–88

Jamison, Leslie, 148, 151
Japanese Americans. *See Korematsu v. United States* (1944)

Jeppson, Sophia, 5
Jones Act (Merchant Marine Act) (1920), 258
Junta de Supervisión y Administración Financiera para Puerto Rico, 258

Kaine, Tim, 99
Katrina (hurricane), 252
Kendzior, Sarah, 116–17
Kidd, Ian James, 234
Kind, Amy, 135
Klein, Melanie, 4
Kline, Neal A., 104, 194
knowledge: affective gaslighting and, 136–37; feminist philosophical approaches on, 3, 4, 5–6
Korematsu v. United States (1944), 197–201, 204–6, 207, 253
Kuromiya, Yosh, 208n3

LA Times (newspaper), 107–10
Lacan, Jacques, 97–98
Langton, Rae, 10–11, 83n5
Leder, Drew, 242–43
legitimating narratives, 77
Lloyd, Elisabeth, 57n12
Lorde, Audre, 157, 170n14
Lovaas, Ivar, 47
Lugones, María, 155, 169n4

Mackinnon, Catherine, 10
manipulative gaslighting, 65–66, 70–71, 78–82, 130, 132–33
Manne, Kate: on epistemic injustice, 127–28; on himpathy, 142; on misogyny, 80–81; on moral gaslighting, 13, 104–20, 131–33, 149, 161–62; on patriarchy, 140–41; on structural gaslighting, 130
Manningham, Bella, 121n7
María (hurricane): disaster response and, 256–61, **259**, *262*; impact on Portorico of, 249–51; racio-colonial capitalism and, 252, 265–67; structural gaslighting and, 251, 255–56, 261–67
Martinas, Sharon, 207n1
Matheson, Benjamin, 168n2
"Matriarch" image, 28–30
McDonald, CeCe, 56n9
McKenzie, Mia, 180
McKinnon, Rachel. *See* Ivy, Veronica (Rachel McKinnon)
McMahan, Jeff, 49–51
medical gaslighting: concept of, 231–36, 254–55; as epistemic injustice, 232–36, 255; harms of, 236–45; as hermeneutical injustice, 235–36; as testimonial injustice, 233–34
medical model of disability, 45
Medina, José, 88–89, 99, 168n2
Meehan, John, 107–10
Merchant Marine Act (Jones Act) (1920), 258
Merleau-Ponty, Maurice, 241–42
#MeToo movement, 4, 6–7, 8–9, 103, 118, 141
Mills, Charles, 74–77, 91–92, 95, 99, 100
miscarriage, 222–23
misogynoir, 30, 32–33
misogyny, 80–81, 103, 113, 118, 128, 131–33
mispronouning, 178, 181–88, 214–15, 216–17, 218, 220, 221
Mock, Janet, 187
Moi, Toril, 97–98
moral gaslighting: concept of, 13, 104–20, 127, 131–33, 137–38; affective gaslighting and, 143; anger gaslighting and, 149, 161–62; structural gaslighting and, 116–18
moral judgments, 218–20
Morgan, Piers, 187

narrative complicity, 24, 32–34, 36, 48, 51
Native Americans, 52–55
neoliberal coloniality, 266
New England Journal of Medicine (journal), 236
New York Times (newspaper), 49–51, 195, 213, 265
Newell, Debra, 107–10
NIH Revitalization Act (1993), 235
NitroMed, 39–42
nonconsensual sex, 141–42
Norman, Abby, 237–39, 240, 243–44
"Normative Isolation: The Dynamics of Power and Authority in Gaslighting" (Bagnoli), 13
Nott, Josiah, 37–38

Office of Information and Regulatory Affairs (OIRA), 260–61
Office of Management and Budget (OMB), 260–61, 264
Omi, Michael, 195–96, 206
Origgi, Gloria, 91
Ostrove, Joan, 180, 187
Oxford English Dictionary, 6–7, 104, 193–94

Palestine, 24
patriarchy: affective gaslighting and, 137; disability and, 45; moral gaslighting and, 118, 132–33, 140–41; structural gaslighting and, 26, 28–30
Pence, Mike, 98–99
pernicious ignorance, 10–11
The Phenomenology of Perception (Merleau-Ponty), 241–42
Pohlhaus, Gaile, Jr.: on controlling image of dominance, 224–25; on epistemic gaslighting, 66; on structural gaslighting, 65, 72; on white ignorance, 74–75; on willful hermeneutical ignorance, 184
political philosophy, 72–73
posttraumatic stress disorder (PTSD), 178
post-truth, 4, 6–7
power: affective gaslighting and, 136–37; anger and, 155–56, 166; credibility and, 128–29; cultural gaslighting and, 78; feminist philosophical approaches on, 3, 4, 5–6; manipulative gaslighting and, 79–80, 130; moral gaslighting and, 115–16, 119–20; as necessary condition for gaslighting, 71; racio-colonial capitalism and, 253; sexism and, 128–29; white ignorance and, 76. *See also* social power
Pratt, Richard, 54
projective identification, 4, 12
PROMESA (Puerto Rico Oversight, Management, and Economic Stability Act) (2016), 258
ProPublica, 46
Pryor, Richard, 98–99
psychoanalysis, 1–2, 5, 12, 95–98
psychology and psychiatry, 3–4, 5
Psychology Today (magazine), 47
Puerto Rico. *See* María (hurricane)
Puerto Rico Oversight, Management, and Economic Stability Act (PROMESA, 2016), 258

Quijano, Aníbal, 268n4

race and racism: medical gaslighting and, 232, 235, 236; scientific racism and, 25, 26, 37–44; slavery and, 37–38, 40, 92, 94, 252, 255, 266; white ignorance and, 74–77, 91–92. *See also* racial capitalism; racial gaslighting; white settler colonialism; white supremacy

racecraft, 25, 30–32, 37, 44, 45. *See also* scientific racism
racial capitalism, 25, 40, 57n17, 252. *See also* racio-colonial capitalism
racial contract, 74–77, 91–92, 95, 100
Racial Formation in the United States (Omi and Winant), 195–96
racial gaslighting: concept of, 24, 65, 75, 117, 194–95, 223, 253; *Commonwealth of Kentucky v. Braden* (1955) and, 197–98, 201–5, **203**, 207, 223–24, 253; *Korematsu v. United States* (1944) and, 197–201, 204–6, 207, 253; Palestine and, 24; process of, 195–98, **203**, 204–7
racial spectacles: concept of, 196–97, 206–7, 223–24, 253; *Commonwealth of Kentucky v. Braden* (1955) and, 202–3; *Korematsu v. United States* (1944) and, 199–201
racio-colonial capitalism, 251–54, 265–67
radical behaviorism, 47
rape and rape culture, 93–95, 99–100, 141–43
Richards, Jennifer Smith, 46
Rihanna, 32–33
Roberts, Dorothy, 25–26, 36, 38–39, 40–41
Roberts, Tuesda, 194
Robinson, Cedric, 252
Roosevelt, Franklin D., 198
Ruíz, Elena: on cultural gaslighting, 12–13, 24–25, 77–78, 81–82, 117, 231, 255; on epistemic apartheid, 41; on epistemic gaslighting, 66; on narrative framing, 264; on silencing, 89; on structural gaslighting, 65, 72, 251, 254–55; on structural trauma, 26–28

Scarry, Elaine, 242

Schmitt, David, 57n12
science, 25–26, 34–37
scientific racism, 25, 26, 37–44
self-doubt: Abramson on, 82n3; affective gaslighting and, 137; manipulative gaslighting and, 130, 133–34; medical gaslighting and, 233, 238, 239–41, 243; testimonial injustice and, 88
self-help culture, 33
Seneca, 169n9
Serwer, Adam, 106
sexism: manipulative gaslighting and, 132–33; medical gaslighting and, 232, 233–34, 235–39; power and, 128–29. *See also* misogyny
sexual abuse, 49–51. *See also* rape and rape culture
Shabot, Sara Cohen, 222–23
shame, 137–39, 141–43
silencing, 4, 9, 10–11, 83n5, 89, 95–96
Singer, Peter, 49–51
Slatman, Jenny, 241–42
slave medicine, 37–38
slavery, 37–38, 40, 92, 94, 252, 255, 266
social epistemology, 1–2, 7–8, 9–12
social imaginary: concept of, 90–95; credibility and, 93–95, 100–101; epistemic injustice and, 89–90; hysteria and, 95–101
social model of disability, 45
social power: concept of, 1, 8, 87; epistemic injustice and, 9–10; manipulative gaslighting and, 70–71; medical gaslighting and, 232; social imaginary and, 91–95
Sommerville, Diane Miller, 94
SoVerano 2019 protest, 270n16
Spear, Andrew, 12
Srinivasan, Amia, 165–66, 168n2
Stanley-Becker, Isaac, 43

Stark, Cynthia: on epistemic injustice, 127–28; on manipulative gaslighting, 66, 70–71, 79–81, 130, 132–33; on structural gaslighting, 223–25; on varieties of gaslighting, 213–23
Steinem, Gloria, 148, 151
Stern, Robin, 219–20, 221
Stonewall Riot (1969), 179
Straub, Adam, 265
structural gaslighting: concept of, 9–10, 12, 13–14, 23–30, 65–66, 72, 231; controlling image of dominance and, 224–25; epistemic gaslighting as, 74–79; interpersonal gaslighting and, 23–24, 65–66, 71–82, 251; manipulative gaslighting as, 78–82; María (hurricane) and, 251, 255–56, 261–67; medical gaslighting and, 231–32; moral gaslighting and, 116–18; narrative complicity and, 24, 32–34, 36, 48, 51; naturalization of disability as, 24, 25, 26, 36–37, 43–55; racecraft as, 25, 30–32, 37, 44, 45; racio-colonial capitalism and, 251–54; science and, 25–26, 34–37; scientific racism as, 25, 26, 37–44. *See also* cultural gaslighting; racial gaslighting
structural trauma, 26–28
Stubblefield, Anna, 49–51
Succession (TV show), 113
Sweet, Paige L., 104, 117–18, 121–22n9

The Talented Mr. Ripley (Highsmith), 166–67, 178, 182–83
Taller Salud, 268n1
testimonial injustice: concept of, 150–51, 239–41; agency and, 11; example of, 222; Fricker on, 9–10, 73, 83n5, 88–89, 109, 128, 166, 178, 182–83, 185, 239–41; Ivy on, 68–70, 177–78, 180, 182–88; medical gaslighting as, 233–34; rape culture and, 141; social imaginary and, 92–93
testimonial quieting, 109, 183
testimonial smothering, 171n27
Thomas, Laura, 169n7
TMZ (blog), 32–33
tone policing, 195
Traister, Rebecca, 163, 165
trans women: mispronouning and, 178, 181–88, 214–15, 216–17, 218, 220, 221; narrative complicity and, 56n11; use of term, 188–89n3
trans* epistemology, 179–88
trauma: epistemic violence and, 178; medical gaslighting and, 243–44; structural gaslighting and, 26–28
Tremain, Shelley, 24, 25–26, 36, 44–45, 48, 52
triangulation, 160
Trump, Donald: crowd size and, 214–15, 216, 217, 218, 220, 221; as gaslighter, 116–18; María (hurricane) and, 261–64, 267; misogyny and, 131; social imaginary and, 98–100
truthfulness, 216–17
Tulsa Race Riot (1921), 208n6
Turner, Brock, 141
"Turning Up the Lights on Gaslighting" (Abramson), 12, 13–14, 66–68

uptake, 148–49, 153–55, 156–60, 162–67
US Department of Housing and Urban Development (HUD), 250, 256–58, 260–61, 264–65

victim blaming, 33

victimhood, 142
Vogue (magazine), 232

Wade family. See *Commonwealth of Kentucky v. Braden* (1955)
Wall Street Journal (newspaper), 265
Washington Post (newspaper), 213
Weinshel, Edward M., 3–4
white feminism, 33, 253–54
white ignorance, 74–77, 91–92
white settler colonialism: cultural gaslighting and, 12–13, 24–25, 77–78, 81–82, 117, 118; disability and, 45, 52–55; social imaginary and, 91–92; structural gaslighting and, 26–28, 251–54
white supremacy: anger gaslighting and, 161–62; definition of, 207n1; disability and, 45, 49–51, 52–55; racecraft and, 25, 30–32, 37, 44, 45; racial gaslighting and, 24–25, 196–98, 200–201, 202–8; scientific racism and, 25, 26, 37–44; structural gaslighting and, 26–34, 251–54
Whitney, Shiloh, 140–41
"Who Is the Victim in the Anna Stubblefield Case?" (Singer and McMahan), 49–51
willful hermeneutical ignorance, 184
Williams, Serena, 232
Willison, Charley, 257
Winant, Howard, 195–96, 206
Women's March (2017), 195

Young, Iris Marion, 168n2

Zambrana, Rocío, 266
Zevallos, Zuleyka, 195

www.ingramcontent.com/pod-product-compliance
Ingram Content Group UK Ltd.
Pitfield, Milton Keynes, MK11 3LW, UK
UKHW031835210225
455389UK00005B/28